D0147736

Dominant Ideologies

Dominant Ideologies

edited by

NICHOLAS ABERCROMBIE

STEPHEN HILL

BRYAN S. TURNER

London
UNWIN HYMAN
Boston   Sydney   Wellington

Published by the Academic Division of
Unwin Hyman Ltd
15/17 Broadwick Street, London W1V 1FP, UK

Unwin Hyman Inc.,
8 Winchester Place, Winchester, Mass. 01890, USA

Allen & Unwin (Australia) Ltd,
8 Napier Street, North Sydney, NSW 2060, Australia

Allen & Unwin (New Zealand) Ltd in association with the
Port Nicholson Press Ltd,
Compusales Building, 75 Ghuznee Street, Wellington 1, New Zealand

First published in 1990

British Library Cataloguing in Publication Data

Dominant ideologies
1. Capitalist societies
I. Abercrombie, Nicholas   II. Hill, Stephen *1946–*
III. Turner, Bryan S. (Bryan Stanley) *1945–*
330.122
ISBN 0-04-301298-1
ISBN 0-04-301299-X pbk.

Typeset in 10 on 12 point Bembo by Fotographics (Bedford) Ltd
and printed in Great Britain by Billing and Sons Limited, Worcester

Contents

Acknowledgements

We would like to thank Gordon Smith of Unwin Hyman who has supported our exploration of the sociology of ideology over a period of years, and our contributors, some of whom waited patiently for their chapters to appear in print.

Contributors

The editors have jointly published *The Dominant Ideology Thesis* (1980), *Penguin Dictionary of Sociology* (1984, 1987) and *Sovereign Individuals of Capitalism* (1986).

Nicholas Abercrombie: Born 1944 in Great Britain. Studied Politics, Philosophy and Economics at Oxford University (BA in 1966), Sociology at the London School of Economics (M.Sc. in 1968) and was awarded a PhD in Sociology at Lancaster University in 1983. He is a Reader at Lancaster University. Author of articles in social theory, sociology of knowledge and sociology of culture, and of *Class, Structure and Knowledge* (1980), *Capital, Labour and the Middle Classes* (1983) (with J. Urry), and *Contemporary British Society* (1988) (with A. Warde and others). Co-editor of *Enterprise Culture* (1990) (with R. Keat) and *Social Change in Modern Britain* (1990) (with A. Warde).

Stephen Hill: Born 1946 in Great Britain. Studied History at Balliol College, Oxford and Sociology at the London School of Economics (M.Sc. in 1968 and PhD in 1973). He is Reader in Sociology at the London School of Economics and author of *The Dockers* (1976) and *Competition and Control at Work* (1981). Author of a number of articles on the sociology of work and employment.

Scott Lash: Born in Chicago, Illinois in 1945, he received his BS from the University of Michigan and PhD in Sociology from the London School of Economics in 1980; he is currently Senior Lecturer in sociology at Lancaster University. He has published *The Militant Worker* (1984), *The End of Organized Capitalism* (1987) (with J. Urry), *Max Weber Rationality and Modernity* (1987) (co-edited with S. Whimster), and *The Sociology of Postmodernism* (1990), He is an Alexander von Humboldt Fellow at the Institut für Soziologie at the Freie Universitat, Berlin. He has published many articles on sociological theory and postmodernism.

Ephraim J. Nimni: Born in Buenos Aires, Argentina in 1947. Graduated in Sociology and Political Sciences at the Hebrew

University, Jerusalem; MA in the Sociology of Latin America (University of Essex), PhD in Sociology (University of Hull). He has taught sociology at the University of Keele and Politics at the Flinders University of South Australia. He is lecturer in Political Sociology, School of Political Science, University of New South Wales, Sydney, Australia. His principal research interests are nationalism, Austro-Marxism, and political theory. He recently published (1989) 'Marx, Engels and the national question', *Science & Society*, vol. 53, no. 3, pp. 297–326.

Jan Pakulski: Born in 1950 in Poland. Studied Sociology at the University of Warsaw (MA in Sociology in 1973) and at the Australian National University in Canberra (PhD in Sociology in 1980). Visiting Fellow in the Russian Research Centre, Harvard University in 1982 and St Antony's College, Oxford in 1982 and 1986. He is currently Senior Lecturer in Sociology at the University of Tasmania, Hobart, Tasmania. He has published a number of articles and monographs on political elites, ideology and social movements.

Roland Robertson: Born in Great Britain in 1938. He was Professor of Sociology at the University of York (1970–4) and has been Professor of Sociology at the University of Pittsburgh since 1973. His publications include *International Systems and the Modernization of Societies* (1968) (with P. Nettl), *The Sociological Interpretation of Religion* (1969), *The Sociology of Religion* (1969) (editor), *Deviance Crime and Socio-Legal Control* (1973) (with L. Taylor), *Meaning and Change* (1978), *Identity and Authority* (1980) (co-edited with B. Holzner), and *Church-State Relations* (1986) (with T. Robbins). He is the author of many articles on sociological theory, comparative religion, modernization and globalization.

Bryan S. Turner: Born in Great Britain in 1945, PhD University of Leeds (1970) and D. Litt. the Flinders University of South Australia (1986). He was Professor of Sociology at Flinders University (1982–8), Guest Professor and Alexander von Humboldt Fellow at Bielefeld University, West Germany (1987–8), Professor of General Social Science at the University of Utrecht, The Netherlands (1988–90) and is now Professor of Sociology, University of Essex. He is a Fellow of the Academy of Social Sciences in Australia. His recent publications include *Citizenship and Capitalism* (1986), *Equality* (1986), *Medical Power and Social Knowledge* (1987), *Status* (1988) and *Max Weber on Economy and Society* (1989) (with R. J. Holton). He has published a number of articles on the sociology of religion, social theory and historical sociology.

Anthony Woodiwiss: Born 1945 in Great Britain. BA (Leeds), M.Sc. (London), PhD (Essex). He is a lecturer in Sociology and fellow of the Centre for the Study of Contemporary Japan at the University of Essex. He has been the Visiting Professor of Sociology at Dokkyo University. He is the author of *Social Theory After Post-Modernism* (1990) and *Rights v Conspiracy* (1990). He is completing a study of the development of Japanese labour law.

Preface

How do societies cohere? This question has long concerned those with an interest in the nature of social life and still informs modern social science. Coherence seems especially problematic in societies with a capitalist form of economic organization. Capitalism requires the co-operation of capital and labour as factors of production, both benefit from this relationship, yet in the same moment they face each other as competing interests that pull in different directions. Because modern capitalism is found mainly where individuals have extensive formal freedoms and in political democracies where access to power is relatively open, authoritarian regulation by the state is rarely an option to maintain stability. Various explanations have been proposed for the continued integrity of capitalist societies in the face of their internal pressures towards instability, but there is no agreed solution. The lines of analysis are clear, however. The prevalence of the polar opposites of values versus pragmatism, ideology versus interests, consensus versus coercion points to the major division of opinion, which is between those who believe that an overarching and powerful common culture binds together people who otherwise have incommensurable interests, and those who do not. The former group includes culturalists of a Marxist or Parsonian persuasion, the latter is more heterogeneous. It embraces rational choice theorists, the phenomenological view of the constraints of everyday life, and accounts which more explicitly recognize non-normative forms of social power.

In 1980 we published *The Dominant Ideology Thesis* as a contribution to this discussion about the stability of capitalist society. We argued against a view that was then fashionable among Marxists, namely that the dominant class which controlled capital also successfully set the dominant values of society in such a way as to win the consent of subordinates to a system which advanced dominant interests, while obscuring the fact that this was so, a view we called the dominant ideology thesis. We similarly challenged an established sociological analysis that social consensus resulted from common values. We analysed the contemporary and historical evidence, mainly in Britain, and showed that the main role of ideology was to preserve the coherence of the dominant class itself, that subordinates challenged the interests of this class and were not greatly affected by their ideology, and that the relative stability of society was best explained by factors other than the internalization of a common culture, whether this be a class ideology or other values. We demonstrated that the role of culture had to be found by empirical investigation and could not be assumed a priori on the basis of some theoretical predilection.

We have commissioned the papers collected here in order to advance the analysis of ideology in a comparative and historical perspective. Our hope is to illuminate the range of experience in other societies, the extent to which there is a common pattern, and how far Britain is typical. We asked the contributors briefly to consider four issues, so as to maintain a thematic unity to the volume as a whole. First, what is the dominant ideology? Second, what effect does this have on the dominant class? Third, what effect does it have on subordinate classes? Fourth, what is the apparatus of its transmission?

The volume covers a range of different capitalist societies, including familiar cases and others which are discussed less often. We have included two examples of white settler societies – Australia and Argentina – whose inclusion into the capitalist world system shares certain common features, but whose political histories are very different. Japan, Germany and America are the core of the modern global economy, yet they too have very different historical roots. We pay special attention to recent changes in Britain, because the first decade of Thatcherism was an interesting test case of ideological hegemony. Finally, we present a study of a state socialist society, namely Poland, on the grounds that ideology would be expected to have a different role in this social system. These chapters are mainly empirical in focus and contribute directly to an understanding of cultural forms in different societies. We hope that they will also set the way for future study in the sociology of culture and ideology that is both empirically grounded and comparative in perspective.

Nicholas Abercrombie
Stephen Hill
Bryan S. Turner
October 1989

Dominant
Ideologies

CHAPTER

1

Britain:
The Dominant Ideology
Thesis after a decade

STEPHEN HILL

Economism and empiricism

The Dominant Ideology Thesis (Abercrombie, Hill and Turner, 1980) had its gestation during that period – which with hindsight was comparatively brief – when the intellectual climate of British sociology was influenced by new forms of Marxism, notably structural Marxism. Louis Althusser's reading of the concept of ideology (1971), and the parallel concerns of writers as otherwise diverse as Gramsci and Miliband to identify ideological systems arising out of capitalism as an economic mode of production, gave a distinctly materialistic, even economistic, cast to our discussion. Despite the similarity of tone, our own position was developed in opposition to the shibboleths of the time and we put forward a distinctive twist to existing Marxist theory. On the one hand, we endorsed a broadly historical–materialist approach to the analysis of ideology. On the other, our different evaluation of Marx and Engels's account of the 'ruling ideas' in *The German Ideology* led us to turn much of conventional Marxism on its head. Many aspects of the prevalent Marxist view of ideology, such as the notion of the fetishism of commodities, had already been criticized elsewhere (Abercrombie, 1980). Our unusual relationship to Marxism was reflected in some of the criticism levelled against our argument and various commentators clearly had difficulty in locating our position. A statement of the main features of our argument is necessary for the purpose of clarification.

We challenged the then conventional Marxist argument that the stability of capitalism could be explained by reference to the existence of a dominant ideology which had the consequence of incorporating the working class into the capitalist system, whether by leading them to accept false beliefs, by obscuring the real character of economic exploitation in capitalism, or by blocking the development of oppositional ideas. We contested this view on the grounds that the empirical evidence available did not support the thesis and, in addition, that there were theoretical problems with such a dominant ideology thesis. Our critique was thus both theoretical and empirical in focus. We then reversed the convention and argued that ideology does have significant effects but these are primarily on the dominant rather than the subordinate class. What has been important for the stability of capitalism is the coherence of the dominant class itself, and ideology has played a major role in securing this. The Marxist position was criticized for its failure to analyse the apparatus or mechanisms by which dominant beliefs were transmitted and how such beliefs were received by subordinates; and for its assumption that the human subject was an ideological dupe, incapable of independent thought and rational action. While we were critical of much Marxist structuralism, we also felt that there were influential arguments within conventional sociology which were subject to the same criticisms. In particular, we saw a parallel between the analysis of culture in structural functionalism and the analysis of ideology in structural Marxism. Both propounded normative integration as a solution to the Hobbesian problem of social order.

In our empirical investigation of ideology, we wanted to do more than simply assert certain theoretical positions or criticize conventional accounts of ideology. We felt that the theoretical elegance of much Marxist conceptualization often failed to engage in any significant way with the historical evidence or the findings of contemporary empirical sociology. Although there are obvious theoretical and philosophical problems in the analysis of the concepts of ideology and false consciousness, we argued that whether a society did indeed have a dominant ideology and whether this did indeed incorporate subordinates, had to be issues which were, at some stage or at some level, empirically verifiable. In addition, we wanted to go beyond a review of the historical and contemporary evidence, to produce an alternative conceptualization of the possible foundations of capitalist society. In short, we hoped to propose a solution to the

Hobbesian problem of order which did not rest upon an appeal to the idea of a dominant ideology or culture and which did not treat the human subject as a dupe. Our proposal was mainly drawn from the works of Marx. The stability of capitalism rests primarily on the dull compulsion of the economic relations of everyday life:

> The constant generation of a relative surplus population keeps the law of supply and demand of labour, and therefore keeps wages, in a rut that corresponds with the wants of capital. The dull compulsion of economic relations completes the subjection of the labourer to the capitalist. Direct force, outside economic conditions, is of course still used, but only exceptionally.
>
> (Marx, 1974, p. 689)

Despite the significant changes in many features of capitalist society since Marx, we argued that the economic constraint of everyday circumstances still ultimately compels people to work, and at the same time the commitment of subordinates to the system is likely to be characterized by some form of pragmatic acquiescence rather than normative or ideological involvement (following Mann's notion of pragmatic acceptance [1970]). The economic basis of social order has several dimensions. Dull compulsion in the classical sense is seen in the market for labour – people have to enter the labour market if they are to live adequately – and in the labour process internal to enterprises. In modern capitalism, the economic has additional importance because subordinates have a larger material stake in the system than before. We noted that the stream of rewards available from the economy provides an impetus to work within the system and increases the price of replacing it. In a similar vein, we suggested that the complexity of the modern division of labour has increased both the interdependence among subordinates and their dependence on existing social arrangements, with the result that economic dislocation caused by insurrectionary discontent has more immediate and severe costs. This is an aspect of Durkheim's conceptualization of a complex division of labour as leading individuals to depend on each other and thereby fostering system integration which need have no normative dimension. Finally, we emphasized the significance of the solidity and coercive quality of everyday life, manifest as a constraining environment that appears unchangeable to social actors, which should be an element of any explanation of social stability. Although modern capitalism might at times call on the additional support of force or overt ideological justification, we made the claim that the foundation of the social stability of the advanced capitalist societies has been non-normative and mainly economic in character.

The other intellectual tradition which formed a background to the study was the postwar sociological tradition of class analysis in Britain. The primary significance of this for our project was that the empirical research which dealt most systematically with modern ideologies and beliefs had been framed within this perspective. It was marked by a concern with subjective perceptions of class, class inequality and power, and the possibilities of political radicalism. In order to test Marxist theories about the nature of, and support for, ideological systems that supposedly obscured and legitimized capitalism as a mode of production, we had to use evidence that had mainly been collected within this somewhat different problematic. The two theoretical traditions were of course linked, since class analysis dealt with a social structure arising out of the organization of the economy, but the evidence from class analysis was not complete for our purposes. It dealt with social divisions and inequalities deriving from the economy, which was one of our concerns, but was less satisfactory with regard to the economic base which was the main interest. That is, it covered the world of distribution and politics better than property and production. A certain amount of pertinent material was also available elsewhere, notably in studies by industrial sociologists.

The coverage as well as the content of the empirical evidence available in the late 1970s left something to be desired. Subordinate values had been covered quite extensively, mainly in the form of small-scale studies of particular occupational groups or geographical areas, and with a heavy concentration on the manual working class. There was little evidence for the working class on a national scale, however, while middle-class values were documented even more sketchily. There was a shortage of good information on how members of subordinate and, indeed, dominant classes viewed *capitalism*. Nevertheless, we pieced together an account of what the adherents of a dominant ideology thesis regarded as the ideological requirements of capitalism and its pattern of social class inequality, and evaluated these against the range of available evidence. Our discussion concentrated on the ideologies of accumulation, managerialism and state neutrality/welfare, which had been identified as important in Britain.

We also noted the further claim that individualism was the central dimension of dominant ideology, both as an essential requirement of the capitalist mode of production and as an all-pervasive and bourgeois cultural force that legitimized capitalist society. We were unable to pursue this claim in much depth at the time, but subsequently we have assessed aspects of the relationship between individualism and capitalism as a mode of production more carefully (Abercrombie, Hill and Turner, 1986). Our analysis in this later publication is that individualism and capitalism have no necessary or enduring relation: any linkage is entirely contingent. Individualism did give capitalism a particular shape in America and Britain, notably in the early capitalist period, and capitalism in turn shaped individualism by emphasizing its possessive features. However, oriental capitalism and late capitalism in the west bear no particular relationship to individualism; indeed, they flourish best in the absence of an individualistic culture. While collectivism may be an appropriate cultural milieu for capitalism, individualism now degenerates into the culture of individuality, which has little economic effect. We conclude that the capitalist form of economic organization has no need of the bourgeois cultural form of individualism. Indeed, on theoretical as well as empirical grounds, we find that capitalism has no necessary ideological requirements at all. Approaching the issue from another direction, by asking what is strictly and logically required for a 'pure' form of capitalism to maintain itself over time, Coram (1987) also arrives at a similar conclusion: capitalism constrains rational actors (including both the owners and non-owners of the means of production) to pursue certain ends, the pursuit of these ends is sufficient to explain the operation and reproduction of the system of production, thus capitalism has no ideological or cultural conditions of existence.

Capitalism involves the production and exchange of commodities with the aim of accumulating a surplus value, that is, profit. Profit is realized in the market, and some part of this profit is reinvested in order to maintain the conditions of future accumulation. As a mode of production, its particular features are commodified labour, the separation of labour from the means of subsistence, and exclusive property rights in the means of production and the products of the labour process (Abercrombie, Hill and Turner, 1986, p. 87). It is likely that accumulation, as the essence of capitalism, will be culturally endorsed in dominant values in historically existing capitalist societies, and the position taken here is that its legitimation is constitutive of actual ideologies of capitalism. However, aspects of accumulation, notably the appropriation of profit by the owners of the capital stock, may well be contested by subordinates, although with little effect on the stability of the economy as the present chapter shows.

Developments over the last ten years have implications for the original study. New empirical information from large-scale survey research on attitudes, beliefs and values relates to its analysis and suggests new issues for consideration. Changes in the real world of the British political economy in the first decade of Thatcherism appear to have challenged the earlier conclusions about the nature and significance of ideology. Finally, sociological thinking on issues of class, politics and culture has advanced considerably. How well has *The Dominant Ideology Thesis* stood the test of time?

Attitudes, beliefs and values in Britain

The publication of *British Social Attitudes* annually since 1984, in particular the fourth report edited by Jowell *et al.* (1987), the reports of the British part of the European Values Study (Abrams *et al.* [eds], 1985) and the study of class beliefs carried out by G. Marshall *et al.* (1988), and the greater use of opinion poll data in a variety of sociological studies, have gone some way to filling the gaps noted above. Before this material is discussed, however, the appropriateness of using surveys must be considered briefly, since some critics believe strongly that this sort of evidence is of little use to the study of ideology (Rootes, 1981; Hall, 1988). The justification of using survey evidence is in part one of practicality: there are no other data available on a national basis and across all social groups. It would be desirable to have more evidence of attitudes, beliefs and values collected by in-depth and discursive methods rather than as responses to a predefined and possibly restricted range of items in a standardized interview schedule, and data collected by such methods will be cited at various points. Nevertheless, trading the depth available in what are inevitably small-scale studies of limited groups of individuals for the coverage of surveys does not mean the latter have little or no validity. There is also a theoretical issue involved in such criticism, namely that ideology is held to be embedded in practices and as such is not amenable to any method that concentrates on attitudes and beliefs. Our disagreement with this view has been made clear previously (Abercrombie, Hill and Turner, 1980; 1983). The position taken in this chapter is that ideology includes beliefs in people's heads, and these may be discovered by conventional methods of empirical investigation.

The evidence of the 1980s is that subordinate groups still subscribe widely to a radical-egalitarian and oppositional ideology. Most people recognize that social conflict is endemic. Indeed, the Gallup Polls' political index for the years 1964–84 shows a steady increase in the proportion of people who think there is a 'class struggle' in Britain, rising from 48 to 74 per cent (Abercrombie and Warde, *et al.*, 1988, p. 165). G. Marshall *et al.* also report the view, found across their whole sample, that British society is riven by social conflict. This perception of conflict is fuelled by a desire for the redistribution of income and wealth (1988, pp. 151–6). Respondents from lower social classes see greater class divisions and are more concerned with distributive justice than those from higher classes; nevertheless, the extent of radical egalitarianism among the latter is also unexpectedly high. Half of the respondents agreed that there is still a dominant class which controls both the economic and the political system, and a lower class which has no control at all over economic and political affairs (1988, pp. 143–4). The authors find this result quite striking, since they had deliberately formulated their question in a way that invited disagreement, in order to prompt people to report how they felt the class structure had in fact changed. Those who disagreed did so because they felt that political and other citizenship rights had grown, rather than that society had become more equal and class less salient. *British Social Attitudes* reports endorsement of the statements that wealth is shared unfairly, the rich have one law while there is another for the poor, managers and workers are on opposite sides, business benefits owners at the expense of the poor (Heath and Topf, 1987). Economic and social radicalism are strongest among the working class but a sizeable minority of the managerial, professional and administrative class – the 'salariat' – is also radical (Heath and Topf, 1987). Both surveys document cynicism about the political process. There is a belief that, while greater social justice could be engineered by political means, in fact the political process will not deliver the goods and people acting politically are fairly powerless. These who are radical on economic and social issues are the most cynical politically (Heath and Topf, 1987).

The surveys still focus mainly on distributional and political issues, but they do present some interesting data on production and the nature of the economic system. First, G. Marshall *et al.* find people place the major line of social conflict in the economy, between employers and employees (1988, p. 151). *British Social Attitudes* reports that a large majority of the working class and a substantial minority of the 'salariat' take this view (Heath and Topf, 1987). Second, most people seem to accept that the making of profits is the legitimate goal of economic activity, but they disagree that the use to which profits are put at present is correct: 55 per cent report that profits go to shareholders in the form of dividends and to top managers in the form of salary bonuses, but only 4 per cent think that this is how profits *should* be used. The preference of the majority is for reinvestment in machinery, training, research and development, and a fairly sizeable minority for distribution as employee benefits (Collins, 1987). The proportion of the salariat reporting that profits do at present go to shareholders and top managers is higher than in the two other major social classes (working and routine non-manual).[1] Nevertheless, only 4 per cent of the salariat approve of profits being used in this way, which is identical to the other groups.[2] Third, people have a growing preference for employee participation in managerial decision-making within companies and believe that government should legislate for this component of economic citizenship; the proportion agreeing that 'the government should give workers more say in running the places where they work' increased from 56 to 80 per cent between 1974 and 1986 (Heath and Topf, 1987). There are minor class differences, with the working class endorsing the idea more strongly in 1986.[3] When asked about greater participation in the form of profit-sharing, 80 per cent of the population say that business should indeed share more of its profits with its employees (Collins, 1987), with all these groups in agreement as to its desirability.

G. Marshall *et al.* emphasize that most of their respondents do accept, or are at least resigned to, the capitalist mode of production, and that their concern for greater distributional justice is not incompatible with modern capitalism (1988, p. 153). They conclude:

> there is little evidence of British working-class participation in a consensus about agreed principles governing distributional issues . . . this would seem to lend support to the claim made by Abercrombie, Hill and Turner that the social order in capitalist societies does not depend on agreement about a dominant ideology.
>
> (1988, p. 222)

I do not disagree with this conclusion. Nevertheless, the various data just cited do raise the question of exactly *what* is being endorsed, if capitalism is accepted in any positive sense rather than being accepted simply with resignation. While people appear to endorse certain of the economic imperatives of a capitalist economy, they also dispute the structure of economic rights and the distribution of financial rewards and social power which follow in the British system. The reproduction of capital and private profit-making are central to the accumulation process in the capitalist mode of production, and together constitute the ideology of accumulation. The evidence from the 1980s does show a widespread endorsement of accumulation for the purpose of reproduction, since corporate profitability is sanctioned and reinvestment is given a high priority. But there is scarcely any support for the priority of the private property rights of the *owners* of the capital stock to benefit from the profits of their investment: their rights are held to be far less legitimate than the claims of firms and their employees to a larger share of these profits. Similarly, the managerial ideology which justifies the rights of non-owners to dominance in the economy is contested. First, respondents see employment as the site of a fundamental social conflict. Second, their demand for legislation for employee participation suggests that they do not wholly subscribe to legitimatory beliefs which justify managerial privilege in terms of managers' special, technocratic competence and their role as the servants of capital.

The service and upper classes

New research shows the complexity of, and raises interesting questions about, the belief systems of the higher echelons of the class structure. The Goldthorpe social class I comprises higher-grade managers, professionals and administrators, and large proprietors. Class II includes the lower grades of these occupations, plus higher technicians and the supervisors of non-manual employees. Jointly, these constitute the 'service' class for Goldthorpe and for G. Marshall and his colleagues, and in a slightly modified form the 'salariat' for the authors of *British Social Attitudes*. The data on socioeconomic beliefs show that a substantial proportion of the service class tends towards oppositional and radical-egalitarian values – between a quarter and a half of the relevant respondents on a range of issues (Jowell *et al*. [eds], 1987, p. 186; G. Marshall *et al*., 1988, p. 180). It is particularly striking that around two-thirds of both class I and II respondents state that the distribution of income and wealth is unfair. Nearly a third of class I cite wealth that is acquired too easily and unearned income as the major components of this unfairness, which is the largest proportion to give this reply in any social class, while a fifth cite the size of the gap between high and low incomes (G. Marshall *et al*., 1988, p. 186). The fact that only 4 per cent of the service-class respondents in the *British Social Attitudes* data set endorsed the existing distribution of profit to owners and top managers shows their critical stance on this issue also.

The potential of managerial, professional and administrative personnel to promote radical–egalitarian ideologies, whether these be old–style socialism or new forms of cultural and political radicalism, has largely been discounted recently. Goldthorpe argues that the service class already is, or will at least become, an essentially conservative force in modern society, because its members have 'a substantial stake in the *status quo*' (1982, p. 180). The radicalism of the minority may turn out to be a temporary phenomenon, of course, reflecting the diverse social origins of the members of the present service class which has yet to mature as a class and reach a stable state of self-reproduction and closure to outsiders. Members of the service class who have been upwardly mobile from the working class are indeed considerably more likely to vote Labour than are those who have been born into this class (G. Marshall *et al.*, 1988, p. 240). The fact remains, however, that as yet a lot of people located towards the top of the class structure do not subscribe to parts of the dominant ideology.

In Goldthorpe's view, meritocracy is likely to be the major legitimatory ideology used by the service class to resist any move towards greater distributional equality, that is against any challenge from below. It now seems equally plausible, however, that meritocracy could have a legitimatory function within the context of any distributional conflict at the *top*, that is, between the relatively propertyless senior employee and the owners of private capital who draw *rentier* profits and who may have inherited wealth.

It is not clear where the service class would be expected to stand in relation to the dominant ideology, apart from managerialism (which includes meritocracy). As a whole, the modern service class is not the successor of the old dominant or upper class. Even class I on its own is too large and too heterogeneous with regard to occupation, income and wealth, economic and social influence. The traditional view of social dominance, which we followed, sees this as deriving from ownership of productive property. The declining importance of individual private property as a productive force was put forward as a reason to anticipate that the old dominant ideology might lose its hold on the higher social classes, resulting in a greater plurality of beliefs. It makes sense, however, to distinguish an elite stratum within the service class, which has a distinct relationship to property.

Research published in the 1980s regarding the ownership and control of Britain's top 250 companies in 1976 documents how the old system of personal possession has largely been superseded by the modern system of impersonal possession (Scott and Griff, 1984; Scott, 1986). Personal possession has not completely disappeared, of course, and the continuing centrality of entrepreneurial capital – both individually and family owned – in a small number of large companies is evident. Nevertheless, even in the dominant form of impersonal possession,

> enterprises are linked to one another through chains of control which do not originate in the personal wealth of individuals and families. Rather, these chains are never-ending circles of connection . . . In a system of impersonal possession, enterprises are subject to the constraints inherent in the network of connections between enterprises, which are created by interweaving chains of intercorporate relations.
>
> (Scott, 1986, p. 1)

This primary network of capital relations is supplemented by another form of intercorporate linkage, namely networks of interlocking directorships which are mainly centred on the major banks. These personal relations link different company boards, provide channels of information across the corporate world and link firms to the major capital brokers (Scott, 1986, p. 120).

We originally noted that many senior managers, even if they are propertyless at the outset, will have accumulated substantial personal wealth out of disposable income in the course of their careers and should be receptive to the full ideology of accumulation. Developments in the remuneration of top managers in the 1980s, which have included a dramatic increase in salaries, bonuses and other performance-related payments, and the spread of schemes for share ownership, indicate that this personal capital stake will have grown substantially. The assets of the wealthiest sections of the population include substantial investments in equities and land as well as home ownership (Stark, 1988, pp. 26–7), and top managers are presumably likely to follow the same pattern of asset holding.

In the light of both recent work on company shareholdings and modern theorizations of class (for example, Wright [1985] and Goldthorpe [1982]), another relationship between senior managers and capital ownership should now be emphasized. Top executives who are members of company boards are the direct agents of the owners of the capital stock and serve these owners, both legally and in practice. The older 'managerialist' argument, that the dispersed ownership of company shares gives top management the effective possession of capital, is qualified by the evidence of the concentration of impersonal possession. Even where there is sufficient dispersion that no single majority or minority controller emerges, the presence of constellations of interest means that several shareholders acting jointly are able, if they wish, to exercise control. On the other hand, boards are normally allowed considerable freedom to exercise the functions of ownership, and control is more constraining than directing, with the effect that directors are both the servants of, and participants in, impersonal possession. Moreover, directors will in turn exercise the ownership function directly, if their own organizations control stock in others. These dimensions of ownership are supplemented by a pattern of social relations which links board members into a community of business leaders.

The apparent separation of the ownership and management of productive capital which followed the growth of professionally managed companies does not, therefore, place all managers in the same position *vis-à-vis* ownership. I would expect a variety of interests among the managerial segment of the service class, which reflects the degree to which managers share in the different aspects of capital ownership. There are variations in the direct, personal stake people have by virtue of their own wealth, the extent to which they exercise the functions of ownership on behalf of impersonal capital, and the degree to which they are part of or in contact with the network of controllers. Those further down corporate hierarchies have at the same time less personal capital and more attenuated links with ownership and the network of business leaders than those at the top.

Definitions of elites vary widely, but most would include those who are economically dominant because they participate in the strategic control of productive capital, and their immediate families. In Britain, this means the directors of the large companies, societies and corporations which comprise the 'monopoly' sector of the economy, say the top 1,000 firms; and perhaps top executives just below the main board in the largest of these. It also includes the owners of large-scale entrepreneurial capital and real estate. Most individuals within the economic elite do themselves possess substantial personal wealth, whether inherited or accumulated in the course of a career, but their dominance is due in most cases to their control of impersonal property rather than their own personal capital. Those who wish to retain the notion of an upper class extend this central grouping to include an outer fringe of people of substantial personal property who have chosen occupations outside the business arena, and who are linked to the centre by kinship and shared social and educational backgrounds (Scott, 1982, pp. 124–5). They tend to be found in politics, the civil service and other influential high-status occupations. The modern upper class is largely hidden in the national random samples which underpin research into social stratification and social values; if this fairly narrow definition of the upper class is used, which comprises between 0.1 and 0.2 per cent of the population, then only between 5 and 10 members would appear in a random sample of 5,000 people (Scott, 1982, p. 124).

There is a long-established gap in the study of ideology in Britain, namely the dearth of direct information at the individual level about the values of the upper class. Recent surveys have failed to document these values, for the reason just noted. In fact, it is generally very difficult to persuade members of elite groups to participate in social research of any kind. However, two studies based on small samples of business leaders do provide some evidence of beliefs among this segment of the economic elite. Fidler (1981) was successful in interviewing 110 directors in the 1970s, mainly chief executives, and including a number who were retired. In the mid-1980s, I interviewed 48 directors on the boards of 12 major companies in the course of research on the role of boards of directors, and some of the findings are reported here. The interviews were with a mix of executive and non-executive directors, were semi-structured and lasted about an hour. In addition, respondents completed a short, standardized questionnaire. These interviews were designed to help close the gap noted above and throw some light on the attitudes, beliefs and values of the economic elite, as well as to provide information about boards.

These main board directors were unanimous in their belief that the role of a board is above all to serve the interests of shareholders. This belief is both a statement of fact, in the sense that this is what boards do, and of principle, in that this is what boards ought to do. A board serves the owners by maximizing the sustainable return on assets and providing a good flow of dividends, and, in so far as this can be influenced by what the company does, by maintaining or increasing the price of the shares. There were occasional criticisms of owners, mainly of the financial intermediary institutions, that their time frame was not the same as that needed to run a business and their concern with half-yearly results might lead to an undue emphasis on short-term profitability rather than longer-term success, but the right of the owners to make these demands on a company was not questioned. Faced with a choice between maintaining dividends or a course of action that might be in the longer-term interests of the company but would lower earnings in the short term, the common expectation was that a board would normally maintain dividends, unless it could get the endorsement of its larger shareholders. Other constituencies, including customers, employees and the community, have an interest in a company that a board needs to consider, nevertheless its primary frame of reference is profitability for the owners of its stock. The centrality of shareholders was also noted by Fidler (1981, pp. 117–43). Whereas public opinion contests the legitimacy of giving priority to shareholders, as was noted above, the leaders of large businesses do endorse the structure of economic rights inherent in capitalism.

Three of the companies were controlled by family interests that owned more than half the stock. Members of the families had seats on the board and were closely involved in the direction of the business. The others had more widely dispersed shareholdings. Directors of five companies believed that their ownership was so widely dispersed as to make them effectively immune to outside influence, unless a considerable number of institutions combined together. Outside the family-controlled firms, directors saw themselves as having great discretion to control their businesses. That is, they were participants in the use as well as the servants of impersonal possession.

In the non-family firms I tried to get an idea of how important the larger shareholders were felt to be as a constraint on management. Specific information was hard to come by, given the sensitivity of the topic and the fact that a limited number of directors on each board have dealings with shareholders (usually the chairman, chief executive, finance director and some non-executives). However, in general it appears that major initiatives that might affect shareholders' financial interests, notably capital restructuring, substantial acquisitions that depress earnings or dilute the equity, or a significant change of direction in the business, would be tested for their acceptability on occasion. All the companies maintained a regular dialogue with stockbrokers and the financial institutions, including both existing and potential shareholders, and boards used these occasions to inform the financial community in general terms how they saw the future direction of their businesses and to judge the reaction of these investors. Fidler also found a significant amount of communication between chairmen or chief executives and such outsiders (1981, pp. 139–43). On commercially sensitive issues and where giving information would breach prior disclosure regulations, the external, non-executive directors of these companies could have a major role within the board itself as surrogates for shareholder opinion. In one company the chairman had been appointed at the instigation of a group of financial institutions to reverse a long record of poor performance, but elsewhere the non-executives were independent of any shareholder. Many were chosen because of their stature in the City and Whitehall and because they were part of the network of social relations that makes up the community of business leaders, and thus they had a well-developed sense of how institutional shareholders thought. Moreover, both executive and non-executive directors saw the non-executives as having a special obligation to protect the interests of shareholders in general. The common view was that the board of a company whose business was performing well and was understood by the City would be left completely alone by its shareholders. Conversely, companies that performed badly over a period could expect institutional shareholders to sell their stock, which is the preferred course of action by the institutions in these circumstances. If the institutions were unwilling to take the loss, then they would first put informal pressure on the chairman, chief executive and leading non-executive directors to take remedial action, and in the last resort organize themselves to replace the board (a rare occurrence).

The evidence from the attitude surveys cited earlier is that most people are critical of the levels of remuneration received by those at the top of big businesses. Top salaries had begun to attract adverse publicity in the press and other media in the mid-1980s, and I asked directors what they thought about these levels of remuneration and whether they were justified. I met no one who thought it wrong for chief executives to be paid the sums reported in the press. The unanimous view was that these salaries represented both the market rate and the value of chief executives to their firms, that bonus elements which boosted already substantial basic salaries would reflect the contribution made by chief executives to profitability and that top UK salaries were generally rather low in comparison with those in Europe and the USA. As on the issue of shareholders' rights to profits, top businessmen have a distinct view of how the rewards of a successful business should be distributed.

The Thatcherite project of freeing the economy to allow markets to work more efficiently and breaking with welfare corporatism (which is discussed more fully in the next section) was broadly endorsed. All directors agreed that, on balance, Thatcherism was good for British business and a necessary development for capitalism to thrive. The previous combination of unsuccessful government intervention in the economy, attempts to engineer full employment, higher taxation, irresponsible use of their strength by trade unions, and inflation, was regarded as endangering accumulation and managerialism. A principled commitment to free markets was a major value. Half the sample also volunteered their concern that some of the social aspects and effects of Thatcherite policies were more extreme than they really cared for.

There was unanimous agreement that more employee participation would be desirable. There was an equally unanimous rejection of government making any type of participation statutory, in contrast to public opinion on this issue, and of employee representation on the main boards of companies (three directors said that employees might be able to contribute usefully on the boards of subsidiaries). Participation in the sense of better communications, the greater involvement of employees in their companies (including ownership of company shares), and in problem-solving arenas like quality circles was mainly what these directors wanted to see. Participation that involved joint decision-making or otherwise encroached on the right to manage was not favoured. The issue of board-level representation was still seen as a live one even after the disappearance of the Bullock proposals in Britain, because companies were aware of the possibility that the European Community might endorse some variant of the Vredling scheme for member states, and it was rejected most vehemently.

Meritocracy is undoubtedly a major component of these directors' beliefs. I asked them if they had any views about the proportionately large numbers of top businessmen who had been educated outside the state system in 'public' schools. Most expressed surprise that I should have this impression, since they themselves were not aware that this was the case (in fact, half the people I interviewed had been to public schools). While they believed that I might know things that they did not as the result of my travels around British board rooms, they also thought they saw a hidden agenda in my question, namely that I was referring to the role of the old-boy network and to the power of members of the establishment to advance the careers of their offspring. These assumptions were universally contested as explanations of what happened inside industry – although some people said acerbically that they did fit the merchant banks and other parts of the City – and the primacy of individual merit was continually emphasized. If the educational background was as I said, then this could be explained by the independent sector providing a higher quality of education and character formation which helped in later life. Four-fifths of those with children were presently educating at least one child privately, or had done so in the past, mainly because of these perceived advantages of independent schools. Social origins were deemed to be irrelevant within the world of business, since people could only get to the top if they had the appropriate talents. Moreover, with one exception, people thought the British class system had become more fluid over the previous thirty years, and most believed upwards social mobility was far easier for individuals with drive and ability.

In order to throw some light on the issue of inherited wealth, which meets with disapproval from a significant minority of the service class and seems difficult as well to square with meritocracy, I asked these directors whether they agreed that government ought to tax inherited wealth more heavily so as to reduce the taxes people had to pay on the income they earned in their jobs. This formulation was chosen to pose a trade-off between the interests of those who inherit private capital and those who depend on their ability to earn. Despite their commitment to meritocracy, however, seven out of ten directors disagreed with heavier inheritance taxes which would lower income tax. Regardless of their own social-class origins and the circumstances of their families of origin, which were diverse, the great majority of directors chose to support the traditional rights of those with property to pass their capital across the generations. We originally pointed to the tension between inheritance and achievement and suggested that business leaders might nevertheless adhere to both principles given the lack of consistency in the ideology itself. Other rights were also endorsed by these directors, including the rights of those who can afford it to buy education for their children and medical care which are not available to the less well-off, and the right to own more than one house when others have none (this last right to property often being contested by subordinate groups).

In sum, most of these directors of major British companies did subscribe to the bulk of the dominant ideology. They endorsed accumulation, including the full panoply of private property rights, and managerialism, with its notions of managerial rights and meritocratic individualism. But their commitment to market freedoms led them to question welfare corporatism, even though many were also somewhat uneasy about the social consequences of Thatcherism. Given the low level of popular support for many aspects of the dominant ideology, these findings indicate that the values of the business elite differ quite substantially from those of the public at large, including much of the service class. In addition, the business elite clearly differs from the rest of the service class in the control it has of impersonal capital, and in its integration into the intercorporate networks of capital relations and social relations within the community of business leaders.

Finally, there is new evidence from the national surveys on another important aspect of service-class culture. This is the area of personal morality. We suggested in 1980 that the depersonalization of productive property in the contemporary economy meant that the cultural values which had promoted the integrity of bourgeois and aristocratic families, and thus the transmission of capital across generations, would have less economic relevance. Therefore one would anticipate a fragmentation of the traditional personal–familial morality which was largely Christian in origin and a pluralization of life-worlds. Evidence of this development was found mainly in the fact of changing institutional practices regarding divorce and remarriage, abortion, homosexuality, and the writings of those interested in the sociology of religion, rather than in information about individuals' attitudes and beliefs. Recent investigations now show that attitudes and beliefs are indeed congruent with the earlier evidence and, moreover, that traditional personal morality is least strong at the top of the social hierarchy.

The European Values Study finds a dimension of moral outlook that ranges along a continuum from 'strict' to 'liberal' or 'permissive'. In the area of personal and sexual morality, the upper middle class is more permissive than the lower middle or working class on divorce, abortion, homosexuality and prostitution (Phillips and Harding, 1985). These class categories are derived from market research classifications that do not match exactly the Goldthorpe scales. *British Social Attitudes* finds that higher social class and a higher educational level are associated with support for the 'permissive' options on items relating to pre- and extra-marital sexual relations, homosexuality, pornography (Harding, 1988). Libertarianism in this area is also associated with a libertarian civic culture – which Heath and Topf call a political culture – regarding issues of law and order, dutifulness and discipline, civil rights and traditional morality, which marks off predominantly working-class authoritarians from a somewhat more libertarian service class (Heath and Topf, 1987; Harding, 1988).

This last finding, that traditional morality in personal and familial matters and a traditional-authoritarian civic culture relate to form a fairly coherent and distinct set of beliefs, is a significant feature of recent empirical research (e.g. Himmelweit *et al.*, 1985, pp. 138–59). It extends analysis away from the customary interest in issues of work, class and power, towards a more complete description of values. Moral traditionalism, ranging from authoritarian to libertarian positions, is different from economic and social egalitarianism, and cuts across this. One result is a different class distribution of the two dimensions; another is that radical egalitarians may be moral traditionalists while economic and social conservatives may be libertarians.

Thatcherism

A notable feature of the 1980s was the movement for ideological renewal, often labelled 'Thatcherism'. This development must be addressed, first because Thatcherism seems to be associated with a redefinition of the dominant ideology, and secondly because a number of commentators have ascribed effects to it that seem to challenge the arguments about the ineffectiveness of ideology.

At the level of institutional practices, the dominant ideology has now been made more coherent by stripping the values of early capitalism of some of those later accretions which blurred, even contradicted the pristine philosophy. The contradictions we noted in 1980 have been attenuated by various changes in public policy. These include: the easing of many restrictions on the use and transfer of property; the freeing-up of markets by the withdrawal of the state from the economy and the use of state power to weaken producer cartels, particularly trade unions, in the labour market; the transfer of publicly held assets to private hands; the endorsement of greater material inequality as reflecting the different market capacities of individuals; the end of the commitment to full employment as the major goal of economic management; and the reduced scope of public welfare, while retaining a basic floor of rights. The social basis of this neo-classical, economic liberalism in the entrepreneurial middle class of small proprietors, and the part played by grass-roots activists in maintaining it as a political force within the Conservative Party during this party's so-called 'corporatist' era, have been well documented (Gamble, 1974; Scase and Goffee, 1982).

Political commentators have claimed that the new political programme of the 1980s marked a radical break with a postwar political consensus based on collectivism (e.g. Jenkins, 1987), or, as some Conservative politicians would have it, on socialism (Rentoul, 1989, pp. 2–3). This is greatly to overstate the case, however. On the one hand, changes in government policy have expressed a long-standing and significant strand of thinking within the Conservative Party. On the other, the view that the postwar era through to 1979 was characterized by a political consensus of welfare corporatism is

mistaken. Belief in the original postwar settlement of full employment and extensive tax-based welfare payments had greatly
weakened among Conservative politicians by the end of the 1950s,
and the view that these social rights were incompatible with economic
imperatives was widespread, but political realities meant such dissent
could rarely be voiced publicly (Middlemas, 1986; Schwarz, 1987).
A similar retreat from the postwar consensus was to be found among
other state institutions, notably the Treasury and the Bank of
England. While Heath managed to win limited Conservative
parliamentary support for a qualitatively different version of the
settlement in the 1960s, this proved to be fragile (Schwarz, 1987).
Moreover, Thatcherism is largely consistent with the dominant
ideology. The principles of accumulation, managerialism and
individualism have been emphasized. The state is still presented as
being neutral between interests; indeed, the claim is that the state has
been restored to neutrality after the previous tilt to labour. The view
that social rights should now be restricted to a minimum floor of
rights and that market mechanisms are always to be preferred to
administrative interventions is, however, a more significant
deviation.

   With the benefit of hindsight, it is clear that the welfare consensus
had been more strongly contested among the institutions that
represented dominant interests. While we stressed its contradictory
relationship to the other ideological principles, I believe we should
have examined more carefully the claim that the postwar settlement
was an ideological mystification of the role of the state in promoting
capitalism that was fully endorsed by the governmental and business
elites. Whatever its popular support, many people at the top were far
more disenchanted with it than sociologists realized at the time. Its
rise to prominence in the political culture was in part a product of
popular struggles to extend social citizenship rights, so we should
have appreciated the likely implications for dominant beliefs of what
T. H. Marshall (1950) had already shown: whereas the prior extension
of civil and political citizenship rights had not undermined capitalism
and had advanced 'class abatement', the social citizenship of welfare
threatened to undermine the principles on which the economy was
based.

   Behind the Thatcherite project is the endorsement of a more
fundamental philosophical position. This asserts the moral superiority
of the independence of individuals from reliance on others, and
contains the judgement that there is a widespread popular preference
for such independence. This has justified the strengthening of the

market freedoms advocated by economic liberals, because these are believed to be based on, and to preserve, individual freedom. The same emphasis on the primacy of individual rights is to be found in a radical interpretation of the Christian moral tradition which largely ignores communality or social obligation (Rentoul, 1989, p. 144). Conservative politicians are given to talking as though Thatcherism has revolutionized popular perceptions of the individual (Rentoul, 1989, pp. 1–10). But there is no evidence that this basic value was ever overwhelmed by the values of collectivism, nor that the choice of collective means to advance individual interests is incompatible with it. On the other hand, Thatcherism also gives weight to moral traditionalism, that is to authoritarian civic values and conventional morality, alongside its commitment to personal freedom. This combination, of liberal market freedoms in economic life and illiberal restrictions on personal and civil freedoms in the social and political realms, has frequently been remarked (Gray, 1986, p. 42; Hall, 1988, pp. 85–6). It resembles the capitalist ideology of mid-nineteenth-century Britain.

Hall asserts that Thatcherism has been remarkably effective in establishing ideological dominance over the people of Britain and has won support across all social classes (1988, pp. 6–7). Electoral victories have followed from this capture of the ideological high ground. Hall's description of this hegemonic project and its success, albeit qualified by his insistence that hegeomony is not complete, is in effect a restatement of a dominant ideology thesis. Unfortunately, like most other subscribers to the thesis, he concentrates on content analysis of the ideological message without any informed investigation of how this message is received, and thus falls into the trap of uncritically attributing effects to ideologies. The evidence cited above on attitudes and values in the 1980s, which is reinforced by other findings from these same sources, opinion polls and in-depth interviews, that most people still subscribe to the welfare compromise and a 'dependency' culture, shows how restricted a purchase Thatcherism has on the lower classes and that it is contested by significant numbers even among the service class. Analyses of the relevant data by Jowell and Topf (1988), Crewe (1989) and Rentoul (1989) – who also uses material from open-ended interviews with a small sample of ex-Labour voters – indicate that most government policies embodying the values of the revived 'enterprise' culture have little popular support, apart from some of the legal changes to the framework of industrial relations and the conduct of trade unions and the sale of publicly owned housing to private individuals at discounted prices. There is no evidence either of a real change in employees' attitudes and values at the workplace, despite the publicity given to the 'new realism' in industrial relations (Kelly and Kelly, 1991).

There is a well-established view that nationalism is an important component of the dominant ideology and has the negative function of preventing the clear expression of radical beliefs even if it does not positively commit people to endorse dominant values (Bottomore, 1980). A recent examination of the hold that the British monarchy has on the popular imagination sees monarchy and nationalism as indissolubly linked, with the Crown being deliberately promoted as a symbol of British national unity in the nineteenth century in order to weaken internal divisions based on class and the separate nationalisms of the component nations (Nairn, 1988). An ideology of national unity focused on the Crown conceals the domination of an upper class composed of the hereditary, landed elite and the controllers of financial and commercial capital (1988, pp. 235–45). Nairn believes that nationalism sponsored from above and infused with monarchism works against the formulation and acceptance of popular democratic ideologies, let alone ideologies of radical class action, unlike the nationalism from below found in other societies (1988, pp. 133–7; 386–91). Against this line of analysis, our argument is that nationalism has been a counter-ideology in opposition to dominant values on occasion and therefore the claim for its inclusion in the dominant ideology is far from clear-cut (Abercrombie, Hill and Turner, 1983). Nevertheless, the Thatcher era has indeed brought nationalism to the forefront in a way which seems to support those who concentrate on its ideological potential. In particular, the way in which Thatcherism articulated nationalistic sentiments during and after the Falklands' campaign was widely seen at the time to be a major explanation of the sudden and dramatic revival in the political fortune of the Conservative Party during 1982, which culminated in electoral victory in 1983. This was apparently a clear example of ideology having the most concrete of effects.

Considerable controversy now exists among students of political behaviour as to the real effect of the Falklands in 1982–3, and the estimates of the effect have been downgraded progressively. Crewe (1985) and Dunleavy and Husbands (1985) regarded the Falklands' campaign as transforming popular support for the Conservative government, as measured by public opinion polls, and the latter estimate that it produced a long-term benefit of over 16 percentage points through to the election of June 1983 (1985, pp. 153–4).

Subsequent investigators have produced considerably lower estimates. Clarke *et al.* (1986) find a sharp jump in popularity which persisted through to April 1983, by which time the Falklands had produced a shift to the Conservatives in excess of 7 percentage points. Norpoth (1987) reports a gradual rise in support which tapered off slowly to leave a Falklands' factor worth about 6 points in June 1983. Sanders *et al.* (1987) calculate that the maximum effect was just under 3 points, that it lasted for only three months and disappeared in August 1982, and that the Falklands were irrelevant to the 1983 election. They claim support from Heath *et al.*'s survey-based study of the 1983 election, which concluded that the Falklands were of limited importance (1985, p. 162). The variation among the estimates reflects mainly the way the models are specified, notably which independent economic and political event variables are included. Sanders *et al.* claim that the addition of a wider range of macro-economic variables than are used in the other investigations, which jointly determine what they call 'personal economic expectations', best explains the various movements in Conservative popularity between 1979 and 1983. The government's sudden jump in the polls in Spring 1982 should be attributed to the Budget of that year and the effects this had on voters' actual and anticipated prosperity, rather than the Falklands' issue.

The linkage between ideologies, popular beliefs and political behaviour is weak, except among the core partisan supporters of the major political parties. Whether one is talking about the triumph of the values of economic liberalism or the power of nationalistic sentiments, there were few signs of changing public attitudes in the 1980s to suggest that Thatcherism was successful in its programme of cultural engineering. Nor do the electoral successes of the Conservative Party indicate widespread endorsement of its pro-gramme, given that its share of the popular vote was only 44 per cent in 1979 and declined to just over 42 per cent in 1983 and 1987, all of which were poor results when compared with previous Conservative victories. These results are further diminished when placed in the context of the long-term occupational shift towards a more 'middle-class' electorate which has increased the proportion of likely Conservative voters. The conventional political wisdom that non-ideological variables are of major importance for non-partisans is more plausible than ideological hegemony. In particular, changes in the material welfare of the majority of the electorate remain a major determinant of voting. Other purely political factors, such as the growth of new parties which split the non-Conservative vote and the

internal divisions within the Labour Party in the mid–1980s, also had
their impact on political behaviour.

Material interests

The materialistic cast of our opposition to a misplaced emphasis on
the ideological and cultural realms came across most strongly in the
analysis of the dull compulsion of economic relations. But other
reasons for the relative stability of modern capitalist society were also
advanced. One was the importance of economic interest. We
suggested, albeit briefly, that an appraisal of the material benefits of
capitalism might well lead self-interested individuals to tolerate this
form of economic organization, since, despite its distributional
inequalities, it provides a better stream of rewards for most people in
the advanced capitalist world than other existing systems. People are
likely to have an interest in its continuation, even though they may
see serious faults in the social order that has been built on this
economic base and, to judge from the research done in the 1980s,
consider egalitarian reform of the social and economic structure to be
desirable. The point about the benefits of capitalism is obvious,
although it has been disputed by some critics of the system.

Renewed interest in rational choice models of human action has
given an impetus to this style of explanation of social behaviour in
terms of interests. This assumes the essentially rational pursuit of
valued ends by individuals, with these ends normally being defined
as access to resources. Coram (1987) has shown theoretically that
rational behaviour is on its own sufficient to explain the reproduction
of capitalism over time, as noted above. Further, he provides a game-
theoretical model of our more empirically based view that ideology
and values are unimportant for the acquiescence of subordinates. The
claim of advocates of ideological hegemony is that, if the non-owners
of the means of production were properly aware of their real interests,
they would prefer a different economic and social structure and would
realize that they share a common interest with other non-owners in
creating this preferred state. Even if one starts with the most favourable
assumptions, first that there are no social mechanisms distorting
preference or blocking rationality, i.e. that dominant values or
ideology are not hegemonic and have no effects on subordinates'
consciousness, and second that subordinates have a clear interest in
bringing about a non-capitalist society, Coram suggests that it would
still not be rational for any individual to join in the destruction of

capitalism. His argument, following Przeworski, is that the costs of the transition from capitalism to socialism, resulting from disruption to production and investment strikes, look to be so high that self-interested individuals would choose to combine together to improve their material conditions within capitalism rather than to replace it. It therefore seems reasonable in my opinion to draw the following conclusion: when there is compulsion to work and it is not rational to join a revolutionary combination, then participation in the existing system while trying to change its current distribution of benefits is indeed the more rational strategy for subordinates.

The existence of personal stakes in the rising material prosperity which contemporary capitalism provides has regularly been cited in academic and political accounts of what are believed to be significant shifts in the values of the British working class. The embourgeoise-ment thesis of the late 1950s and early 1960s, that affluent sections of the working class were losing their communal, collectivist and radical culture as the result of greater prosperity, and tending to adopt middle-class life-styles which promoted an individualistic, privatized outlook and support for the Conservative Party, was shown to be misconceived twenty years ago. Affluent workers had not absorbed middle-class life-styles and values. Nor were the stereotypes of traditional workers accurate, since they failed to recognize that elements of individualism, instrumentalism and privatism were always to be found in working-class culture. Embourgeoisement reappeared as an issue in the 1980s, with Conservative politicians claiming that the considerable extension of home and share owner-ship gave the mass of the population a new stake in private property. The real interests of a property-owning democracy and not ideo-logical distortion meant people should endorse the individual self-interest and free-market values that underpin capitalist society. The view of certain political commentators that new sectoral cleavages were superseding class in the determination of political behaviour, notably that the ownership of property would predispose working-class voters towards the Conservative Party, echoed the claims of the politicians.

Even the second time around embourgeoisement remains mis-conceived, both empirically and theoretically. The evidence that working-class values are ' stable and that many middle-class individuals are more collectivist and radical than was once believed, has been discussed. It is worth noting here that, while instrumental-ism is an important dimension of values, there is also a strand of altruism and principled commitment in popular culture (Rentoul,

1989). In the analysis of their survey data, moreover, G. Marshall *et al.* have found that the ownership of property makes little difference to voting intention, and class still remains far and away the most powerful explanatory variable (1988, pp. 248–54).

The theoretical issue relates to self-interest. Are individual interests necessarily better served by individual rather than collective strategies for gaining command over resources? Are free markets always to be preferred to non-markets or fettered markets? Collective and market-restricting solutions are optimal in a number of cases. British experience shows that monopsony provides cheaper access to resources, both through scale economies and because a monopoly purchaser (e.g. the state) representing individuals collectively is able to exploit the sellers of goods and services. The National Health Service is an example of collective provision being cheaper than private, partly as a result of its ability to contain costs including salaries. Collective provision is also rational for individuals when an adequate private provision cannot be completely guaranteed, particularly in the long term and when risks are unpredictable. This is the case, for example, with private provision for health, unemploy-ment and retirement. Collective strategies that restrict market freedoms also benefit the majority who cannot succeed in the competition among individuals for access to scarce resources, where by definition only a minority can win. Trade unions, for example, have often been effective in raising the wages of their members above what the majority might have achieved as individuals. Finally, a major impediment to rational and effective collective solutions is the familiar problem of free riders. But this problem, of course, is one that the state as the ultimate repository of legitimate coercion is uniquely capable of solving.

To emphasize materialism is not to endorse the view that rising prosperity has necessary long-term consequences for party political partisanship and identification with the dominant ideology. It does, however, suggest some acceptance of an economic and social system which delivers material benefits, and the appropriateness of distri-butional struggle. The absence of a real alternative contributes to acceptance, and in 1980 we suggested that the manifest inadequacies of the Soviet Union and other state-socialist societies meant socialism was a powerful negative example. The future development of socialism in the era of economic restructuring and political reform raises intriguing possibilities in this regard. Some see in these events the triumph of liberal values, even leading perhaps to the transition from socialism to capitalism, but other outcomes are possible.

Should any of the present socialist societies attain levels of efficiency comparable to capitalism and match its consumption advantages, while retaining a significant degree of social ownership, developing existing economic citizenship rights of employees in the enterprise and continuing to provide many services on a public, non-market basis, then socialist economic organization might come to be viewed in a different light in the West in future. This is, of course, highly speculative and the outcome of reform remains uncertain. Nevertheless, given the absence of any moral commitment to capitalism, disenchantment with the way profits are distributed under private ownership, and the absence of effective participation in power at work in Britain, it is not totally fanciful to suggest that a new model of socialism might have a wider appeal than the old.

Citizenship

Popular consent and the stability of capitalist society have also been explained in political terms, with reference to the notion of citizenship, and analysis of this phenomenon has enjoyed a new currency in recent years (Turner, 1986; Hindess, 1987; Mann, 1987; Barbalet, 1988). Citizenship is the participation in the national community of all members on an equal basis and as an absolute right. T. H. Marshall (1950; 1972) propounded the familiar and now widely accepted categorization of citizenship rights into their civil, political and social forms. He also noted the importance of another set of rights to industrial citizenship, which he described as 'secondary' in the sense that they derived from trade unions collectively exercising the individual civil rights of their members. He did not, however, present a fully developed notion of economic citizenship, in which employees possess rights to participate in economic power analogous to the rights of political citizenship. All these citizenship rights have an implicit political dimension, since it appears to be the state which ultimately guarantees and enforces rights. While there may be some difference of opinion as to their origin, for example, whether they are mainly the outcome of popular struggle (Turner, 1986) or ruling-class strategies (Mann, 1987), there is no disagreement about the political character of rights. Citizenship thus appears to have implications for the analysis of social order and reproduction. Indeed, Turner has suggested that the materialism of our original joint work, which I have reaffirmed and elaborated in this chapter, should be supplemented by a greater recognition of this political dimension (1986, pp. xi–xii).

Analysis of the claims of those who take citizenship seriously as an explanation of social order and the stability of capitalist society reveals three ways in which these rights are supposed to work. First, access to full citizenship rights promotes moral cohesion and the sense of communal solidarity. This means that citizenship has a normative or ideological force (Lockwood, 1974). T. H. Marshall was explicit that the sense of community was based on an 'autonomous ethical system' (1972, p. 109) and 'loyalty to a civilization which is a common possession' (1950, p. 41), which indicates the role he gave to normative integration into a common culture. In a variant of this perspective, Bendix (1964, p. 73) suggested that the historical demand of the British working class for political rights contributed to the decline of oppositional socialist ideology, because the desire for inclusion in the political community of the nation led to the integration of subordinates into an existing political culture which supported capitalism. Second, political and social rights, and the secondary system of industrial citizenship, ameliorate the inequalities and antagonisms characteristic of a capitalist economy (Lockwood, 1974; T. H. Marshall, 1950). An important aspect of this is that citizenship may thereby contribute to the flow of material rewards to subordinates, via the welfare system and collective bargaining. Third, the civil and political rights of citizenship channel conflicts into agreed political processes, and when subordinate groups try to advance their interests they do so by following the legal and political rules of the game (Dahrendorf, 1959; Mann, 1987).

But the role of citizenship in the maintenance of social order and the stable reproduction of capitalism is by no means clear-cut. There is a considerable body of theory and evidence that points to the contradictory nature of citizenship and to outcomes that exacerbate class antagonisms and social disorder and destabilize the economy. T. H. Marshall (1950) saw a contradiction between the principles of citizenship and class, which the development of political and social rights would intensify. Participation in political power highlights the absence of an equivalent right to participate in economic power, and one might add that industrial citizenship rights have indeed failed to provide effective economic citizenship. Social rights to full employment and welfare also cut across the market principles of capitalism and the material inequalities that these generate. Thus the politics of equality clash with the economics of inequality. Marshall himself was sceptical that the stability of a system containing this contradiction would be sustainable in the long run. However, he seems to have anticipated a further extension of citizenship rights leading to a qualitatively different type of society, and not the curtailment of social and industrial rights that eventually transpired in the political programme of Thatcherism.

Diagnoses of the ills of the British political economy common in the late 1970s also referred, explicitly or implicitly, to the contradictions of citizenship. Goldthorpe (1978) cited citizenship as a cause of the chaotic industrial relations and wage inflation that destabilized the British economy. Employees struggled to expand their citizenship rights against the rights of capital in the sphere of production, seeking more influence at work and higher pay. Meanwhile, the successful institutionalization of political and social rights in the state meant that government appeared no longer to have the option of using unemployment to weaken employees in their dealings with employers. The view found widely among politicians and academic commentators, that governments had become 'overloaded' in many Western democracies, implicitly put part of the blame on citizenship. Citizens came to have excessive expectations of government, demanding levels of public expenditure that the economy was unable to finance and other taxpayers were anyway unwilling to pay for, and social policies that threatened the organization of the economy. The fact of universal political rights obliged government to try to respond to popular demands, yet it was unable to do so because of economic constraints and because many demands came from different groups and were contradictory. Brittan (1975), for example, argued that representative democracy – i.e. political citizenship – contained the seeds of its own collapse, first because it generated excessive expectations, secondly because of the disruptive effects of interest-group competition in the market-place. He was particularly concerned with the ability of one interest group, the trade union movement, to use the political process to advance the interests of employees in the market-place at the cost of the good of the economy as a whole. Marxists writing within the perspective of the fiscal crisis of the state pointed to similar problems of overload, in this case arising out of the fact that the state served the interests of capital but had also to come to terms with political citizenship. Fiscal crises arose because both capital and the working class put pressure on government to expand expenditures in ways that benefited themselves but were unwilling to pay for these out of their own taxes. The balance of class forces on the state meant that government was unable to force the costs on to one party (Gough, 1979, ch. 7).

In an international comparison of the effects of citizenship on the organized expression of conflict, Mann (1987) has shown how much variation there is among societies. Social order and system stability may be achieved where citizenship rights are relatively under-developed, while elsewhere even quite extensive rights may prove considerably less effective. In the USA, for example, there was an early extension of civil and political citizenship rights but the third stage, the social rights of the welfare state, was never realized. Nor, one might add, have the rights of industrial citizenship been effective for the majority of employees, since trade unionism has never covered more than a limited section of the labour force. Yet class movements have been insignificant in the USA and the constituent components of classes have historically acted as interest groups which fight for their own specific aims according to the legal and political rules of the game. This contrasts with Britain, where broader class movements have always existed alongside interest associations. According to Mann, this is because political citizenship itself was initially a product of class struggle, dissident groups were regularly excluded at least in part from the state at the moment of their emergence, and socialism gained a foothold and remained an attractive ideology in coexistence with liberalism. The subsequent growth of social citizenship did not change this pattern of social struggle by a mixture of interest groups and class movements, although the latter are mainly reformist and constitutionalist. Comparative evidence reinforces the argument that one should not attribute general effects to citizenship rights.

It is also germane to ask whether the existence of formal rights of citizenship has led to an exaggeration of their substance, and even to question the extent of formal rights. It has already been noted that government chose in the 1980s to restrict social and industrial citizenship rights by reducing the scope of welfare, renouncing the official commitment of previous postwar administrations to attempt to maintain full employment, and changing the legislative framework of employment relations with the intention of weakening trade unions in their dealings with employers. The issue of industrial citizenship rights is particularly relevant. A few of the changes imposed by government on the way unions conduct industrial disputes, notably their obligation to ballot members prior to taking action against employers, increased the powers of members to determine their own actions and so extended the substance of citizenship. But the capability of employees organized collectively in trade unions to use their formal rights of industrial citizenship for substantive gains was eroded. The most noticeable effects have been inside workplaces, where managers have successfully rolled back their employees' previous gains in non-wage areas and reasserted their own power and prerogative over all aspects of internal organization. This has been a major curtailment of what was in any case a limited industrial citizenship. Nevertheless, the growth of the British economy and the buoyancy of corporate profitability after 1982 ensured that those people who were in work enjoyed rising real earnings for most of the decade, with the result that trade union weakness did not show as a reduced flow of material rewards to employees. Moreover, government would seem to have violated the conventions of the International Labour Organization (ILO) on a number of occasions and so to have encroached on internationally recognized formal rights. The fundamental right of freedom of association and organization appears to have been infringed by legislation that interferes with the internal administration of trade unions (Undy and Martin, 1984, p. 218) and by the banning of union membership at the governmental organization GCHQ. Other apparent breaches of ILO conventions include the government's legislation to remove the negotiating rights of teachers' trade unions in 1987 and its unilateral derogation of joint committees (i.e. the abolition of several Wages Councils). The decline of effective industrial citizenship is not the result of Thatcherism alone; an existing but hitherto largely unremarked limitation on industrial citizenship came to prominence in the 1980s, when some employers chose to circumvent the collective exercise of rights by sacking strikers and hiring a new labour force. This choice is not available in many other advanced capitalist economies where the rights of employees are protected more assiduously.

Formal and substantive rights may diverge even in the heartland of traditional citizenship, namely political participation. If citizenship has the role attributed to it, then presumably citizens should feel that they do participate in the national community, that their participation can have some effect and that the political process is fair. It is therefore pertinent to note that recent British survey data show a considerable division of popular opinion on the issue of the real effectiveness of political participation. On the one hand, half of G. Marshall *et al.*'s sample agreed that there was a dominant class controlling both the economy *and* the polity to the exclusion of the lower class. Among those who disagreed, approximately 28 per cent of the sample mentioned the extension of political democracy, 9 per cent industrial citizenship and 2 per cent citizenship in the form of the welfare state as one of their reasons for believing that this situation no longer held (proportions calculated from the data presented in G. Marshall *et al.*, 1988, p. 144, Table 6.2). It is also apparent that many people are

cynical about politicians and the responsiveness of the political
process to popular demands (G. Marshall *et al.*, 1988, pp. 161–4;
Heath and Topf, 1987). On the other hand, the evidence also indicates
that people seem more willing now to try to influence Parliament than
they were in the 1950s and are more likely to believe that they might
have an influence: *British Social Attitudes* finds that about half the
population now think they could have some influence on the political
process, by contacting the media or their own MP (Heath and Topf,
1987). Finally, the frequently voiced objection to the British electoral
system, that it leads to the return of governments with substantial
parliamentary majorities which are elected by a minority of voters,
also reduces the effectiveness of political rights. This is most
obviously the case in Scotland, where the great mass of citizens
consistently voted for different governments and policies than they
ended up with during the 1980s. Citizenship in these circumstances
seems to do little to promote the appropriate sense of national
(presumably British) communal solidarity and intensifies a more
local, Scottish communality.

Conclusion

There is indeed still a dominant ideology, and this is not a figment of
the sociological imagination. Those who control capital, who are
dominant in the sense that they direct the leading productive force
and so have real economic power, subscribe to the ideology in most
of its aspects. The shift in the political philosophy of the Conservative
Party and its explicit glorification of capitalist values suggest that the
ideology is dominant in another sense, because more than a decade of
Conservative government seems to have entrenched it even more
firmly in institutions of the state. If the large section of the media
industry which has extolled Thatcherism is added, dominance is
almost complete. Yet the hold of this ideology on the population at
large seems no better assured now than it did ten and more years ago.
The extent of the dissent from key features of the dominant ideology
revealed by modern research is noteworthy and, in the case of the
service class, perhaps even surprising.

One may speculate that dissent could grow. Most people do not
wish to replace capitalism as such, and there are good theoretical
reasons for believing that it would not be rational to do so, but a
modification of the British variant to meet popular interests more
fully may well become part of their agenda. People want greater

access to decision-making in the economy and a greater share of the profits. Accumulation which leads to reinvestment and benefits everyone who works in a company is widely held to be more legitimate than the distribution of surpluses to sectional interests. At the same time, certain groups, notably those with higher education, display a greater willingness and self-confidence to use political citizenship to influence government. There would appear to be an unmet aspiration to have more control over the institutions that have power over people's lives, and to do so in ways that share the benefits more widely.

Notes

1 The proportions are 63 per cent of the salariat, 51 per cent of routine non-manual employees and 52 per cent of the manual working class. I am indebted to Sharon Witherspoon of Social and Community Planning Research for providing me with this more detailed breakdown of the 1986 survey data than is reported in Jowell *et al.* (1987), who restrict their analysis of social-class differences to the issue of conflict. This is also the source of tables 1 and 2 below. For economy of presentation, I have not included the class categories 'petty bourgeoisie' and 'manual foremen', and those who have never had a job.

2 There are, however, some interesting differences on investment and workforce benefits: see Table 1.

Table 1 Where should the profit go?

	salariat (n=336)		routine non-manual (n=329)		manual (n=531)	
	%	%	%	%	%	%
Investment:						
New machinery	38		33		26	
Training	8	65	12	54	13	47
Research	19		9		8	
Workforce benefits:						
Pay rise	12		22		27	
Better conditions	6	18	6	28	8	35
Customer benefit:						
Lower prices	12		14		12	
Shareholders/managers:						
Increased dividends and top management bonuses	4		4		4	
D.K./N.A.	2		1		3	

(Totals do not equal 100 due to rounding.)

Question: Suppose a big British firm made a large profit in a particular year, which one of these things do you think *should* be its first priority?

3   The distribution of responses is given in Table 2.

Table 2   Should government give workers more say?

	salariat (n=298) % %	routine non-manual (n=293) % %	manual (n=439) % %
Definitely should	20 ⎫	22 ⎫	37 ⎫
	⎬ 76	⎬ 77	⎬ 85
Probably should	56 ⎭	55 ⎭	48 ⎭
Should not	23	21	14
D.K./N.A.	1	1	1

(Totals do not equal 100 due to rounding.)

Question: Do you think the government should give workers more say in running the places where they work?

Bibliography

Abercrombie, N. (1980), *Class, Structure and Knowledge: Problems in the Sociology of Knowledge* (Oxford: Blackwell).

Abercrombie, N., Hill, S. and Turner, B. S. (1980), *The Dominant Ideology Thesis* (London: Allen & Unwin).

Abercrombie, N., Hill, S. and Turner, B. S. (1983), 'Determinacy and indeterminacy in the theory of ideology', *New Left Review*, no. 142, pp. 55–66.

Abercrombie, N., Hill, S. and Turner, B. S. (1986), *Sovereign Individuals of Capitalism* (London: Allen & Unwin).

Abercrombie, N. and Warde, A. with Soothill, K., Urry, J. and Walby, S. (1988), *Contemporary British Society* (Cambridge: Polity).

Abrams, M., Gerard, D. and Timms, N. (eds) (1985), *Values and Social Change in Britain* (London: Macmillan).

Althusser, L. (1971), *Lenin and Philosophy and Other Essays* (London: New Left Books).

Barbalet, J. M. (1988), *Citizenship* (Milton Keynes: Open University Press).

Bendix, R. (1964), *Work and Authority in Industry* (Berkeley, Calif.: University of California Press).

Bottomore, T. (1980), 'Foreword' to N. Abercrombie, S. Hill and B. S. Turner, *The Dominant Ideology Thesis* (London: Allen & Unwin).

Brittan, S. (1975), 'The economic contradictions of democracy', *British Journal of Political Science*, vol. 5, no. 1, pp. 129–59.

Clarke, H. D., Stewart, M. C. and Zuk, G. (1986), 'Politics, economics and party popularity in Britain, 1979–83', *Electoral Studies*, vol. 5, no. 2, pp. 123–41.

Collins, M. (1987), 'Business and industry', in R. Jowell, S. Witherspoon and L. Brook (eds), *British Social Attitudes: the 1987 Report* (Aldershot: Gower), pp. 29–44.

Coram, B. T. (1987), 'The tough test and the thin theory: the minimal conditions for capitalism to exist', *British Journal of Sociology*, vol. 38, no. 4, pp. 464–81.

Crewe, I. (1985), 'How to win a landslide without really trying: why the Conservatives won in 1983', in A. Ranney (ed.), *Britain at the Polls, 1983* (Durham, NC: American Enterprise Institute and Duke University Press), pp. 155–96.

Crewe, I. (1989), 'Has the electorate become Thatcherite?', in R. Skidelsky (ed.), *Thatcherism* (London: Chatto), pp. 25–49.

Dahrendorf, R. (1959), *Class and Class Conflict in Industrial Society* (London: Routledge).

Dunleavy, P. and Husbands, C. T. (1985), *British Democracy at the Crossroads: Voting and Party Competition in the 1980s* (London: Allen & Unwin).

Fidler, J. (1981), *The British Business Elite: Its Attitudes to Class, Status and Power* (London: Routledge).

Gamble, A. (1974), *The Conservative Nation* (London: Routledge).

Goldthorpe, J. (1978), 'The current inflation: towards a sociological account', in F. Hirsch and J. Goldthorpe (eds), *The Political Economy of Inflation* (London: Martin Robertson), pp. 186–214.

Goldthorpe, J. (1982), 'On the service class, its formation and future', in A. Giddens and G. Mackenzie (eds), *Social Class and the Division of Labour* (Cambridge: Cambridge University Press), pp. 162–85.

Gough, I. (1979), *The Political Economy of the Welfare State* (London: Macmillan).

Gray, J. (1986), *Liberalism* (Milton Keynes: Open University Press).

Hall, S. (1988), *The Hard Road to Renewal: Thatcherism and the Crisis of the Left* (London: Verso).

Harding, S. (1988), 'Trends in permissiveness', in R. Jowell, S. Witherspoon and L. Brook (eds), *British Social Attitudes: the 5th Report* (Aldershot: Gower), pp. 35–51.

Heath, A., Jowell, R. and Curtice, J. (1985), *How Britain Votes* (Oxford: Oxford University Press).

Heath, A. and Topf, R. (1987), 'Political culture', in R. Jowell, S. Witherspoon and L. Brook (eds), *British Social Attitudes: the 1987 Report* (Aldershot: Gower), pp. 51–67.

Himmelweit, H., Humphreys, P. and Jaeger, M. (1985), *How Voters Decide* (rev. edn) (Milton Keynes: Open University Press).

Hindess, B. (1987), *Freedom, Equality and the Market* (London: Tavistock).

Jenkins, P. (1987), *Mrs Thatcher's Revolution: The Ending of the Socialist Era* (London: Cape).

Jowell, R., Witherspoon, S. and Brook, L. (eds) (1987), *British Social Attitudes: the 1987 Report* (Aldershot: Gower).

Jowell, R. and Topf, R. (1988), 'Trust in the establishment', in R. Jowell, S. Witherspoon and L. Brook (eds), *British Social Attitudes: the 5th Report* (Aldershot: Gower), pp. 109–26.

Kelly, J. and Kelly, C. (1991), ' "Them and Us": A social psychological analysis of the "new industrial relations" ', *British Journal of Industrial Relations*, forthcoming.

Lockwood, D. (1974), 'For T. H. Marshall', *Sociology*, vol. 8, no. 3, pp. 363–7.

Mann, M. (1970), 'The social cohesion of liberal democracy', *American Sociological Review*, vol. 35, no. 3, pp. 423–39.
Mann, M. (1987), 'Ruling class strategies and citizenship', *Sociology*, vol. 21, no. 3, pp. 339–54.
Marshall, G., Newby, H., Rose, D., Vogler, C. (1988), *Social Class in Modern Britain* (London: Hutchinson).
Marshall, T. H. (1950), 'Citizenship and social class', in T. H. Marshall, *Citizenship and Social Class and Other Essays* (Cambridge: Cambridge University Press), p. 1–85.
Marshall, T. H. (1972), 'Value problems of welfare capitalism', reprinted in T. H. Marshall, *The Right to Welfare and Other Essays* (1981) (London: Heinemann), pp. 104–37.
Marx, K. (1974), *Capital*, Vol. 1 (London: Lawrence & Wishart).
Middlemas, K. (1986), *Power, Competition and the State*, Volume 1, *Britain in Search of Balance, 1940–61* (Basingstoke: Macmillan).

Nairn, T. (1988), *The Enchanted Glass: Britain and its Monarchy* (London: Hutchinson Radius).
Norpoth, H. (1987), 'The Falklands War and government popularity in Britain: rally without consequence or surge without decline?', *Electoral Studies*, vol. 6, no. 1, pp. 3–16.

Phillips, D. and Harding, S. (1985), 'The structure of moral values', in M. Abrams, G. Gerard and N. Timms (eds), *Values and Social Change in Britain* (London: Macmillan), pp. 93–108.

Rentoul, J. (1989), *Me and Mine: The Triumph of the New Individualism?* (London: Unwin Hyman).
Rootes, M. (1981), '*The Dominant Ideology Thesis* and its critics', *Sociology*, vol. 15, no. 3, pp. 436–44.

Sanders, D., Ward, H. and Marsh, D. (with Fletcher, T.) (1987) 'Government popularity and the Falklands War; a reassessment', *British Journal of Political Science*, vol. 17, no. 3, pp. 281–313.
Scase, R. and Goffee, R. (1982), *The Entrepreneurial Middle Class* (London: Croom Helm).
Schwarz, B. (1987), 'Conservatives and corporatism', *New Left Review*, no. 166, pp. 107–28.
Scott, J. (1982), *The Upper Classes* (London: Macmillan).

Scott, J. (1986), *Capitalist Property and Financial Power* (Brighton: Wheatsheaf Books).

Scott, J. and Griff, C. (1984), *Directors of Industry: the British Corporate Network 1904–76* (Cambridge: Polity).

Stark, T. (1988), *A New A–Z of Income and Wealth* (London: Fabian Society).

Turner, B. S. (1986), *Citizenship and Capitalism: The Debate over Reformism* (London: Allen & Unwin).

Undy, R. and Martin, R. (1984), *Ballots and Union Democracy* (Oxford: Blackwell).

Wright, E. O. (1985), *Classes* (London: Verso).

CHAPTER

2

Poland: ideology, legitimacy and political domination*

JAN PAKULSKI

The East European 'Soviet-type' societies are entering the post-communist stage of development. Their ideological makeup, as well as the entire social and political structure, are undergoing dramatic changes. In order to understand these changes, a retrospective glance at the pre-1989 ideological configurations in these societies is necessary.

The issue of ideology and ideological domination occupies a more central place in studies of Soviet-type or state-socialist societies than in the mainstream sociological and political analyses of Western capitalism. There are good reasons for this. Soviet-type societies have always been considered as more ideologically shaped than the market-oriented Western democracies, and their evolution has been analysed in the context of changes in the Marxist-Leninist doctrine. This perception has been enhanced by the post-Stalinist developments in the Soviet Union and Eastern Europe. While the establishment of the communist regimes was seen in terms of coercion and totalitarian control, the more recent developments gave rise to different interpretations emphasizing the importance of benevolent paternalism,

---

Editorial note: this chapter was completed before the recent constitutional changes in Poland and the election of a new government which included members of Solidarity in 1989. Minor alterations were made in February 1990 to bring the contents as up-to-date as possible.

persuasion, voluntary consent and, more generally, ideological incorporation.[1]

Poland has always enjoyed the status of a somewhat special case. Strongly Catholic, and with a long tradition of independence, Polish society has long resisted Soviet pressure, and it was among the first to start the process of de-Stalinization in 1955–6. Although socialist ideas had a deep-rooted tradition (represented by the prewar Polish Socialist Party), the Soviet brand of communism and the Bolshevik political practices were strongly resented. The communist authorities installed in 1944–5 therefore faced the delicate task of gaining sufficient popular support to rule without constant resort to violence and without, at the same time, straying from the ideological and political orthodoxy imposed by their Soviet patrons. This problem has never been fully resolved and a gap between the official ideology and popular sentiments has always persisted, despite numerous attempts to bridge it through propaganda, indoctrination and ideological 'concessions'.

This gap, though, until 1989 did not undermine political domination. The process of mutual political and ideological accommodation, speeded up by outbreaks of popular discontent in the 1970s and 1980s, led to a situation which resembled both a social armistice and a marriage of convenience. The ideological aspects of this status quo are particularly interesting since they illustrate both the Polish peculiarities and more general regularities observed in all European Soviet-type societies, prior to the 1989 'revolutions'.

Three aspects of ideology

While the concept of ideology gains increased currency, its meaning is far from clear. As Larrain (1979, p. 13) observed, it is 'one of the most equivocal and elusive concepts one can find in the social sciences; not only because of the variety of theoretical approaches which assign different meanings and functions to it, but also because it is a concept heavily charged with political connotations and widely used in everyday life with the most diverse significations'. Similar vagueness characterizes the concept of 'domination', usually treated as a synonym of unopposed rule.

In order to reduce this diversity and avoid confusion caused by equivocal meanings, we have opted for 'partial' or 'aspectual' definitions equating domination with stable power relations (socio-political stability);[2] and treating ideology as synonymous with, respectively, dominant social values, the 'political formula' (principles of Marxism-Leninism) and legitimacy claims made by the leaders.[3] This helps to address the issues of the scope and effectiveness of ideological domination in a more detailed, systematic and empirically informed fashion within the context of current sociological debates on value consensus, 'end of ideology' and 'legitimation crisis'.

The current sociological analyses, especially those conducted from the functionalist perspective, frequently refer to the dominant *social values*, that is, the values underlying the popular images of good and desirable social order, as bases of ideological consensus and effective domination. In the light of the Polish data, however, the link between the general value consensus, value commitment and sociopolitical stability looked much more complex. Most Poles, especially the younger ones, adhered to a relatively consistent and well-articulated system of 'socialist' values, but this adherence by no means implied endorsement of the nominally socialist regime. On the contrary, the strong affirmation of the 'socialist' values seemed to be associated with vigorous questioning of the political status quo.

Political analyses of Soviet-type societies often emphasized the importance of *Marxism-Leninism* as the governing formula and the basis of political-ideological domination. Domination meant, in this context, widespread acceptance *cum* application of this formula in political action. Again, the results of Polish studies fitted neither the popular image of 'de-ideologization' nor the equally widespread notion of ideological incorporation. Despite some signs of ideological erosion, the principles of Marxism-Leninism continued, until the late 1980s, to form the backbone of the political formula adhered to by the political elite and the top layers of the political-administrative 'apparatus'. But these principles did not permeate mass consciousness and were rarely evoked in public pronouncements made by the leaders. In that sense the Polish data confirmed the 'end of ideology' thesis while at the same time supporting the claims for the importance of *elite* ideological unity for the preservation of the political status quo.[4]

Finally, one has to address the issue of the effectiveness of ideological dominance in Poland in the context of debates about *legitimacy* and *legitimation crisis*.[5] Again, the configuration identified in Poland defies simple generalizations. While effective domination did depend on elite-staff and elite-patron (that is, Soviet) legitimation, it did not seem to rest, as far as the majority of the population was concerned, on normative grounds. The absence of this form of mass ideological incorporation (mass legitimacy), however, had been compensated for – as argued here – by some other mechanisms generating mass compliance. These mechanisms, common to all state socialist societies of Eastern Europe (prior to 1989 'revolutions') are outlined in the final part of the chapter.

The three aspects of ideology distinguished here – by no means exhausting the field of possible interpretations – share some important features. They refer to relatively consistent images and representations about the nature of society and political processes. These images include strong normative components; they are associated with visions of a good society, desirable social order and acceptable (legitimate) authority. Assessment of such claims and beliefs can be made both in terms of their accuracy and in terms of their sociopolitical function, that is, in relation to the reproduction of the dominant sociopolitical order.

The dominant social values

One of the consistent findings of sociological studies and public opinion surveys in Poland throughout the 1970s and 1980s was the existence of a well–articulated, relatively consistent and strongly affirmed system of *social values* associated with an abstract notion of socialism (but *not* the 'real' or existing socialism). The core elements of this system included equality of opportunity, social justice, freedom of expression, participatory democracy, truth (in the relations between the authorities and the citizens), respect for human dignity, and social welfare. As a set of general social values and moral principles underlying an ideal vision of a social order, socialism was generally endorsed and approved. This affirmation is extended to those principles of social organization which were seen as essential for the maintenance of the socialist nature of society: public ownership of the main productive resources (but not land), the welfare model of the state, and redistributive (egalitarian) policies.[6]

However, the endorsement of socialist values and principles, particularly strong among the young members of Polish society, could hardly be seen as a symptom of ideological incorporation. First, these general values and principles were not identified with 'real' socialism or the existing sociopolitical and socioeconomic system. In fact, they were frequently *contrasted* with the actual social order and served as an idiom of criticism and rejection of the status quo. The general level of approval of 'real socialism' (that is, the system existing

in Poland and other Soviet-type societies prior to 1989 'revolutions'),
both as existing social arrangements and as a desirable direction of
social development, had been low, especially among the young,
educated and skilled categories. The two most strongly criticized
aspects had been the limitation of the democratic rights and civil
freedoms and the violations of the principles of social justice in the
distribution of economic rewards.[7]

In stark contrast with the general vision of socialism, the existing
sociopolitical system was associated with the general features which
were either negatively assessed (for example, centralization,
exclusion, limited participation, corruption) or were seen as
unimportant, while many positively evaluated 'socialist' characteristics (like individual freedom, material well-being) have been
frequently attributed to Scandinavian and British societies. Moreover, the crucial political institutions of state socialism – the party,
the government, the Sejm – were criticized mainly by those who most
strongly affirmed socialist values, i.e. the majority of young rank-
and-file employees who supported Solidarity. By contrast, the
highest credibility rates were scored by institutions and organizations
which were either neutral or linked with political dissent (the Catholic
Church, Solidarity).

It is also clear that the system of economic rewards (pattern of
socioeconomic inequalities) was seen by the majority of Poles as
incompatible with the cherished principle of social justice. These
deviations from the accepted norm were not perceived as marginal or
accidental; they combined in social consciousness with political
restrictions into a vision of a bias coded into the central institutions
of 'existing socialism'.[8]

There are three interpretations – all probably partly accurate – of
this seemingly paradoxical pattern of attitudes. The first one links the
general endorsement of 'socialist' values and principles with successful
indoctrination and propaganda. As pointed out by Wesolowski and
Mach (1986), the crucial message of the post Second World war
propaganda campaigns was the superiority of 'socialist values' and
the 'socialist model of society'. These campaigns were partly
successful. General socialist principles were endorsed by the
majority, at least on the abstract level; but the authorities failed to
convince the people that the existing sociopolitical system succeeded
in the realization of these values. With the passage of time, more and
more people started to see the reality as divorced from these
principles, and each confrontation between the two increased the
sense of disappointment and frustration.

Therefore the general commitment to socialist values, which was shared – on a more superficial level – by the rulers and many of the ruled, had mixed effects as far as sociopolitical stability was concerned. On the one hand, it fuelled popular discontent by revealing the failure of the authorities to live up to the professed principles. On the other hand, however, it played a cementing role by channelling anger and frustration into non-transformative directions. The common use of the socialist idiom hindered a clear articulation of conflicting views and interests. Moreover, since all sides in the conflicts had declared support for 'socialist principles', critical attention frequently focused on marginal and trivial matters and some superficial issues, such as leadership styles, corruption and welfare policies. Such criticisms, as pointed out by Polish sociologists, could be easily diffused through personnel reshuffles, scapegoating and minor policy changes – the strategies which were successfully adopted by the party leaders throughout the 1970s. Even after the Solidarity experience, the prevailing public sentiments – especially the attachment to egalitarian policies and the paternalistic–distributive model of the state – did favour liberal social transformations and were seen as obstacles to deep market reforms.[9]

The strong exposure to propaganda – which constantly referred to socialist values and principles – also resulted in a linguistic incompetence, that is, an inability to articulate dissent in terms other than those used by the official language (Staniszkis, 1979). Such a linguistic–conceptual limitation undoubtedly affected public pronouncements and was partly responsible for the long-lasting popularity of the socialist idiom among both the supporters and the critics of the status quo.

There is another interpretation, one which points to the vagueness of the term 'socialism'. The word lost its specific meaning and changed into a general positive label applied indiscriminately in all contexts as a synonym of everything good and desirable. Sociological studies showed that the content of the term included most of the elements identified also as national social values and traditions. This value assimilation was also prompted by attempts of communist propaganda to link socialism with 'Polishness' – attempts which proved partly successful. Paradoxically, it may also have been caused by a stubborn resistance by Poles to what was seen by them as an imposition of foreign social values. This resistance took the form of a gradual domestication of foreign values and concepts by means of their reinterpretation in line with the national values and assimilation into an acceptable national value package.[10]

The net result of these processes was that while most Poles accept that socialism is generally good, they mean by it a wide variety of things and most of these things were quite different from, and incompatible with, the official images and practices of 'real' socialism. This placed the rulers in a difficult position. They were not only opposed and criticized by the majority of their nominal ideological constituency – the 'socialist working class' – but are also opposed and criticized in the name of the very values and principles which served as official legitimators of their rule.

This brings us to the third partial explanation of the long-lasting popularity of the socialist idiom in terms of pragmatic and tactical considerations. Many opponents and critics of the regime chose the language of socialist principles as a safe idiom of dissent. Such a language made their criticism more difficult to counter, since it precluded their being labelled as 'ideological enemies'. Opposition in terms of liberal or conservative values and principles would have increased vulnerability for such accusations (and would have provoked strong repressive measures).

Although these tactical considerations undoutedly played some role in the articulation of mass protest and dissent in Poland, it was clear that the demands formulated by workers in the 1970s and 1980s were inspired by a genuine commitment to the values and principles closely associated with the concept of socialism. Strong commitment to these general principles has sharpened and radicalized social and political conflicts. It has transformed them into ethical-political conflicts, that is, conflicts about moral *and* political values.

Such conflicts differ dramatically from conflicts about group or factional interests. The value-laden nature – typical of all mass protest movements – makes accommodation difficult, partly because it weakens communication between the sides and partly because it leads to a blending of the political demands with moral postulates, thus narrowing the scope of possible compromises. In the case of Poland, it must also be remembered, this ethicization and sharpening of conflict were initiated and aggravated by another mobilizing factor – the collapse of the economy and the rapid reduction of the standard of living, throughout the 1980s.

This brings us to the more general issue of the relationship between general value commitment and the stability of the sociopolitical order. This relationship, placed at the centre of the sociological debates about the dominant ideology, seems to be much more complex than suggested by the advocates and critics of the dominant ideology thesis. Stability of the sociopolitical order (or its absence) can hardly be explained in terms of value-consensus and value-commitment (or its failure). This is because there is no necessary link between general and abstract social values (such as equality, justice, freedom, etc.) on the one hand, and the principles of social and political organization as expressed in concrete institutional arrangements, on the other. As Bauman (1984) and Offe (1985) pointed out, the same general social values may serve as bases for both the affirmation and rejection of a sociopolitical system. What is crucial from the point of view of political domination (stability) is not necessarily *what* values are cherished, but how the values are interpreted, that is, translated in the social consciousness into the *principles* of sociopolitical organization (the institutional pattern), the *norms* regulating organizational activities, and actual *policies*. The strategic ideological battles, therefore, occur not between different value systems, but in the process of the social translation of values into institutional principles, organizational norms and policies. Effective systems of domination are characterized by the relative congruence between these four elements combined with a moderate level of commitment. Such a moderate level of commitment indicates the existence of a taken-for-granted fit between the general values, institutional principles, organizational norms and policies. The widespread acknowledgement of such a fit prevents values from being mobilized and entering the agenda of public debates as standards of assessment of institutions, norms and policies.

The loose link between value consensus and sociopolitical stability is also due to a well-documented gap between the general value commitments people declare and their actual behaviour. This gap was particularly deep in Poland in the 1982–88 period when what people thought differed from what they actually did (Rychard, forthcoming). Polish leaders recognized and incorporated this fact into the 'normalization' strategy. They relied on pragmatic compliance and passive tolerance, rather than sincere and genuine ideological-normative support. This was reflected in the propaganda language of this period which avoided references to values and principles and stressed the non-sentimental foundations of the political order.

Marxism–Leninism and 'real socialism'

There is another context within which the issue of ideology and domination in Soviet-type societies has been discussed: the context of the 'end of ideology' debates. In this context, ideology has been equated with the political doctrine of Marxism–Leninism, or rather the specific interpretation of this doctrine serving as the political formula and the official *Weltanschauung* of the East European communist elites, prior to the 1989 'revolutions'.

Although the 'end of ideology' theme was formulated in the 1950s and 1960s, it has undergone a remarkable renaissance in recent years. The wave of the post-Maoist reforms in China, followed by the reformist drive in Eastern Europe and the USSR, have revived interest in the 'pragmatization' and 'de-ideologization' of communist politics.

There seems to be a consensus among political observers that in Eastern Europe Marxism–Leninism failed as a popular *Weltanschauung*. Particularly in Poland, where over 90 per cent of the population declare themselves as believers, the impact of the doctrine has always been very limited. There, to an even greater extent than in other East European societies, the main tenets of Marxism–Leninism were gradually transforming into

> ritual messages and signals, meant to be only formally respected. The citizens (and even members of the Communist Party) are not expected to believe in the correctness of the contents of ideological postulates but simply to respect them outwardly: to refrain from criticizing them publicly, and to behave in practice according to ideological signals roughly in the way a driver respects road signs. Those who fulfil those requirements are not asked by the regime to display any measure of internal identification with official ideology in private life. (Mlynar, 1984, p. 22)

This process was associated with, on the one hand, an increasing organized public pressure for liberalization and, on the other hand, an increased tolerance on the part of the authorities for unorthodox policies and various creative developments in the public sphere. In the case of Poland, the former trend resulted in the formation of the free union movement, the unofficial culture, as well as the whole range of semi-official public initiatives sponsored mainly by the Church. On the government side, the massive movement of political 'renewal' in 1980/81 has fostered a degree of pragmatism combined with considerable factional divisions. This further increased the flexibility of the official doctrine at the expense of its coherence and identity.

These two processes and their dramatic 1989 *finale* may be seen by the advocates of the 'end of ideology' thesis as convincing evidence of the formalization, ossification and public irrelevance of the doctrine. But such an interpretation would miss two important points: the temporary reassertion of ideological orthodoxy (mainly within the elite and the party apparatus) especially after the military suppression of Solidarity in 1982–88, and the determined efforts of the communist reformists formally to incorporate even the most radical programmes into the existing doctrinal formulas. Thus, although formalized and rejected by the mass public, the doctrine remained – as the unifying political formula for the elites and the apparatuses – an important component of elite identity and an important foundation of the sociopolitical order, prior to the revolutionary changes in 1989/90.[11]

Paradoxically, one may say, the importance of the ideological-doctrinal formula as the basis of elite unity and the main condition of Soviet sponsorship grew proportionally to the de-ideologization of the general population and the erosion of mass legitimacy among the East European publics. Weakening mass support increased the importance of internal cohesion in the leadership and the apparatus. It also strengthened the indirect Soviet control. The Soviet patrons prefer leaders enjoying less popular affection than, for example, Tito; they also prefer party programmes generating less ideological effervescence than the 'Prague spring' and the 1980–1 reforms in Poland. Thus the reduction of Marxism-Leninism throughout the 1960s and 70s to a ritualized, formal and largely 'internal' (that is, used within the elite and the top political-administrative staff) political formula seemed to suit the interests of all major political actors.

Before it was transformed into an 'internal' and ritualized political formula, the Marxist-Leninist doctrine had been carefully sanitized. All revolutionary and anti-statist references had been removed or played down. The central thesis on the 'inevitable transformation to communism' and 'the historical mission of the proletariat' had been translated to mean a dictatorship by the party-state leadership. Transition into communism had been interpreted as a prolonged process consisting of many stages, including 'advanced socialism'; and 'classlessness' had been pronounced as compatible with the persistence of considerable socioeconomic inequalities. 'Democratic centralism' had been equated with the centralized party control over policies, personnel and recruitment procedures (the 'nomenklatura' system); and 'proletarian internationalism' had become a synonym of the Soviet hegemony. At the very heart of the doctrine rested the teleological justifications for the *étatisation* of social life. The state became a major tool of the ongoing social reconstruction, and its authority was derived from the party's mission to construct an (advanced) socialist society. This mission was realized through the party programme. Serious objections to this programme were symptoms of political-ideological deviations: 'revisionism' (if advocating more far-reaching reforms) or 'dogmatism' (if opposed to the party-sponsored reforms).[12]

While in public pronouncements the doctrinal references were rather rare, in the internal elite circles and among the staff they were very frequent and important. They signalled loyalty and – in the case of divisions – political allegiances and became part of a hermetic language in which terms and references obtained new meanings transparent only to the insiders and more experienced observers of the political process. This gave rise to a new form of political-ideological hermeneutics practised by the specialists and the informed part of the lay public.

Three elements in the doctrine seemed to be particularly important: the reference to 'the logic of history' (including the role of the state as the party's tool of social reconstruction); the Leninist principles of 'democratic centralism'; and the notion of 'the unity of the socialist camp' ('proletarian internationalism'). They formed the core of the ruling formula up until the late 1980s. Open questioning of any of them by elite members signalled serious dissent and possible Soviet intervention.

The core elements of the formula had an important self-explanatory and self-justifying function. References to 'historical necessity', 'objective laws', 'universal principles' served officially to justify frequent disregard for tradition, ethical norms and laws. They depicted social institutions and policies as the articulation of 'higher' historical necessities. Insight into this 'higher' level of reality was acquired through the 'proper' cognitive perspective provided by the doctrine. Thus both the reality and the epistemological basis of its construction became internal to the doctrine, producing a character-istic sense of closure, *a-priorism* and insensitivity to the real world (Staniszkis, 1985–6). In a similar way one could see the practical-political centrality of the other principles: of 'democratic centralism' and 'proletarian internationalism'. They constituted not only the articles of faith but also, and more importantly, the practical – that is, evoked in everyday political arguments – justifications for centralized control and dependence of Soviet sponsorship. Therefore what was most strongly guarded was not so much the theoretical foundations of these core principles, as the *exclusive right* of the elites to interpret them and translate them into party programmes.

Finally, the political doctrine performed also an important pre-emptive or dog-in-the-manger function by blocking the articulation of alternative (especially oppositional) world-views. As Rigby (1986, p. 6) pointed out,

> After decades of immersion in it, few can escape its power over their cognitive process, and indeed, few, perhaps, are aware of that power . . . To employ a different metaphor, it constitutes a charmed circle of the mind from which only the exceptional individual can escape.

There were some escape routes – religion (especially in Poland) was perhaps the most important one – but an open acknowledgement of escapist intentions leads inevitably to political demotion.

To reiterate: in spite of the fact that the depth of social penetration and its impact on the mass consciousness in Eastern Europe were rather low, the Marxist-Leninist doctrine has not ceased to play an important political role until 1989. In a sanitized and truncated form it continued to be an important ideological force unifying the leadership and securing Soviet support. Marxist-Leninist principles structured elite consciousness by providing justifications for their rule and by blocking the articulation of alternative world-views. They organized elite experience by giving it a certain degree of cohesion and a specific 'monadic' quality, pierced only temporarily during acute social and political crises.

The response of the Polish leaders to the recent sociopolitical crises provided the best evidence of the strength and stability of the political formula. The official assessments of the dramatic events of 1970, 1976 and 1980 – contained in the two internal reports – were strikingly ideological. The diagnoses of maladies leading to the eruptions of mass discontent were heavily coated in doctrinal terms and references. They pointed to 'ideological distortions', 'violations of the Leninist principles', 'voluntarism' and insufficient commitment to ideological principles. The therapies proposed by the reports included above all reassertions of ideological principles.[13]

These were not merely rhetorical figures. In the aftermath of the 1970, 1976 and 1980 revolts in Poland (and, it may be added, in Czechoslovakia after 1968 and in the Soviet Union under the reformist leadership of Mr Gorbachev) ideological 'renewal' formed an essential ingredient of the 'normalization' programmes. This involved purges in the elite and the political-administrative appara-tuses, the strengthening of ideological indoctrination and the tightening of political discipline. Such forcible reassertions of the ideological-political principles affected the mass public to a much lesser extent; they were usually limited to the essential ideological constituency – the elite and 'nomenklatura' positions.

Domination and legitimacy

The third aspect of ideology dealt with here is legitimacy, that is, the normative foundations of the sociopolitical order. Ideological domination, from that perspective, is synonymous with legitimation proper, which involves mass acceptance of legitimating claims made by the rulers and voluntary consent by the ruled. Such consent, based on normative acceptance of the sociopolitical order and the right of the rulers to issue binding commands, results in dutiful subordination and has been seen as a necessary ingredient of any stable polity (Weber, 1978, pp. 36–7, 263–5).

Explanations of sociopolitical stability in Soviet-type societies in terms of legitimation of post-revolutionary regimes have been popular since the late 1950s. De-Stalinization, combined with the general intellectual *détente* which followed the Cold War, changed the way of thinking about Soviet-type regimes. A growing number of scholars gradually abandoned the totalitarian paradigm which accounted for sociopolitical stability mainly in terms of mass coercion and manipulation. The alternative models (the bureaucratic, the neo-traditional, and the developmental) stressed, by contrast, the importance of mass consent and voluntary compliance – the attributes of legitimate authority. The bases of the alleged mass legitimacy were variously identified in the national traditions, charismatic appeal of the leaders, legalism and/or commitment to political-ideological goals and programmes.[14]

The legitimacy approaches, in turn, have been subjected to growing criticism which picks out their theoretical weaknesses and the absence of empirical support. The critics point to the frequent confusion between legitimation proper, on the one hand, and various forms of compliance based on expediency (fear of sanctions and expectations of rewards), fatalism (lack of viable alternatives, helplessness) and sheer discipline (routine), on the other. They are also criticized for the tendency to conflate legitimation with the popularity of some leaders (like Tito and Gomulka) and for identifying the actual (that is, granted) legitimacy with legitimacy claims made by the communist authorities. While all leaders make such claims, only some have acquired legitimacy, and there is strong evidence suggesting that in countries like Poland the regimes have failed to generate mass normative consent even before the 1989 changes.[15]

The failure to legitimate Soviet-type regimes in Eastern Europe, prompted the communist leaders to adopt three parallel strategies (all of them resulting in non-legitimate domination). First, some of them gave up their attempts to legitimate the crucial elements of the sociopolitical system – such as 'the leading role of the party', 'democratic centralism' and 'proletarian internationalism' – and started to issue *substitute claims* (often in a covert form) which refer to some more acceptable (but peripheral) features of the system, some popular policies and/or leadership styles. In Poland, for example, such claims included the programme of reconstruction following the Second World War, the acquisition of the Western Territories, land reform, broad welfare measures, respect for national symbols, consumerism (in the 1970s) and 'socialist legalism' (in the post-martial law period). Acceptance of such substitute claims led to quasi-legitimacy, that is, partial and conditional consent. Second, the East European leaders skilfully manipulated the system of economic and political sanctions, systematically rewarding conformism and punishing dissent.[16] This resulted in pragmatically based compliance which, unlike legitimation proper, was largely devoid of normative foundations. Third, throughout the 1970s and 80s all Soviet-type rulers increasingly resorted to indirect domination based on manipulation of the circumstances under which people act. This form of domination, resting on indirect control rather than commands, decreased the importance of legitimation. All three strategies, it must be stressed again, stabilized the regimes without legitimizing them.

Critical reassessments of the post-totalitarian legitimacy interpretations are themselves a result of certain historical experiences. The suppression of the Hungarian Revolution of 1956, the Soviet invasion of Czechoslovakia in 1968 and the violent repression of the Solidarity movement in Poland and the sudden collapse of the communist regimes in 1989, have stimulated interest in the non-ideological aspects of domination. Studies of these events have helped to highlight the difficulties in legitimizing partocratic rule, and they prompted studies of non-legitimate, non-ideological, forms of exerting power and securing mass compliance.

(i) Problems with legitimation

The East European communist leaders have faced much more serious difficulties in legitimizing their rule than their Western counterparts.

For a start, their ruling aspirations (and the scope of control they required) were much broader than the aspirations of even the most reformist Western leaders. The massive social reconstruction undertaken by the East European regimes could not be accomplished within the constraints of traditions, market pressures and parliamentary democratic institutions. Consequently, all these obstacles were either eliminated or seriously curtailed, thus dramatically increasing the rulers' control over social processes.

Such measures, however, also increased the demands for explicit and convincing justifications. These justifications had to cover much broader aspects of ruling, including not only the goals and directions of change, but also the newly formed power structure, the socio-economic system and the whole historical vision the implementation of which they were supposed to serve. The rulers had to justify destruction of market mechanisms, erosion of privacy (including familial relations and religious beliefs) and serious limitation of civil rights and personal freedoms. As Kolakowski (1985, p. 137) observed, after the communist takeover 'ideological norms were established for everything: what we should think about the theory of relativity, which styles of music were correct and which unacceptable, and what width trousers satisfied socialist requirements'. Although these totalitarian tendencies were subsequently reduced, and most of them remained in the sphere of aspirations rather than accomplishments, they nevertheless set an agenda for an ideological reinterpretation of reality which was unparalleled in its scope and depth.

It must also be remembered that the programmes of social reconstruction imposed by the East European communists, unlike the party programmes in the liberal-democratic regimes, had an unlimited time-span. The communist elites saw themselves as the agents transforming society into the final stage of social development, so their historical mission was never accomplished (Lamentowicz, 1983, p. 13). This eschatological dimension of party programmes increased the need for 'deep' and comprehensive legitimation.

Additional difficulty was related to the very origins of the East European regimes. With few exceptions, they were imposed with the aid of the Red Army on largely unwilling, and/or indifferent populations. This imposition was particularly painful in Poland – a nation with a long tradition of resistance to Russian and Soviet expansion, and a strong indigenous socialist movement hostile to the Bolshevik practices. In Stalin's words, it was a society as fit for communism as a cow for riding. The Marxist-Leninist doctrine was unpopular and the local communist movement was almost non-existent. The anti-Russian and anti-Soviet sentiments, fuelled by fresh memories of the 1920–1 war, the Ribentrop-Molotow pact, the Katyn massacre, and mass deportations to Siberia and Central Asia in the 1940s, made Stalinist institutions and policies highly unpalatable. The opposition was strengthened by vigorous religiosity, especially among the peasants, and the deep attachment to democratic traditions incorporated into the ethos of the workers and the urban intelligentsia.

Under such conditions the chances of mass legitimation were close to nil – the fact which the communist authorities soon recognized, and largely accepted. On the other hand, however, the public also had to learn to live with the acute legitimacy deficit. This led to a mutual adaptation – an adaptation accomplished without mass legitimation of the actual sociopolitical system.

(ii)   The evolution of legitimacy claims – from social revolution to geopolitics

The position of the communist authorities in Poland in 1944–5 was rather difficult. Their indigenous support was weak, they were perceived as Soviet agents and they found themselves competing with the established political forces of the underground state and the legalized political forces of the Polish Socialist Party (PPS) and the Peasant Party (PSL). In that situation their first priority was to gain a minimum public acceptance, thus preventing active opposition to the political-administrative takeover.

They largely succeeded in doing that. Although the takeover tactic involved, especially in the initial stage, violence and threats, the use of violence was selective and relatively rare. But it was well publicized, thus warning people of the grave consequences of active opposition. The propaganda machine left no doubts as to what happened to the 'fascist lackeys' and the 'drivelling midgets of reaction' (popular labels for all opponents ranging from the ex-Home Army fighters to the supporters of the initially legalized oppositional Peasant Party). Such propaganda did not need to be believed in order to be effective as a deterrent of active dissent. It relied on fear and expediency rather than moral convictions.

At the same time the party-controlled mass media emphasized the achievements of the communist-sponsored Polish armed forces in the war effort and the restoration of the Polish state, and promised wide-ranging social reforms. In an attempt to widen social support, the stress was laid on the 'open door' policy: who is not against us, is with us.[17]

The legitimation claims in the takeover stage had four distinctive features. First, they were relatively undifferentiated. Similar messages were directed to all the audiences: the sympathizers, the opponents and the uncommitted public. Second, they were pragmatic and non-doctrinal. References to 'communism', 'Marxism-Leninism', 'revolution', 'class conflict', etc., were carefully avoided or reduced to general slogans of social justice. The stress was laid on the postwar reconstruction and the security of the state within the new borders. Third, appeals for support were addressed to the inclusive and unspecific 'democratic forces' and 'Polish patriots' were treated as a natural constituency of the communist-controlled leadership. The ideological requirements were minimal; behavioural conformism was sufficient. Finally, the appeals were future-oriented. They promised not only economic reconstruction, but also democratic and egalitarian reforms involving the collective social elevation of all the working people.

These claims, it must be stressed again, were quite popular among the general public, but they failed to generate mass legitimacy. They created expectations which were difficult to satisfy, and were increasingly at odds with the reality. Consequently, even people who initially supported the programmes of the communist-led social reconstruction, soon started to treat the claims with a mixture of scepticism and indifference.

Thus, as a result of these initial failures in developing mass legitimacy, the communist leaders relied on conditional tolerance rather than generalized normative acceptance. Moreover, this conditional tolerance was never comprehensive. Some policies, such as the land reform, the rebuilding of Warsaw, the reconstruction of the Western Territories, were widely accepted; other measures, such as suppression of democratic organizations and persecution of ex-freedom fighters, were bitterly contested. What is more important, the central elements of the gradually emerging political–administrative structure – depicted by the propaganda as preconditions for the popular policies – were rejected. Widespread dissent among the intellectuals, mass stoppages by industrial workers, and the enthusiastic support for the oppositional Peasant Party in the countryside, were good evidence of these attitudes. Even among the party members and the political–administrative apparatus the political consciousness was low, as testified by frequent and massive purges.[18]

In the 1950s both the content of the claims and the methods of their dissemination started to change. Coercion and threats were replaced by persuasion and manipulation conducted through a massive party-controlled 'preceptoral system'. The communist-controlled tutelary machine extended far beyond the institutions of censorship and propaganda proper and covered all mass media, the entire educational system and the institutions of administration. Its operation, taking the form of mass campaigns, was backed by a broad range of sanctions ranging from retrenchment and blacklisting to imprisonment. These indoctrination campaigns were partly successful, but they also provoked strong resistance which forced the rulers into a series of concessions and retreats: abandoning the mass collectivization drive, practising tolerance of the Church and religion and showing respect for national symbols. The enthusiastic endorsements of Gomulka's 'Polish road to socialism' were, in that sense, a mass no-confidence vote cast *against* the crucial elements of the Stalinist and political system and policies.[19]

After the early 1960s the nature of legitimacy claims started to change quite rapidly. The previously undifferentiated appeals were replaced by specialized messages addressed to specific audiences, mainly selected groups of industrial workers. The attempts at mass indoctrination were largely abandoned, and the emphasis was shifted to, on the one hand, buying off the support of certain strategic social categories and, on the other, the ideological screening and education of the apparatus. The language of mass pronouncements became de-ideologized, stressing achievements in the areas of industrialization, literacy and the rising standard of living. This pragmatization of mass appeals reached its peak during Gierek's secretaryship. The main slogan, 'Let Poland grow stronger and people live better', addressed principally to industrial workers, marked what amounted to an ideological revolution *à rebour*. Justifications for ruling referred almost exclusively to the growing standard of living, new consumption opportunities and technological progress – all to be achieved here and now.

The dramatic collapse of Gierek's programme and the suppression of Solidarity did not lead to the revival of mass ideological appeals. General Jaruzelski, like his predecessor, avoided doctrinal references in public pronouncements and carefully adjusted appeals to specific constituencies. While the restoration of the political-administrative apparatus in 1982–88 proceeded under strong doctrinal-ideological slogans – 'return to the Leninist principles' and 'ideological renewal' – the appeals addressed to the mass public were relatively free of doctrinal elements. The crucial claims included the geopolitical argument – in terms of *raison d'état*; the reformist one, promising a pragmatic and meritocratic re-structuring of the economic administration; and the legalist one, announcing the restoration of 'socialist legalism'. The first appealed to the sense of realism and sober calculation of political risks involving a possible Soviet intervention and civil war. In a fashion similar to the market and technocratic arguments used by Western leaders, it depicted the existing socio-political configurations as given, determined by factors (in this case the geopolitical location of Poland) which were outside political control. The major policy decisions were under such conditions no longer a matter of political choice but, to paraphrase Habermas (1971, p. 105), an 'objective exigency which must be obeyed by any politics oriented towards functional needs' (in this case, the geopolitical realities). The reformist claim was based on similar non-ideological reasoning. It promises the improvement of the living standards through limiting political-ideological constraints in production and personnel policies. The legalist one offers consistency and predictability in applying sanctions; but above all it stressed the need for discipline and outlined the limits to tolerated dissent. All three claims – the geopolitical, the reformist and the legalist – were pragmatic and stripped of normative overtones. They had no doctrinal references. Instead, they contained hidden threats (Soviet invasion, individual sanctions) and promises of rewards (political stability, rising productivity and increased consumption). They were also backed by widely applied repressive measures executed by the well-developed repressive apparatuses of the militia, the army and the special courts (Swidlicki, 1987).

(iii) Social differentiation

A simple distinction between 'the rulers' and 'the masses' (the people) is in line with the popular – and largely accurate – image of conflict in Poland dividing 'them' from 'us'. On the most general level, this dichotomy fits well the data on social consciousness, especially at the time of heightened political conflicts in the 1970s and early 80s. Sociological studies and public opinion surveys conducted in the early and mid-1980s showed a major split in political attitudes which goes roughly along administrative/political lines separating the top party-state personnel from the rest of the people. This was most conspicuous in the case of attitudes to the central elements of the political-administrative system in Poland: the monopolistic rule by the party-state elite, centralism and restriction of civil freedoms.[20]

This picture, however, needs a slight correction to fit better the configurations forming on the eve of the 1989 'revolution'. First, the political–ideological divisions become more complex. The category of the rulers, as well as their supporters, started to show a further division between those who accepted the political-administrative system on ideological-doctrinal grounds, and those who accepted it for other reasons – be it self-interest, expediency and/or fear. Most observers assessed the latter category as larger than the former and pointed to the fit between the motives for pragmatic compliance and the arguments of the official propaganda (Marody, 1986, p. 76; Rychard, 1985, 1987). The pragmatic supporters started to form the main target category in the attempts by the communist authorities to strengthen their position.

The categories of 'the people' and 'opponents' contained similar internal divisions. They included a sizeable group of active political dissenters and their supporters – mainly young, educated and skilled blue- and white-collar workers – who rejected the system on the grounds of principle, and took part in occasional demonstrations and clandestine activities (mainly publishing and distributing under-ground literature). But the majority, estimated in the mid-1980s at about 50 per cent of the population, rejected the sociopolitical system without becoming actively involved in opposition. Their compliance was grounded in helplessness, fear, expediency and sheer discipline. This grumbling majority, increasingly withdrawing from the public arena into private concerns and family life, became the main target of the propaganda. In order to secure their compliance, the rulers did not need to convince them about the virtues of socialism, party rule, democratic centralism and friendship with the Soviet Union. Instead, they were persuaded that there was no viable alternative to the present system, that active opposition was hopeless and dangerous and that compliance was likely to be rewarded. This was the audience to which the messages of 'brutal realism' were addressed, in 1982–88, stressing the dangers of political, economic and ecological catastrophe.[21] The effectiveness of these messages depended largely on their cognitive, rather than their normative, content, and on the ability of the rulers to back their words with deeds. The resulting sociopolitical stability thus depended not on the normative acceptance of the regime but on discipline and widespread conviction that, to put it bluntly, conformism paid and opposition was not worth the risk.

Conclusions: the pillars of the social order

As we have argued throughout this chapter, the major mechanisms stabilizing the sociopolitical order in Poland were only partly ideological. Ideology – understood as a system of doctrinally derived normative justifications of the system – played an important role as a political formula unifying the communist elites and the top layers of the political-administrative apparata. It was also important in legitimizing the rulers in the eyes of their crucial external constituency – the Soviet leaders. In that sense the political formula of Marxism-Leninism continued to be a central pillar of the sociopolitical order, until the 1989 change. Ideological disintegration of the elite-apparatus and the loss of Soviet support heralded the collapse of the regime and started a massive social transformation.

As the 1989 events proved, the ideological incorporation did not reach very deep. The lower ranks of the apparata, and the vast majority of the public, accepted the system for more pragmatic and non-ideological reasons. In the case of Poland, as we argued, this pragmatic acceptance extended even to the majority of the political-administrative officials. Their compliance rested on pragmatic grounds – institutional involvement, expectations of rewards, fear of sanctions and fatalistic helplessness.[22]

Such domination rested on a mixture of pragmatic tolerance and fatalistic withdrawal. Its symbolic reflections – the geopolitical argument, the propaganda of brutal realism, thinly veiled threats, and promises of reforms – were stripped of normative elements, de-ideologized and constantly backed by widely publicized sanctions. These sanctions, combined with the propaganda of brutal realism, had a double function. They deterred, but also informed and appealed: informed about the limits to tolerated nonconformism and about the grave consequences of dissent; and appealed to sober calculations, expediency, individual interests and the collective sense of realism.

Should such claims, and the beliefs and attitudes they appealed to, be considered as a form of mass legitimation and/or ideological incorporation? It is argued throughout this chapter that they should not. The beliefs and representations analysed here were non-normative, peripheral from the point of view of the system and effective only when backed by sanctions. When the sanctions weakened, the whole edifice collapsed like a house of cards.

Notes

1 See, for example, Jowitt, 1975; Rigby, 1980, 1984; Lewis, 1982; Brown, 1984.
2 Domination refers to 'the probability that a command with a specific content will be obeyed by a given group of persons' (Weber, 1978, p. 53). It is more specific than 'power' (it does not include coercion) and involves both legitimate and non-legitimate forms.
3 This chapter is exclusively concerned with ideology in politics and not ideology in knowledge (that is, epistemological questions of truth and scientific validity).
4 See, for example, Abercrombie, Hill and Turner, 1980; Rothchild, 1977; Field and Higley, 1980.
5 General reviews of these legitimacy interpretations can be found in Rigby and Feher, 1982; and Lewis, 1984. Critical assessment is offered in Pakulski, 1986, 1988; Staniszkis, forthcoming; and Rychard, 1986, 1987. Interpretations of the Polish crises in terms of legitimacy crisis can be found in Lamentowicz, 1983, 1988; K. Nowak, forthcoming; and Wesolowski and Mach, 1986.
6 Adamski *et al.*, 1981; S. Nowak, 1979; McGregor, 1984; Mason, 1985; Marody, 1986, forthcoming; Rychard, 1987.
7 The approval rates of the central principles of exclusive party rule and 'democratic centralism' oscillated between 4 per cent (among students) and 21 per cent (among workers), and they reached their nadir after the imposition of martial law and the banning of the Solidarity union. See Adamski *et al.*, 1981, 1982; Marody, 1986, esp. pp. 6–10; McGregor, 1984; Nelson, 1984; Mason, 1985; Rychard, 1985, 1987; *Tygodnik Mazowsze*, 1986.
8 Perceptions of, and attitudes to, socioeconomic inequalities have been analysed in Wnuk-Lipinski, 1987; and Wesolowski and Mach, 1986.
9 Rychard, 1987; Staniszkis, 1985–6, forthcoming; Tarkowski, forthcoming.
10 On the blurred meaning of the term 'socialism', see: Marody, 1986, pp. 17–20; and *Tygodnik Mazowsze*, 1986. The value convergence is discussed in S. Nowak, 1979; Adamski *et al.*, 1981, 1982; McGregor, 1984.
11 Arato, 1982; Brunner, 1982; Pakulski, 1988.
12 See, for example, Brunner, 1982; Suchor, 1984; Lamentowicz, 1988; Pakulski, 1988.
13 The so-called Kubiak Report covered the period of the 1960s and 1970s. It was subject to numerous changes. Fragments of the earlier versions were published in *Survey* (1982); the sanitized version was published in the party journal *Nowe Drogi* in autumn 1982. The so-called Grabski Report dealt with the period of the late 1970s and early 1980s. It appeared to be too hot to handle and was never formally released. Fragments of the Report, leaked from the Central Committee of the Polish United Worker's Party (PUWP), were published underground and republished by the Institut Literacki in Paris (see *Protokoly*, 1986).
14 For the most comprehensive review of the literature on legitimation problems in communist states see: Rigby, 1980, 1982; Lewis, 1984; Pakulski, 1988.

15   Critical assessments of legitimacy arguments in relation to Soviet-type
     societies can be found in Brunner, 1982; Feher, 1982; Wright, 1984;
     Lomax, 1984; Fulbrook, 1987; Rychard and Sutek, 1988 and Pakulski,
     1986, 1988. For the assessment of the Polish situation, see in particular
     Marody, 1986, forthcoming; Wesolowski and Mach, 1986; and
     Rychard, forthcoming.
16   For the review of legitimacy claims in Poland and their evolution in the
     last forty years, see Lamentowicz, 1983, 1988; and Wesolowski and
     Mach, 1986. The issue of legalism is discussed in Swidlicki, 1987.
17   Kersten, 1986; Kostecki, 1982; Zenczykowski, 1982; Lamentowicz,
     1983.
18   Kostecki, 1982; Kersten, 1986; Socha, 1980.
19   Gomulka was seen as a victim of Stalinism, as a Polish patriot opposing
     Soviet influence, and as a reformer advocating democratization. These
     perceptions were false and mass disappointment with Gomulka's
     policies led to growing opposition and his downfall in 1970.
20   One study showed that the leading role of the party was accepted by over
     two out of three of directors and deputy directors of large plants and
     nearly nine out of ten party secretaries. Among the employees and non-
     party members the acceptance rates were about one in four and one in
     five respectively (Rychard, 1985, p. 14). See also Adamski *et al.*, 1981,
     1982; Kostecki and Mrela, 1982; Mason, 1985; Marody, 1986; Rychard,
     1987.
21   The most notorious exponent of such statements was the government
     spokesman, Mr Jerzy Urban. He was well known for his cynical remark
     that even in the case of economic sanctions the government will feed itself.
22   One should also mention studies which stress the importance of non-
     legitimate (and, generally, non-ideological) forms of domination in
     Western capitalist societies: Mann, 1975; Mayntz, 1975; Abercrombie,
     Hill and Turner, 1980.

Bibliography

Abercrombie, N., Hill, S. and Turner, B. S. (1980), *The Dominant Ideology
    Thesis* (London: Allen & Unwin).
Adamski, W. *et al.* (1981), *Polacy 1980* (Warsaw); some of the results were
    published in English ('Poles 1980: results of survey research') in (1982),
    Sisiphus III (Warsaw: IFiS, Polish Academy of Sciences).
Adamski, W. *et al.* (1982), *Polacy 1981* (Warsaw); for a critical review of the
    interpretation, see Powiorski, 1983.
Arato, A. (1982), 'Critical sociology and authoritarian state socialism', in
    J. B. Thompson and D. Held (eds), *Habermas: Critical Debates* (London:
    Macmillan), pp. 196–218.

Bauman, Z. (1984), 'Review symposium on Soviet-type societies', *Telos*,
    vol. 60, pp. 173–8.
Brown, A. (1984), 'Political power and the Soviet state: Western and Soviet
    perspectives', in N. Harding (ed.), *The State in Socialist Society* (Oxford:
    Macmillan and St Antony's College), pp. 51–103.

Brunner, G. (1982), 'Legitimation doctrines and legitimation procedures in East European Systems', in T. H. Rigby and F. Feher (eds), *Legitimation in Communist States* (London: Macmillan and St Antony's College), pp. 27–44.

Feher, F. (1982), 'Paternalism as a mode of legitimation in Soviet-type societies', in T. H. Rigby and F. Feher (eds), *Political Legitimation in Communist States* (London: Macmillan and St Antony's College), pp. 64–81.
Feher, F., Heller, A. and Markus, G. (1983), *Dictatorship Over Needs* (Oxford: Blackwell).
Field, G. L. and Higley, J. (1980), *Elitism* (London: Routledge & Kegan Paul).
Fulbrook, M. (1987), 'Political legitimation in East and West Germany', *Comparative Studies in Society and History*, vol. 29, no. 2, April, pp. 211–44.

Habermas, J. (1971), *Legitimation Crisis* (London: Heinemann).

Jowitt, K. (1975), 'Inclusion and mobilization in European Leninist regimes', *World Politics*, vol. XXVIII, pp. 69–96.

Kersten, K. (1986), *Narodziny systemu władzy, Polska 1943–48* (The birth of the power system. Poland 1943–48) (Paris: Libella).
Kolakowski, L. (1985), 'Communism as a cultural formation', *Survey*, no. 2 (125), vol. 29, Summer, pp. 136–48.
Kostecki, M. J. (1982), 'Organizacyina Historia PRL' (Organizational history of the Polish People's Republic), typescript in the Polish Academy of Sciences, Institute of Philosophy and Sociology.
Kostecki, M. J. and Mrela, K. (1982), 'Workers and intelligentsia in Poland', *Media, Culture and Society*, vol. 4, no. 3, pp. 225–41.

Lamentowicz, W. (1983), 'Legitimizacja wladzy politycznej w powojennej Polsce' (Legitimization of political power in postwar Poland), *Krytyka*, XIII–XIV (Warsaw and London: Aneks).
Lamentowicz, W. (forthcoming), 'Kulturowe aspekty legitimizacji monocentrycznych struktur politycznych' (Cultural aspects of the legitimation of monocentric political structures), a chapter prepared for *Legitimacy and Beyond*, edited by A. Rychard and A. Sulek.
Larrain, T. (1979), *The Concept of Ideology* (London: Hutchinson).
Lewis, P. G. (1984), 'Legitimation and political crisis: East European developments in the post-Stalinist period', in P. G. Lewis (ed.), *East Europe: Political Crisis and Legitimation* (London: Croom Helm), pp. 1–41.
Lomax, B. (1984), 'Hungary – the quest for legitimacy', in P. G. Lewis (ed.), *Eastern Europe: Political Crisis and Legitimation* (London and Sydney: Croom Helm), pp. 68–110.

McGregor, J. P. (1984), 'Polish public opinion in a time of crisis', *Comparative Politics*, vol. 17, no. 1, pp. 17–35.
Mann, M. (1975), 'The ideology of intellectuals and other people in the development of capitalism', in L. N. Lindberg *et al.* (eds), *Stress and Contradiction in Modern Capitalism* (London: D. C. Heath), pp. 275–307.

Markus, M. (1982), 'Overt and covert modes of legitimation in East European societies', in T. H. Rigby and F. Feher (eds), *Political Legitimation in Communist States* (London: Macmillan and St Antony's College), pp. 82–93.

Marody, M. (1986), *Warunki Trwania i Zmiany Ladu Spolecznego w Relacji do Stanu Swiadomosci Spolecznej* (Conditions of persistence and change of the social order in relation to the social consciousness) (Institute of Sociology, University of Warsaw, Warsaw).

Marody, M. (forthcoming), ' "Collective sense" and stability or change of the social order', a chapter prepared for *Legitimacy and Beyond*, edited by A. Rychard and A. Sulek.

Mason, D. S. (1985), *Public Opinion and Political Change in Poland, 1980–82* (London: Blackwell).

Mayntz, R. (1975), 'Legitimacy and the directive capacity of the political system', in L. N. Lindberg *et al.* (eds), *Stress and Contradiction in Modern Capitalism* (London: D. C. Heath), pp. 261–74.

Mlynar, Z. (1984), *The Soviet System Under Brezhnev*, study no. 5, project on 'Crisis in Soviet-type systems' (Vienna).

Nelson, D. N. (1984), 'Charisma, control and coercion: the dilemma of communist leadership', *Comparative Politics*, vol. 17, no. 1, pp. 1–15.

Nowak, K. (forthcoming), 'Three models of legitimation crisis: Poland 1970–85', a chapter prepared for *Legitimacy and Beyond*, edited by A. Rychard and A. Sulek.

Nowak, S. (1979), 'System wartosci spoleczenstwa polskiego' (Value system of the Polish society), *Studia Socjologiczne*, no. 4.

Offe, C. (1985), 'New social movements: challenging the boundaries of institutional politics', *Social Research*, vol. 52, no. 4, Winter, pp. 817–68.

Pakulski, J. (1986), 'Legitimacy and mass compliance: reflections on Max Weber and Soviet-type societies', *British Journal of Political Science*, vol. 16, no. 1, pp. 35–56.

Pakulski, J. (1987), 'Are Soviet-type societies going through legitimation crisis', a paper presented at St Antony's College, Oxford (January).

Pakulski, J. (1988), 'Ideology and political domination: a critical re-appraisal', *International Journal of Comparative Sociology*, vol. 28, no. 00.

Protokoly tzw. Komisji Grabskiego, Tajne dokumenty PZPR (1986) (Protocols of the so-called Grabski Commission. Secret documents of the Polish United Workers Party), Seria Dokumentow, tom 415 (Paris: Instytut Literacki).

Rigby, T. H. (1980), 'A conceptual approach to authority, power and policy in the Soviet Union', in T. H. Rigby, A. Brown and P. Reddaway (eds), *Authority Power and Policy in the USSR: Essays Dedicated to L. Schapiro* (London: Macmillan), pp. 9–33.

Rigby, T. H. (1982), 'Introduction: political legitimation, Weber and communist mono-organizational systems', in T. H. Rigby and F. Feher (eds), *Political Legitimation in Communist States* (London: Macmillan and St Antony's College), pp. 1–26.

Rigby, T. H. (1986), 'The Soviet "system crisis": is it terminal?', mimeo, Department of Political Science, RSSS, The Australian National University.

Rothchild, J. (1977), 'Political legitimacy in contemporary Europe', *Political Science Quarterly*, vol. 92, no. 3, Fall, pp. 487–501.

Rychard, A. (1985), 'Social order in the economy: between rejection and consent', mimeo, Institute of Philosophy and Sociology, Polish Academy of Sciences, Warsaw.

Rychard, A. (1986), 'Legitimation and the stability of social order', mimeo, Institute of Philosophy and Sociology, Polish Academy of Sciences, Warsaw.

Rychard, A. (1987), *Wladza i interesy w gospodarce* (Power and interests in the economy) (Warsaw University Press).

Rychard, A. (forthcoming), 'Who needs legitimization?', a chapter prepared for *Legitimation and Beyond*, edited by A. Rychard and A. Sulek.

Rychard, A. and Sulek, A. (eds) (1988), *Legitymacja; klasyczne teorie i polskie doswiadczenia* (forthcoming in English as *Legitimacy and Beyond*).

Socha, L. (1980), 'O prawach i bezprawiu w Polsce w latach 1944–48' (On laws and lawlessness in Poland, 1944–48), *Krytyka* (London), no. 6.

Staniszkis, J. (1979), 'On some contradictions of socialist society: the case of Poland', *Soviet Studies*, vol. XXXI, no. 2, pp. 167–87.

Staniszkis, J. (forthcoming), 'Stabilizacja bez uprawomocnienia' (Stability without legitimacy), a chapter prepared for *Legitimation and Beyond*, edited by A. Rychard and A. Sulek.

Staniszkis, J. (1985–6), 'Forms of reasoning as ideology', *Telos*, vol. 66, pp. 67–80.

Suchor, L. (1984), *Contribution to the analysis of the conservative features of the ideology of Real Socialism*, study no. 4, research project 'Crises in Soviet-type systems' directed by Zdenek Mlynar.

Survey (1982), 'The Kubiak report', vol. 25, no. 3 (16).

Swidlicki, A. (1987), *Political Trials in Poland: 1981–1986* (London: Croom Helm).

Tarkowski, J. (forthcoming), 'Economic efficiency as the substitute for legitimacy in the post-war Poland', a chapter prepared for *Legitimation and Beyond* edited by A. Rychard and A. Sulek, forthcoming.

Tygodnik Mazowsze (1986), Solidarity underground newspaper, 'Robotnicy w polowie lat 80-tych' (Polish workers in mid-1980s), results of the sociological surveys conducted by sociologists from Poznan, no. 157, 6 February.

Weber, M. (1978), *Economy and Society* (Berkeley, Calif.: University of California Press).

Wesolowski, W. and Mach, B. W. (1986), *Systemowe Funkcie Ruchliwosci Spolecznej w Polsce* (Systemic functions of social mobility in Poland), Instytut Filozofii i Sociologii, Polska Akademia Nauk (Warszawa). The English language version 'Unfulfilled systemic functions of social mobility: I. a theoretical perspective; II. the Polish case') can be found in *International Sociology*, vol. 1, March and June 1986.

Wnuk-Lipinski, E. (1987), *Nierownosci i uposledzenia w swiadomosci spolecznej* (Inequalities and social handicaps in the social consciousness) (Warsaw: IFiS, Polish Academy of Sciences).
Wright, M. (1984), 'Ideology and power in the Czechoslowak political system', in P. G. Lewis (ed.), *Eastern Europe: Political Crisis and Legitimation* (London and Sydney: Croom Helm).

Zenczykowski, T. (1982), *Dramatyczny rok 1945* (The Dramatic Year 1945) (London: Polonia).

CHAPTER

3

Coercion as ideology: the German case

SCOTT LASH

For well over a decade students have been introduced to the theory of ideology via Louis Althusser's classic distinction between coercion and ideology. Althusser, drawing on Gramsci's much-needed correction of Lenin's political reductionism, taught us that there were, on the one hand, ideological state apparatuses and, on the other, coercive state apparatuses and that these two categories were mutually exclusive and exhaustive. I want, in the pages that follow, to give Althusser's distinction a rather different twist. I want to claim that coercion *itself* can be a dominant ideology.

I develop this argument through a brief examination of the German case. The main claim is that coercion, or 'statism', has consistently been the distinctive ideology of the ruling class in Germany. I do not hold that there has not been a plurality of ruling class ideologies in Germany, but I do hold that to understand what most distinguishes the ideologies of the German ruling classes from those in other countries one must turn to statism. And the best way I can support my claim is via the outline of an historical sociology history of ideology among the German ruling classes.

This chapter begins with a lengthy discussion of the historical origins of statism as a distinctive ideology in Germany. Here, like Ralf Dahrendorf (1980), I argue that these origins lie in the desynchronized development of society and polity in Germany. But unlike Dahrendorf, who maintains that the peculiarities of the Germans are due to too much modernization in the economy and too little in politics, I claim that quite the reverse has been the problem – i.e.

a too *rapidly* modernizing state coexisting with a still pre-modern society.

The second section turns to the era of industrial capitalism and the German bourgeoisie in the nineteenth century and the first half of the twentieth. In this context I point to the ideological persistence of Germany's previous consolidation as a social formation with an overdeveloped state and underdeveloped civil society. This already existing ideological predisposition among the bourgeoisie was then overdetermined by the splicing together under Bismarck of policies that were, at once, nationalist and statist *and* liberal and modernizing. Subsequently, from Bismarck's 'conservative turn' through the years of the Third Reich, statist values came to dominate universalist ones among the middle classes.

A third and concluding section claims that the state continues to be paradigmatic for ideological struggles in today's Germany. But that now, from the normative consensus in the postwar decades through the political philosophy of the late twentieth-century Green movement, it is *anti*-statism that sets discursive agendas.

Political backwardness in perspective

Alexander Gerschenkron in *Economic Backwardness in Historical Perspective* (1962) showed that there were advantages in economic backwardness. Early industrialization in countries like England, he observed, created obstacles for further modernization after a certain historical point. In comparison, later industrializers, such as Germany and Russia, were not faced with such obstacles, and after this point they could then modernize at a greater speed than could early industrializers. Much the same case can be made for the effects of 'political backwardness'. That is, it might well be that political backwardness can be, at a specific historical juncture, an advantage for rapid subsequent political modernization. This, we shall see below, is precisely what took place in the case of Germany.

Post-medieval Germany was notoriously and consistently 'politically backward'. First and foremost in this was the unusually late development of absolutism (Anderson, 1974). Absolutism was only put on the political agenda in Germany centuries later than in England, France and Spain, in the aftermath of the Thirty Years War (1618–48). The engineering of the absolutist state in Prussia was carried out mainly under Frederick William (the Great Elector, 1640–88), Frederick William I (1713–40) and Frederick II (Frederick the Great, 1740–86). At the beginning of this period, not only was Germany not in existence, ·but neither, properly speaking, was Prussia. The Great Elector was leader of Brandenburg, itself an electorate of the Holy Roman Empire. Prussia was a duchy, one among many principalities of the Electorate of Brandenburg. The Electors of Brandenburg, who had accepted the Reformation in 1539, acquired the Duchy of Prussia only in 1618. And even then the duchy remained under Polish suzerainty until well into the reign of the Great Elector (Hubatsch, 1985, pp. 81–4).

Brandenburg did not have the status of a 'state' or a 'country' in the sense of England, France, or Spain. Its lack of corporate definition was reflected in the fact that it was but an *electorate* of the Holy Roman Empire. Only in 1701 did Prussia itself acquire a royal crown when Frederick I, the son of the Great Elector, was crowned king in Prussia. Only from 1740 was the territory Brandenburg covered known as Prussia/Silesia. And it was finally Frederick the Great who was crowned first king of Prussia in 1772. Not only was Brandenburg not anything like an absolutist state until the mid-seventeenth century, it was even more decentralized than a *Ständesstaat* (i.e. the state poised midway between feudalism and absolutism, governed by assemblies of nobles). It was only a collection of principalities, *each* of which was a *Ständesstaat* (Poggi, 1978). Given such a context, Frederick William, the Elector of Brandenburg, was clever enough to parley a set of family agreements into the achievement of suzerainty over this dispersed lot of heterogeneous principalities. This suzerainty he was able to convert into absolutist sovereignty through the illegal (without consultation of the territorial assemblies) introduction of a standing army and centralized taxation (Craig, 1955, pp. 1–21).

Second, Germany was politically retarded in the weak and late development of a *noblesse de robe*. In the west, from the twelfth through the fourteenth centuries a reorganization of royal households took place leading to the creation of offices carrying out royal functions, such as the Exchequer for Taxation, or in England the Chancery and in France *parlements*, which fulfilled judicial functions. As these offices gained autonomy from the royal household, they became subject to purchase and/or inheritance. It was was the *noblesse de robe*, or the courier nobility, who purchased these offices and in doing so constituted a quasi-independent bureaucracy of *officiers*. This social status group was crucial in countries further west in the development of the modernizing, absolutist state. And this courtier class of office-holders was much weaker in Brandenburg/Prussia than in these other countries (Rosenberg, 1966, pp. 51–7).

A third aspect of political retardation was the very late final termination of serfdom. The institution of serfdom was all but unknown in the knightly-monastic Prussian state of the thirteenth and fourteenth centuries, founded by the Teutonic Order. Subsequently, however, the Hohenzollern acquisition of Brandenburg was accompanied by the instatement of serfdom under the local tyranny of the East Elbian Junkers. Conditions for this were set by the beginnings of a profitable market in grain exports to the west. In western countries the *noblesse de robe* formed an absolutist alliance with monarchs against the rural *noblesse d'epée* who were the basis of the *Standesstaat*. In the German-speaking territories, the weakness of the *noblesse de robe* bolstered the landed Junkers, and enabled *their* entry into an absolutist alliance based on lord-serf relations. In the event, serfdom was made ever more coercive through the seventeenth and eighteenth centuries, before its lightening and abolition only in the 1794 Preussiche Allgemeine Landrecht and the 1807 Stein-Hardenberg reforms (Braun, 1975, pp. 249–60).

Concomitant with this was the actual *decline* of town life in Germany from the sixteenth through the eighteenth centuries. When urban life resumed in the eighteenth century it was largely in the shape of army-dominated garrison towns. Moreover, guilds and monopolies persisted to a very late date, vitiated again by the 1794 legislation and the Stein-Hardenberg measures, but persisting in fact well into the nineteenth century (Meinecke, 1977, pp. 69–89). Even as late as the Weimar Republic, when social insurance was introduced for white-collar workers, it was set up on a 'corporate' basis, apart from the insurance of manual workers (Kocka, 1977).

Officiers and commissaires

Paradoxically this very political backwardness permitted the forced paced modernization of the state after the Thirty Years War. This was based on the development of a modern civil service, i.e. a bureaucracy, not of '*officiers*' from the courtier nobility, but of '*commissaires*'. Much as the *parlements* were dominated by the French *officier* bureaucracy, the *Regierungen* served as institutional sites for their Prussian counterparts. The *Regierungen* were primarily supreme courts of law, standing effectively against the private law jurisdictions of the landed nobility, and buoyed by the *jus publicum* of Roman law, received in Brandenburg in the sixteenth century (Rosenburg, 1966, p. 128). The shift from *officier* to commissaire bureaucracy was a step in the direction of a fuller absolutism for the Prussian state. The *officier* bureaucracy with its purchased and hereditary offices was partly independent (though not as independent as the rural nobility) of the monarch while the commissaire bureaucracy was fully dependent on him. It was also a big step in the direction of modernization in (1) its creation of a set of 'legal-rational', impersonal and internally consistent rules for the regulation of the bureaucracy itself; (2) the creation of general norms regulating the administrative practices of the bureaucracy; and (3) the creation of a systematically coherent set of administrative districts (Fischer and Lundgreen, 1975, pp. 520–4).

The Great Elector initiated this process with the reconstitution of the Brandenburg Privy Council in 1651. These were basically salaried tax collectors, fully dependent on and loyal to the king. The main agent of the creation of a modern commissaire civil service and in effect the Prussian state was, however, Frederick William I. Pivotal here were his reforms which introduced the *Landrate* and *Steuerrate* as replacements for the old *Regierungen*. The *Regierungen* functioned on the geographical basis of the old Hohenzollern principalities, which were previously the realms of rule of the territorial estates assemblies. These were transformed into administrative provinces, themselves divided into districts and administered by the new commissaires. The *Landrat* was a part-time official, who doubled as police chief for rural administrative districts, but mainly had fiscal and military (conscription and *corvées*) responsibilities. The *Steuerrat*, with similar functions, replaced the *Regierungen* in the towns. These new commissaires numbered a few dozen in the 1660s but a few hundred by 1740. Whereas the old *Regierungen* were independent men of substance, often established jurists and civilian nobles, the new modern civil servants were often from petit bourgeois backgrounds or were impecunious former military officers and had none of the potential autonomy of men of independent means. Further, in the middle of the eighteenth century, measures were introduced to bring the judicial elite of the *Regierungen* into the framework of the modern civil service, through the introduction of examinations, university training and the payment of a high salary as replacement for the private fees they had previously charged (Fischer and Lundgreen, 1975, pp. 511–17).

The pre-eminently *modern* nature of this bureaucracy becomes particularly clear when placed in comparative perspective. Though the commissaire principle may have originated in France, the entrenched position of the Parisian *noblesse de robe* prevented its pervasion on anything like the Prussian scale. As for Britain, a

commissaire bureaucracy was introduced only with the civil service
reforms of the 1850s. Sales in offices of army commissions here were
abolished only in 1872 (Rosenberg, 1966, pp. 50–2). And the
replacement of traditional by 'rationalized' administrative districts
was largely the work of Keith Joseph in the Heath government of the
early 1970s.

Having explained the origins of a precociously modernized state in
the context of political backwardness in Germany, we can see how
this setting became, as Hegel famously speculated, political home for
large portions of the bourgeoisie (Kocka, 1987). In comparison with
the west, German bourgeois identity formation was, then, not so
much linked with economic practices and still less linked with
parliamentary experience, but more directly connected with
experience in the state apparatus itself. It makes sense to speak of
national bourgeoisies as divided into two fractions, based on
Bourdieu's (1984) categories of 'economic' and 'cultural' capital.
Contemporary German social historians refer to these two fractions
as the *Wirtschaftsburgertum* and the *Bildungsburgertum*. Whereas in
Britain, France, the Netherlands and the USA, the *Wirtschaftsburgertum* has played the hegemonic institutional and cultural role, in
Germany, as Lepsius (1987) has argued, this hegemonic place belongs
to the *Bildungsburgertum*. Lepsius further divides the *Bildungsburgertum*
into fractions comprised of those employed by the state (civil
servants) and self-employed professionals (1987, pp. 82–5). Here we
see that the civil servants have a numerical and cultural predominance
in Germany that is unmatched elsewhere. Thus only in Germany does
that fraction of the bourgeoisie who themselves work inside the state
apparatus have a dominant position within the middle classes as a
whole. The largest category of participants even in the German liberal
movements of the nineteenth century and the early twentieth – i.e.
that portion of the middle classes who most enthusiastically
advocated the autonomy of civil society from the state – were
themselves civil servants (Sheehan, 1978, p. 119).

Second, the contradictory (overly traditionalist/precociously
modernist) nature of the German polity fostered statist ideology
among the aristocracy. This was a polity trying to skip, as it were,
not one but two stages of development. It was a polity that proceeded
directly from ideal-typical feudalism to the modern, commissaire,
bureaucratic state, while skipping stages of the *Ständesstaat* and
courtier absolutism. How then was the rural nobility reconciled with
the fact of the modern state? The Junkers' brute presence was simply
too strong for the Hohenzollerns to initiate the transition towards

absolutism against them, so they had instead to integrate them and promote their identification with the state at every step of the way. This they did through the offer of a whole range of concessions. These concessions included: (1) economic measures such as the increased severity of serfdom, and favourable foreign trade policies; (2) the maintenance of the legal powers of the rural nobles on their own lands; (3) the reinforcement of Junker power in local politics, in county and district assemblies (*Kreistage*); (4) the introduction and extension of Junker power in the civil service. Even under Frederick William I, the proportion of nobles in high positions in the bureaucracy increased; substantial numbers of them did not have to sit the otherwise obligatory examinations. Nobles were particularly prominent among the *Landrate*. Career trajectories from squire to army officer to *Landrat* to board president to minister were not uncommon. Finally of course there was Junker privilege within the army (Ritter, 1968, pp. 158–61; Bendix, 1978).

Third, and perhaps most important in terms of how this precociously modern polity promoted statist ideology, is the extraordinary salience of the state itself. If one were notionally to divide a set of western eighteenth- and nineteenth-century social formations into comparative weightings of state and civil society, one would find a preponderance of civil society in most cases, but an overwhelming preponderance of state in Germany. To understand this peculiarly German historical disarticulation of state and civil society it is helpful to draw on some concepts put forward by Michel Foucault.

The non-appearance of the social

Foucault has periodized the history of power into two main epochs – a pre-modern epoch of the 'juridico-discursive power' of the absolutist state, and that of modern power, which he dates from the end of the eighteenth century. In this formulation, juridico-discursive power is exercised from above in a sort of hypostatized political body, while modern power instead is lodged immanently in the social. Juridico-discursive power is exercised from a transcendent instance and is repressive, while modern power is exercised immanently in the 'capillaries' of the social and is not repressive but 'productive'. The logical implication of Foucault's schemata is that in (absolutist) pre-modernity, the social is insignificant in comparison with the state and exists primarily to reproduce the state; while in modernity it is the social which becomes the dominant instance and the state comes to exist predominantly to reproduce the social (Foucault, 1980). What is important for our purposes here is that, whereas elsewhere in the west modernity spelled the new predominance of the social over the state, in Germany state hegemony persisted for at least a century even into the epoch of modernity. Foucault further characterizes modern power, very much in the way that Weber understood legal-rational *Herrschaft*, in terms of its ability to 'normalize', to 'individuate' and to 'regiment'. The models in this context for Foucault are the confessional and the army. What we should note in this regard is that the German state possessed normalizing, regimenting and individuating power long before the epoch of modernity. We should note that in Germany a precociously modern state exercised hegemony over civil society and hence reinforced statism as a dominant ideology, long after it ought to have ceased doing so.

Foucault also attached importance to the concept of 'cameralism' (Gordon, 1987). Cameralism is the issue which Hegel broached in *The Philosophy of Right* under the notion of 'Polizei'. Cameralism can be understood as the characteristic set of institutions and norms which are used by the absolutist state in order to reproduce itself. These norms and institutions function in both the internal (domestic) and external (foreign policy) environments of the state. German cameralism was distinctive because of its pre-eminently *military* nature. The army played a crucial role in structuring the shape of the state: a very large proportion of state personnel was involved in military activity; the new eighteenth-century public law bureaucracy was modelled along martial lines; while under Frederick William I and Frederick the Great top generals commonly served as chairmen of royal special committees (Ritter, 1968, pp. 129 ff.). It also structured civil society. The eighteenth-century resurrection of the Prussian city took shape largely on the model of the garrison town. In 1840, more than half of Prussia's 3.8 million urban civilians lived in towns which doubled as garrisons (Blackbourn and Eley, 1984, p. 242). Army officers were on municipal committees in these towns. Military commanders worked with *Steuerrate* to control local retail trade and food prices. The military also served supremely as an apparatus for the *dissemination* of statist ideology. First it had a highly visible presence in the day-to-day running of domestic affairs. Local populations must have been affected by the common experience of unpunished insolent behaviour of soldiers to civilians. Second, it instilled military virtues in young men during their inordinately long tour of obligatory military service (Craig, 1955, pp. 42–6, 80–1). Third, the myth and reality of the *Fronterlebnis* played a key role in fuelling nationalism.

'Rights' and statism

The contradictory concatenation of backwardness and modernity in the polity, which we have addressed, is duplicated in the notion of 'rights' that prevailed in German thought. Leonard Krieger shows in his often neglected classic, *The German Idea of Freedom* (1957), how such a conception of rights is supremely statist in character. The kind of rights at issue here are not private rights of contract and property, but *political* rights of constitutional law. The point is that long after notions of popular political rights had become widespread in the west, the German concept of rights remained, not the rights of the people, but those of the prince or the state.

In this context, the era of princely absolutism of the Holy Roman Empire was crucial. Prior to this, political rights were very much the 'chartered liberties' of the medieval corporations. From the early modern period, these, as well as the private rights of the landed nobility, came to be 'grafted onto the sovereign powers of those corporations which became territorial states' (ibid., p. 6). That is, only when the princes were able to gain sovereignty in their own territories did they gain princely rights (as electors) in the Holy Roman Empire. Under princely absolutism came the reception of Roman law. This enabled princes to consolidate their powers over the previously dominant private law regime which buoyed the local landed nobility and their estates. The reception of Roman law also meant that the principality was juridically a part of the Holy Roman Empire of the German nation. We saw that state absolutism of the late seventeenth and eighteenth centuries succeeded through the incorporation of the claims of the landed aristocracy. And we shall see below that nineteenth-century bureaucratic statism thrived through the incorporation of the rights' claims of the middle classes. Similarly, princely absolutism succeeded through the incorporation of the claims of local aristocracies. The post-medieval prince was to mediate, between the First Reich, on the one hand, and his own subjects, on the other. He thus incorporated rights *vis-à-vis* the former as well as the latter.

A rather similar pattern emerges in *doctrines* of constitutional law. In absolutist natural law doctrines, western thinkers such as Hobbes, Grotius and Bodin took it as axiomatic that independent natural individuals had to cede their rights to the sovereign, who was then to be the main bearer of rights. Among Germans such as Pufendorf, Thomasius, Leibniz and Wolff there were two ultimately enduring differences from the classic doctrines. The first was that, where the classic analyses dealt very much in polarities of state and individual, the German theorists underscored the mediating role of territorial estates and corporations. Pufendorf, for instance, between a theory of the state and an anthropology of natural individuals, had a doctrine of society which stood halfway between state and individual. For him this 'society' was corporatist and hierarchically structured and effectively mediated 'the unitary sovereign's representation of the rights of independent natural individuals' (ibid., pp. 50–1).

The second difference was that the Germans saw the state as a means to perfect the morality of the individual. Thus the individual for Leibniz and Wolff was not the Hobbesian brute, but was morally perfectible. And rights in the state of nature were not the Hobbesian rights to everything and anything at all, but rights which gave individuals the freedom to fulfil their duties to perfect themselves morally. The presumption in this was that duties were in an important sense prior to rights. It was equally, as Thomasius underlined, that the state was to be the individual's guide to the 'social moral principle' (ibid., pp. 62–3; Strauss, 1953).

These differences left an imprint on later, 'popular' doctrines of natural rights. Kant and Hegel, in their radical problematization of subjectivity and popular sovereignty, did parallel Locke and Enlightenment constitutional theorists. Kant, however, left the door open to state sovereignty in his own assumptions of human perfectibility. *The Critique of Pure Reason* counterposed a moral realm of 'reason', to which he assigned the idea of 'free civil constitution', to the 'empirical' realm of experience. The latter was also the realm of theory, including the logical categories of the understanding (Beck, 1965, pp. 9–10).

Kant's constitutional theory is a subset of his ethics. Natural law ethics from its point of origin in the Stoics has derived its postulates from the principles of reason in the human intellect (Strauss, 1953). What is meant by natural law depends of course on what is meant by reason and what is meant by nature. For theorists such as Hobbes and Grotius, the assumption was that the state of nature was brutish. For Locke and later for Montesquieu and Blackstone, the natural order exhibits rationality and not violent and radical contingency. In Locke's *Two Treatises* published in 1689 the state of nature was assumed to be social and peaceable. Kant's (like Rousseau's) notion of nature diverges from both these discordant views. He, like Aquinas, drew on Aristotelian teleology, assuming that a being has his/her own *telos* and is thus perfectible through following his/her own nature (Finnis, 1980, pp. 32–6).

Kant's nature implants capacities into humans, who themselves are half sensual and half rational, though reason is usually a servant of the passions. The exception to this rule of course is moral action in which rational means are regulated by rational ends. What then are the means by which the passions are to be regulated by pure practical reason? For Aquinas this source was divine. For Kant, as for Rousseau, it is through obedience to some sort of 'rational will'. Kant, however, shied away from any of the radical democratic implications of Rousseau's view. He did not believe in the right of individuals to resist even unjust political regimes. His ideal constitution was a vague combination of monarchical and popular sovereignty (Cassirer, 1955, pp. 263–74). The logical consequence of these assumptions is that the state itself would play a pivotal role in the shaping of Kantian moral subjectivity.

Not only Kant, but more importantly Hegel, whose ethics, in contestation of Kantian abstraction were more properly a political philosophy, assigned a determining role to the state in shaping moral perfectibility. Unlike absolutist natural law theory, Kant did not stress the role of hierarchical estates and corporations as mediating bodies between the individual and the state. Hegel, however, brought the estates and corporations back in his *Philosophy of Right* as a neo-romanticist correction of Kant's abstract morality.

Statism is again present in the nineteenth- and early twentieth-century theory of the *Rechtsstaat* (the state whose basis is legality). Though some have identified the *Rechtsstaat* with popular sovereignty, neither parliamentary rule nor any fundamental notion of individual rights is inherent in the concept. The *Rechtsstaat* does necessarily presume a certain measure of accountability of the state to law. But this does not entail accountability to universalist tenets of human rights, nor even a partial accountability of the executive to the legislature such as is assumed in the US constitution. It entails only a certain accountability of executive to the judiciary and to a set of legally prescribed procedural rules (Hart, 1961). Hence the Austrian legal positivist Hans Kelsen (1949) could argue that even Hitler's (though not Stalin's) state operated in the framework of legality. In most interpretations of the *Rechtsstaat*, much as in previous German constitutional theory, rights were understood to inhere more in the state itself than in the individual (Kirchheimer and Neumann, 1987). In a nation of jurists, where a legal training was (and still is) essential to obtain the most varied sets of positions in the civil service, this sort of – whether *rechtsstaatlich* or legal-positivist – jurisprudence was conducive to statist ideology. On this count alone, along with the military, legal training, the legal profession and the civil service bureaucracy must figure as a crucial apparatus for the dissemination of Germany's distinctive ideology.

Statist modernism

A bourgeois public sphere

Contrary to the claims of many who have explained German exceptionalism via the relative insubstantiality of the German middle classes, there is a host of evidence which points to bourgeois dominance of nineteenth-century Germany and hence to the bourgeoisie as the pivotal vehicle of statist ideology. There is evidence that the German bourgeoisie was not only the motive force of a muscularly modernizing economy, but was also instrumental in the creation and domination of a universalistic public sphere. The beginnings of a political public sphere can be identified as early as the last quarter of the eighteenth century, with the mushrooming of a communications network based around magazines, newspapers, lodges, clubs and scientific societies. Particularly important were the societies and their associational life, not the least among the professions, which was established, in contrast to the old regime, on a non-corporate basis. These were indeed voluntary organizations, or *Vereine*, into which the middle classes streamed. From about 1815 choral associations and gymnastics clubs appeared on a significant scale. Bourgeois sporting associations came to replace, for example, the aristocratic hunt. Duelling associations, again dominated by the middle classes, centred around notions of honour and duty and had little to do with the aristocratic model of the duel (Ruppert, 1984, pp. 113–17).

From the mid-nineteenth century a whole set of philanthropic organizations began to flourish, whose membership was again overwhelmingly drawn from both *Besitz* and *Bildungsbürgertum*; that is, from fractions of the bourgeoisie, grounded, on the one hand, in property, and on the other, in cultural capital. Such organizations not only created a civil society or public sphere in terms of communications structures, but also transformed the shape and use of material public space itself. Hence the aristocratic preserve, for instance, was replaced by the public park. Bourgeois-owned art galleries and public art museums released painters from dependence on aristocratic patronage and threw them on to the markets. Writers as well became free of such patronage and dependent on the revenues of publishers. Nineteenth-century concert halls and museums were no longer financed by the court nobility, but by subscription or by middle-class notables, and their space for the new middle-class audience likewise dramatically increased. The royal menagerie was displaced by the public zoo, for which financial appeals were mounted through middle-class voluntary organizations. Space for new forms of leisure-spending was to be provided through the developments of public restaurants and sidewalk cafés. Spa resorts and great hotels grew to rival the aristocratic hunting party (Blackbourn and Eley, 1984, pp. 197–210).

Such associations came to play a major role even in national politics. The revolution of 1848 was sparked not just by the February days in France; in the summer of 1847 a number of conclaves of professionals and academics had held meetings at which political demands began to be raised. This was the era of the local bourgeois notable (*Honoratorien*). In many towns associational life was a set of constellations around one hub, usually a major club like the local Museum Society or Monday Club or Honoratorien Club. From the mid-century chains of such local groupings crystallized into a national communications network that became the foundation of German liberalism. Local notable politics thus became national politics predicated on assumptions of, for example, equality before the law and rights of association. The key figures here were the very small circle of local notables who dominated local club life. Political organization typically was the liberal electoral committee, created on the eve of an election (ibid., pp. 227–32).

The German bourgeoisie did thus create a universalistic public sphere. Yet this public sphere was created at a much later date than in the west. And it came under attack at a much earlier date. From about the 1870s non-bourgeois social groupings – aristocrats, Catholics, shopkeepers, craftsmen, peasants and industrial workers – began to form their own *Vereine* on a considerable scale. A number of these were outspokenly particularist, traditionalist and anti-Semitic. Further, in local communities a sort of stratificational ladder of *Vereine*, based on invidious distinctions, came into being. Corresponding to this was the beginning of particularization of even the older bourgeois *Vereine*. That the bourgeoisie at this point in time began on a qualitatively greater scale to acquire titles, to buy rural estates and to take their places in reserve officer corps reflects not so much their 'feudalization' as their attempt to create social space between themselves and the quickly consolidating classes beneath them (ibid., p. 235). In any event this new particularist civic quietism among the middle classes put paid to the persistence of any universalistic public sphere into twentieth-century Germany.

The German bourgeoisie, even at their most universalist, subscribed very substantially to statist ideology. This was exemplified, perhaps above all, in their ambiguous conception of popular sovereignty. The fact was that German liberals had no clear idea of what form of governance should replace the statist regime of king and bureaucracy. In the first half of the nineteenth century even in Baden, the German state with the most progressive constitution, parliament in the main served only as a conduit for passing information up from the populace to the government. For most liberals during this period, constitutional monarchy meant that ministers were responsible to law and not to parliament. And many among them supported the awarding of ample emergency powers to the executive (Sheehan, 1978, pp. 8–13).

When the National Assembly convened in Frankfurt following the Revolution of 1848, radicals did back a centralist, democratic form of government, but the moderate majority persisted in vague dualist notions of power-sharing between legislative and executive, with primacy finally given to the princely houses. Indeed the Assembly's initial choice for its leader was an Austrian arch-duke. The final tenets of constitutional law agreed by the Assembly did hold that ministers were to be accountable to parliament, but it unfortunately failed to specify *how* they were to be accountable. Ministers were to be appointed by the Crown and no clear power was created for parliament to force them from office. Ministers and the monarch were to co-sign laws and the latter was granted ample powers to issue decree laws in case of emergency (Hamerow, 1966, pp. 117–36).

In the 1860s and 1870s even this vague notion of popular rule waned among liberals as again only legal, but not parliamentary, accountability of monarch and ministers was called for. With the founding of the Second Reich, not only were monarch and Bismarck not in the least responsible before parliament, but the Reichstag had no powers whatsoever in the initiation of legislation. Further, a Reich's ministers council did not even exist, as Bismarck ruled with a cabinet of Prussian ministers. Yet liberal demands were only for control over the budget, legal guarantees and the right to present the nation's views in parliament. In the event, parliament had control only over the military budget, though Bismarck attempted to devise ways to get around even this (Eyck, 1958, pp. 100–10).

Modernization or particularism?

German liberals, even if they had problems on the issue of parliamentary rule, were, like liberals elsewhere, secularists, constitutionalists and believers in freedom of speech and assembly. They were 'internationalists' and they were free traders. In short they bought the modernization *problematique* lock, stock and barrel. The German state, for all its anti-parliamentary proclivities, was often, itself, on the side of modernization and, in so far as this was the case, already marked liberal symptoms of statism were only made chronic.

By the mid-1860s, as Bismarck began his vast foreign policy offensive in the quest for Schleswig-Holstein, liberals began to see that the type of freedom they wanted was impossible in the absence of national unity. Unity would provide a large and unified market. Centralization, further, would finally erode the particularism and traditionalism of artisans, landowners, peasants and Catholics. And liberals, like Theodor Mommsen, came to support Prussian and then the Reich's foreign policy. Thus began 'the liberal era' in German politics, from the 1866 initial meeting of the Liberal Nationalverein up to the major policy turn at the end of the 1870s (Kehr, 1977, pp. 118–21). Apart from foreign policy, the radical free-trading measures initiated by Hans Delbruck, architect of Bismarck's economic policy, fostered further liberal identification with the state.

Perhaps best illustrative of the measures which brought liberals into the statist fold was the *Kulturkampf*. Liberal support for these anti-Catholic measures cannot simply be written off as reactionary, for organized Catholicism had played rather a reactionary role throughout nineteenth-century Germany. The Congress of Vienna of 1815 brought the restoration of Catholic church power in Germany and organized Catholicism consistently opposed the abolition of guilds, the introduction of freedom of movement and the reinstatement of Jewish emancipation. With the founding of the Catholic People's Party in 1869 and the enunciation of the doctrine of papal infallibility in 1870, both liberals and Bismarck came to see the Church as a threat to unity and modernization. This was the context of Bismarck's October 1871 diatribe versus 'ultramontane and anti-Prussian efforts' and his contention that 'Slavs and Romans in alliance with ultra-montanism seek to uphold barbarism and ignorance and fight everywhere in Europe versus Germanism, which seeks to spread enlightenment' (Evans, 1981, p. 50). Hence his attack three months later on the Catholic Party as 'a mobilization against the state', along with his pronouncement that the very 'idea of a confessional party is dangerous and divisive' (ibid., p. 56).

The actual measures of the *Kulturkampf* were carried out by Adalbert Falk, appointed as Prussian Minister of Religion and Education in 1872. Just before Falk's appointment the Catholic department of the ministry had been abolished in a conflict over teaching the doctrine of papal infallibility in the schools. The first measures taken under Falk were the expulsion of the Jesuits from Prussia and the state assumption of power over the appointment of priests. The high point of the *Kulturkampf* came in February of 1875 with the mass arrests of priests, editors of Catholic publications and Catholic *Zentrumspartei* members. This was accompanied by newspaper confiscations from Catholic publishers and the dissolution of scores of meetings of Catholic organizations (ibid., p. 76). Falk's ultimate aims were the full secularization of the schools and the introduction of obligatory civil marriage. Liberal support of the secular and modernizing aspects of *Kulturkampf* was accompanied by uncritical support for these repressive and statist measures.

Falk's aims were ultimately foiled by the increased weight of conservative, Protestant opinion in Germany towards the end of the 1870s. This was encouraged by Bismarck to amass support for his new political agenda, including the anti-Socialist laws and the erection of substantial tariffs. For this he needed the support of landowners and peasants in rural Protestant areas, the social bases of the Conservative Party founded in 1876. Fearing the loss of Liberal support, especially over the new protectionism, Bismarck mobilized a traditionalist coalition of Catholics and Conservatives behind his new politics. The rural Conservatives had always opposed social modernization; moreover, their agricultural exports were no longer competitive on international markets (Sheehan, 1978, pp. 160–85).

Somewhat less anticipated was that much of political liberalism went along with Bismarck. The anti-Socialist laws occasioned a schism between the two parties of political liberalism, as the minority Progressives opposed the attack on *Rechtsstaatlichkeit*, while the majority National Liberals supported the laws. As for protectionism, both Progressives and most National Liberals initially opposed Bismarck's measures. But high tariffs had become increasingly attractive to heavy industry, as the Ruhr's coal, iron and steel had lost in competitiveness on international markets. Thus, with the resignation of free-trading National Liberal leader Rudolf von Bennigsen and the rise of ultraprotectionists such as Johannes Miquel, even this former keystone of political liberalism had lost its sacred character (Kehr, 1977, pp. 160–63).

The tariffs, the anti-Socialist laws and Bismarck's paternalist social insurance legislation of the early 1880s were the package that mainstream liberalism came to accept. The mood of the country had shifted noticeably to the right, as a string of Liberal successes in Reichstag and Prussian Landtag elections was terminated by the newly strong Conservatives in 1879. By the early 1880s, even the minimalist liberal commitment to legal equality was weakened, as anti-Semitic articles began to appear in the Liberal magazine *Grenzbogen*. Now right-wing National Liberalism began to argue for an alliance with Conservatives against Progressives and Catholics, who were beginning to drop their previous traditional baggage. In 1887 the Centre and the left-liberals defeated Bismarck in his attempt to circumvent parliament by putting through a seven-year military budget. Bismarck responded by dissolving the Reichstag and calling elections, in which Conservatives and National Liberals did indeed make common cause (Sheehan, 1978, pp. 196–8).

Reactionary modernism?

How does one explain this shift of German middle-class politics? In most western countries, from around the turn of the nineteenth century – that is, from what has been called the era of *liberal* capitalism – the principle of the social comes to outweigh the principle of the state. German exceptionalism, I argued above, was largely due to the fact that in German liberal capitalism, the state still dominated the social. Now at some point historically, even in Germany, the principle of the social also comes to take on a very substantial weight. This point in time it seems to me coincides roughly with the rise at the turn of the twentieth century of *organized* capitalism. Organized capitalism, according to Rudolf Hilferding, brings the displacement of free-market assumptions by monopolies, by cartels, by the interventionist state, and by the interpenetration of banks and industry. It is the age of organized interests, of trade unions, of mass social-democratic parties (Lash and Urry, 1987), the associative action of peasants, small businessmen and Catholics. It is the era of imperialism, nationalism and anti-Semitism.

The rise of 'the social' in German organized capitalism is witnessed to the extent that Social Democracy collected 32 per cent of the vote in the Reichstag elections of 1912. It is reflected in the fact that the new imperialism was not the old abstracted statism of governing elites but was rooted in *popular* nationalism. Even liberals in the progressive tradition like Friedrich Naumann and Max Weber were strong imperialists, endorsing popular nationalism in the wake of the First World War and citing national survival as the reason for reform at home. The rise of the social and the popular is further reflected in the fact that nationalism in the Weimar Republic was made legitimate no longer by reference to the monarch but by reference to the people.

Hence all bourgeois parties, to whom the notion 'popular' had previously been anathema, became *Volksparteien*. The National Liberals changed their name to the Deutsche Volkspartei, the Conservatives became the Deutsche Nationale Volkspartei and the Progressives the Deutsche Demokratische Partei (Hunt, 1964).

Further to the west there were also strong pressures, with the rise of organized capitalism, for the bourgeoisie to sacrifice the principles of the Enlightenment on the altar of the new particularisms. But here the longer and deeper experience of a universalistic public sphere prevented the anti-democratic excesses of their German counterparts.

All of this goes a long way in the explanation of what Jeffrey Herf has called the 'reactionary modernism' of the Weimar Republic and Third Reich. According to Herf, reactionary modernism was an ideology widespread among the right in Germany of the 1920s and 1930s which successfully combined a set of contradictory elements into the same coherent thematic (1984, p. 10). What was combined was the *Gemeinschaftlichkeit*, particularism and anti-intellectualism of the early nineteenth-century Romantic reaction with the ethos of technical and aesthetic modernization. Originating in the Weimar Republic analyses and polemics of young populist conservatives in the engineering profession and the work of intellectual figures such as Spengler, Carl Schmitt, Ernst Junger, Heidegger and Sombart, this ideology became the 'common sense' of vulgar politics and everyday life in the Third Reich.

The intellectual tradition of philosophic anthropology has consistently worked from the counterposition of *Kultur* to *Zivilisation*, the concrete and particular to abstraction, and *Gemeinschaft* to *Gesellschaft*. What the reactionary modernists were able to do was to remove technology from the abstract sphere of economic calculability and (cosmopolitan) *Zivilisation* and insert it as integral to the national *Gemeinschaft* of (Germanic) *Kultur*. The new ideology rose out of the experience of the front in the First World War. In this context, technical advance in military hardware lost its connection with abstract economic rationality. The producer also lost its connection with the abstract market, as the Germanic worker-soldier was placed in high relief to the cosmopolitan citizen. The *Gemeinschaft* of battle was 'modernized', not only through its association with technics, but through its aestheticization. Walter Benjamin wrote of the reactionary celebration of war as beauty espoused by Ernst Junger and the Italian futurist Marinetti, where experience of the front was turned into a 'cultic object' and a metaphysical abstraction (ibid., pp. 32 ff.). This was linked with the Faustian infinitization of self, integral to the modernist sensibility. Thus Junger wrote of the inner impulses towards life expressed in battle and through membership of the front's *Blutgemeinschaft*. The *Gemeinschaft* in the new ideology was not, however, the hallowed community of medieval myth but a modernist *Gemeinschaft* of the battle front. It was in this sense a *Gemeinschaft* of the national *state*. It was a *Gemeinschaft* which stemmed not from tradition but from the *invention* of tradition, driven by nationalism and the interests of the German state.

Also formed in the *Fronterlebnis*, and key agents of dissemination of reactionary modernist ideology, were Weimar's new generation of professional engineers. Writing in the journal *Technik und Kultur* of the Verband Deutscher Diplom-Ingenieure, these new militants followed Werner Sombart in his distinction between a Germanic sphere of production and a cosmopolitan and Jewish sphere of circulation. Writing in *Die Tat*, the mazagine most widely read among right-wing intellectuals, engineer ideologues drew on Schopenhauer's parallel distinction between 'visualizing thought', which engineering exemplified, and 'conceptualizing thought' of the abstract intellectual. Again, in the writings of the engineers we see the ideological triptych of technics, aesthetics and war. Thus Ernst Junger drew on Nietzsche to speak of will and beauty as linked to technology. What the engineers had done was to remove the identification of technics with the economy and identify the spirit of the frontline soldier with the 'instinct of technology', and to counterpose the 'technical-creative individual' to the 'calculating capitalist' (ibid., pp. 178–81, 186). At the same time, however, in the persistent espousal of war imagery and the *Blutgemeinschaft*, they had taken the *state* from 'system' and reintegrated it into the life-world.

The aesthetic dimension of this new German ideology was as relentlessly exploited as the technical one. Thus Albert Speer's Bureau of the Beauty of Labour saw the engineer as creative artist. It identified technology with form and *Kultur* in contrast to the formlessness of *Zivilisation*, and used the language of inwardness to cast productive labour in an aestheticist mode. Aesthetic modernist self-infinitization was very much of a piece with (especially bowdlerized) conceptions of *Innerlichkeit*, expressionism, authenticity and vitalism. In this sense Walter Benjamin foreshadowed mass society theory in writing that in fascism the 'masses' do not have 'rights' but 'the chance to express themselves' (ibid., p. 34). Heidegger advocated withdrawal from politics in the interest of self-preservation and held that *innerlich* authenticity was fulfilled by participation, not in the public sphere, but in the national *Volksgemeinschaft*.

What Benjamin feared and Heidegger celebrated is very much what, among our contemporaries, Jean Baudrillard has described as 'implosion' and the 'dissolution of the social'. In Baudrillard's vision of postmodernity the expressive force of the masses' desire is externalized into the 'images', the simulacra of communication and information networks. In this instance the substance of the social, and this too would spell the death of the public sphere, is 'imploded' into the spectacle of consumer culture. In this model it is not the media and digitalized information which reproduce social relations of domination; instead the social has become subordinated to the simulacrum and functions merely in the reproduction of the latter. Unlike Baudrillard's mass society interpretation of postmodernity, Heidegger and Benjamin's mass society is located firmly in the modern (Kroker and Cook, 1988; Lancaster Regionalism Group, 1989, ch. 5). And the public sphere and the social implode, not into networks of media and computers, but into the national *Gemeinschaft* of the Third Reich's state. I will return to this issue in the conclusion to this chapter.

The statist assumptions of reactionary modernism's self-infinitization is illustrated in the world of Third Reich political theorist Carl Schmitt. Schmitt's radical voluntarism, his refusal of causality in favour of teleology, bears comparison on crucial points with the position of Georg Lukács. Both Schmitt and Lukács extended their voluntarism to the practice of *collective* actors, in Schmitt's case the state, in Lukács's the proletariat. Both theorists opposed the Whiggish, mechanistic and evolutionist assumptions of both liberalism and conventional Marxism. Schmitt held that technological progress would bring, not moral betterment, but only a heightening of violent conflict. Hence the state would not wither away but would of necessity play a heightened role as economies modernized. Schmitt was thus, like Weber, an arch-separatist concerning the realm of morality and the realms of politics and law. Like Schmitt, Weber saw a future of heightened power struggles. But unlike Weber, whose ethic of responsibility was grounded in a sober realism, Schmitt celebrated power and struggle as values in themselves (Turner and Factor, 1987).

Whereas many of their contemporaries wanted to reserve *Innerlichkeit* to the aesthetic realm, Schmitt and Lukács were mainly concerned with *political* expressionism. For the young Lukács the result was an extreme left, almost anarchist collective and individualist voluntarism; for Schmitt, the famous doctrine of 'decisionism'. Decisionism contends that 'self-realization is possible only through the exercise of will and decision on the part of the political actor'. In a Sorelian vein it claims that 'political action is a value in itself regardless of the normative justifications attached to it' (Herf, 1984, pp. 44, 118). Decisionism presumes that all political relations are in principle reducible to that of friend versus foe.

Schmitt, E. Böckenförde (1976) argues, must be understood as a Hobbesian. That is, Schmitt's state must above all be protected against internal and external enemies. Each of the above tenets of decisionism for the individual actor holds equally for the state as collective actor. State action, therefore, is a value in itself. Political decisions must be divorced from any normative foundation other than the affirmation of state power. And all political relations for the state can be reduced to that of friend/foe. More programmatically, the actual situation that the state is faced with creates its own legality; emergencies supersede the general norms of the law; and sovereign is he who makes the decision in the emergency situation (Herf, 1984, p. 44; Mommsen, 1984).

The other side of Schmitt's action theory, like Parsons's and Nietzsche's, is an effective functionalism. Thus Schmitt's state is an 'autopoetic', or self-reproducing, system with internal and external environments. The internal environment is not concerned with the economic or with system integration, but with the normative and social integration. Foreign relations for the state is a matter of extended self-reproduction. Similarly, the problem of normative (internal) regulation has very little to do with *Rechtsstaatlichkeit*. It is instead fully to subordinate legal matters, in the context of identification of friend and foe, to the maximization of state power.

How could this statist ideology still dominate in an era of the hegemony of the social? Carl Schmitt's state was 'a militant national political community'. Schmitt may have been a Hobbesian, but Hobbes's state was transcendent, where Schmitt's is concrete and particular. Hobbes's state had little which was militant and surely nothing communal about it. It was, further, questionably even national, or if so in a sense far removed from modern nationalisms. Modernity is indeed the era of the social, but it is also the era of the immanence of power in the social. Paradoxically perhaps, what is distinctive about German modernity, and this is the key ingredient of totalitarianism as well as twentieth-century corporatism, is that this power which is immanent in the social is *state* power.

Whether transcendent or immanent, the persistence of statist ideology throws light on the seemingly unproblematic Nazi conquest of the middle-class electorate from the liberal parties. Statist beliefs –

reinforced by the continued salience of the *Beamten* in the German bourgeoisie – underlay the low level of commitment of Liberals and Nazis to party politics and parliament (Sheehan, 1978, pp. 55–6). Further, the Nazis had the same old enemies – the Sozialdemokratische Partei Deutschlands (SPD) and the Catholics – as the Liberals. Finally both appealed to heightened sentiments of nationalism.

Anti-statism in the federal republic

I have so far not addressed the question of dominant ideologies' impact on the subordinate classes in Germany. There has been considerable interest in this subject. The whole 'legitimation crisis' literature sparked by Offe (1984) and Habermas (1976) was largely grounded in assumptions arising from the original ideological integration of the working class through Bismarck's introduction of social insurance in the 1880s. Here bourgeois strategies entailed a quid pro quo, whereby material benefits were won in exchange for the sacrifice of democratic rights. This sort of argument is, however, not based on the extension of a dominant ideology such as statism to the subordinate classes, but in an alternative set of ruling class strategies. In this sense such arguments dovetail with the view put forth by, for example, Gunther Roth (1963). This is that the ruling class never particularly *wanted* to integrate the proletariat into the dominant system of values, but instead preferred to exclude the working class from civil society altogether. The virtual caste consciousness of *Beamten* and white-collar workers – different unions, different social legislation, more rigid social distinctions – seemed to exclude workers from the norms regulating everyday life (Kocka, 1981, pp. 116–38). The stratified electoral system, the weak role of parliament and the anti-socialist laws effectively excluded the working class from the polity also. Ideological integration of the proletariat did not seem then to be the main strategy of social control, which instead was to be had through a combination of material incentives and outright repression.

Yet statist ideology was not fully without effect. Workers were socialized during military service and by the military's importance in the garrison towns. The volte-face of social democracy and the trade unions on participation in the First World War effort cannot otherwise be understood. Perhaps statism had most impact in working-class allegiance to *Rechtsstaatlichkeit*. Such beliefs in legality partly explain the moderation of workers' committees during the brief Council Republic in the aftermath of the First World War. Given wholesale bourgeois desertion from universalist and constitutionalist values in the Weimar Republic, only the working class remained to uphold the values of bourgeois legality (Moore, 1978). A portion of the politically oriented bourgeoisie, led by Gustav Stresemann, did support the values of legality and entered into a *rechtsstaatlich* class-compromise bloc with the working class during the middle and late 1920s. The fall of the Weimar Republic is, then, partly explicable through the inability of one statist doctrine, *Rechtsstaatlichkeit*, to compete with authoritarian statism amongst the bourgeoisie, as well as the increasing prominence inside the working class of the very *unrechtsstaatlich* Communist movement.

Rechtsstaatlichkeit, however, is very much a two-edged theory. On the one hand, it connotes the legal order of the state. On the other, it signifies the legal protection of the citizen from the state. In the postwar *Bundesrepublik* it is the latter that has had the upper hand. This is exemplified in the prominence of natural law theory in the postwar decade, largely promoted by Roman Catholic political philosophers in de-Nazified universities. It is also evidenced in the frequent allusions, by left and right, to the *Grundrechte* of the West German Republic's constitution (Abendroth, 1975, pp. 174–8). For example, in the debates over the *Berufsverbot* (i.e. the refusal to allow political dissidents to be civil servants) in the middle 1970s, each side cited the constitution's Basic Laws against the other.

Thus can also be understood the ideological impact of contemporary Critical Theory, whose influence among the university-educated lay public should not be underestimated. Some, for example, like Lyotard (1984) and analysts who argue for a lineage from Carl Schmitt to Habermas, find an implicit statism in Critical Theory (Kennedy, 1987). Yet communicative rationality, however 'totalizing', in its very conception is designed to encourage and protect the development of an *Offentlichkeit* in counterposition to the coercive and arbitrary character of the *Obrigkeitsstaat* (Lash, 1985). It may be true that Offe's (1984) conception of a state engaged in pursuing its own interests is conceived in the framework of systems theory. Yet the normative component of systems theory, for Niklas Luhmann (1983) and effectively for Schmitt, has favoured the expanded reproduction of the state. Offe's state, to the contrary, functions against the public interest, in that the entity in its environment most favourable to its self-reproduction is capital itself.

This very anti-statism means, paradoxically, that the state still sets the paradigm for ideological discourse in Germany. For example, today's dominant jurisprudential theory is based on a notion of *Werte*, that is, on a set of universalistic values of legality, autonomy and citizens' rights, grounded in a refusal both of pre-1989 Eastern European statism and memories of the Third Reich. Such values, disseminated today above all by television, are just now coming under attack by neo-conservatives. One front of this challenge has been the *Historikerstreit* (1987) led by conservative academics and Chancellor Kohl's initiative in establishing a national historical museum in Berlin. The conservatives' theme in this is that Germans, like any other nation, should be proud of their history. Against this offensive, Habermas and social democratic historians have countered that the Third Reich experience is quite singular, that its historical lessons are basic to a political culture protecting civil society and the individual against the state.

The significance of this anti-statism is perhaps best illustrated in contemporary Green politics. In pursuing their prime aim of ending human domination over nature, which *is* the 'logic of exterminism', the ecology movement has necessarily posed a radical challenge to both the external and internal powers of the state. The Greens originated in the late 1970s, in the ambience of the disintegration of the quintessentially statist (Marxist-Leninist) K-Gruppe, themselves the heirs of the more radical democratic German student movement of the late 1960s. Also catalytic to their rise was SPD Chancellor Schmidt's support in 1979 for substantially increased deployment of nuclear missiles and increased centralization in education and district government (Spretnak and Capra, 1986, pp. 20–2). The central plank of the Green Party's founding convention was advocacy of a nuclear-free, neutral and decentralized 'Europe of the regions'. The idea is that smaller units of domestic government, on the level of, say, Corsica, or for the Allemannen, would mean more limited capacities for the domestic and foreign exercise of state power (ibid., p. 48).

Internal party regulations of the *Grünen* function to prevent elected representatives from being absorbed into the apparatus of the state. Bundestag and Landestag members are subject to a rotation principle, developed by the *Bürgerinitiativen* (citizens' movements) in municipal government. Thus the Greens have run twice as many candidates as there are winnable places in elections; one candidate acts as legislative assistant to the other, whom he or she will replace halfway through the legislative term. Deputies also must pay one half of their monthly salary into an Ökofund which provides resources, not for the Green Party, but for social-movement groupings such as alternative newspapers, shops and shelters for battered women. The radical accountability of deputies to the party, and hence protection against the former being integrated into the state apparatus, is illustrated in party policy development in Hesse in the mid-1980s. Ideas here were first solicited from the party rank and file on an individual basis; then a programme committee compiled these proposals into a provisional platform; third, this draft document was sent to some 100 local party groups for revisions; and finally the Hesse party assembly met for discussion and debate on six successive weekends to finalize the programme (Langner, 1987).

Some analysts, such as Jeffrey Herf, claim to have detected strains of the old nationalistic *Volksgemeinschaft* in the Greens' putative romanticism. Green philosophy, however, would seem to be polar opposite on almost every count to the reactionary modernists in Herf's account. If the latter displace the state and technics from the realm of abstract rationality and into the life-world, the Greens inversely expel both the state and rapid economic growth back to their starting-place in the realm of formal rationality. Green political philosophy, moreover, would stand fully opposed to the radical voluntarism of the reactionary modernists, on grounds of an implicit hierarchy of man over nature. Instead endorsed is a radically structuralist ecosystems theory, drawing on the writings of Ilya Prirogene, Gregory Bateson, Humberto Maturana and, more recently, Niklas Luhmann. The Greens Federal Programme promotes a 'social ecology', in which hierarchy is rejected, and all systems are seen as interwoven. It calls for human beings to find their place in these 'autopoetic', or *sui generis* and self-reproducing, networks of ecosystems (Eisel, 1987).

Among Green activists the most influential theorist is Rudolf Bahro, who has pushed this rejection of 'agency' further and maintained that the 'logic of exterminism' is built into the very notion of emancipation. Emancipation is, for Bahro (1986, p. 145), a Fichtean and Marxian concept, which assumes the power of the self-infinitizing subject over 'external' nature, over 'internal' nature, and over the 'nature' of the third world and peripheral proletariat. The concept of practice, which 'always intervenes from the standpoint of a constantly limited knowledge into states of equilibrium', should also be rejected (ibid., p. 149). Theories which privilege the individual or collective human subject, Bahro concludes, presuppose a vision of a 'patriarchal dominion over earth', a 'masculine spirituality' which is 'expressed above all in the one-sided orientation of energy "forward" [expansion progressive, etc.] and "upward", towards world appropriation by masculine conquest and towards heaven [away from earth]'. Instead a 'feminine spirituality' is advocated, which is 'directed "backward" and "downward", towards the origin in the mother's womb and the Earth, nature'. To counterpose 'feminine' ecosystems to 'masculine' notions of subjectivity is at the same time to refuse, observes Bahro, a 'suicidal patriarchal civilization' in favour of 'a biophile culture' (ibid., p. 45).

According to Green political philosophy, it is the 'supreme subject', the state, which pre-eminently embodies this 'exterminist' and 'masculine spirituality'. Green politics for some time have been divided between 'Realos' who advocate a 'long march throughout the institutions' and 'Fundis' who instead want to divert resources away from the 'formal sector', away from the 'system', to the 'alternative sector' and the 'life-world'. The driving and motivating ideological basis of the ecology movement, the alternative networks and the *Bürgerinitiativen* is surely the latter, who advocate a fundamental break with the 'core' and establishment of a 'commune network' of horizontally 'communicating peripheries' (Papcke, 1986). This is an unconditional refusal of the 'system' and *eo ipso* a rejection of statist values in two substantial senses. It is first a rejection of the internal functions of the state and the *social* system, comprised of the formal economic sector and a core political framework. In the social system, political power is wielded either in a neo-corporatist manner, through the tripartite convergence of central labour organizations, employers' federations and the state; or through the paradoxically even more interventionist (through anti-union measures, welfare service destruction, attacks on civil liberties, forced privatization) putatively neo-liberal state. The new politics of the life-world would come from those excluded from, or opting out of, the core, from minority ethnicities, peripheral nationalities, welfare recipients, feminists, ecologists, squatters and those involved in alternative work arrangements (see Offe, 1985, pp. 300 ff.).

It is, second, a rejection of the external functions of the state and the *modern world* system of nation-states competing for core status. Green philosopher Johann Galtung castigates dependency and world systems theory as 'western-centric' and holds instead that 'causality will emanate from the Third World' (Bahro, 1986, p. 131). His scenario advocates an *exit* from the world system's core following the advent of popular power. Factors of production would then be redistributed with First World countries moving substantially into agriculture. With the institution of periphery-periphery trade, the notion and reality of 'core' itself would be challenged.

Bahro likens this advocacy of withdrawl from the (statist) social system and world systems to the destruction of the earlier world system of the Roman Empire. He likens his advocacy of autarchic, self-reproducing communes to the monasteries, especially those of the Benedictine Order, that formed on the periphery of the Roman Empire, its power in cinders. The Benedictines and other orders were pivotal, Bahro observes, in establishing the valuation of labour, Christian religion and knowledge as bases for western civilization as well as disseminating these values over a vast geographical area. He envisages contemporary system–rejecting communes as potentially engaged in a similar mission. As in the case of the Benedictines, a 'long phase of accumulation of spiritual force' (Bahro, 1986, p. 98) would be necessary before these communes could properly be established external to the system. This accumulation would depend on a learning process, transforming basic structures of 'deep ideology', whose ideal space would be a 'commune network' of 'communicating peripheries'. Thus a 'common field of energy' would arise, a 'critical mass' which would result in the destabilization of exterminism in both social system and world system.

Thus the discourse of today's ecology movement, in its problematization of the state, remains within the historical and characteristically German ideological paradigm dating from early modern times. Yet it turns on its head the hypertrophied statism bequeathed by Prussian ideology and embodied in the Third Reich reactionary modernism. It calls instead for 'accumulation in the alternative sector', on 'whose foundations a comprehensive network of autonomous (thus anti–statist) base communities can emerge'. This accumulation is not of abstract (Marxist) units of economic value, nor of (Weberian) units of bureaucratic administration. It is to be an accumulation of new values, of 'deep ideology', and a refusal of statist rationality, of social and world systems, in all their guises.

Conclusions

What are the implications then of the particularities of the German case for the more general sociological study of ideology and discourse? The chapter contains implications, for example, for how ideology might be defined. Its central assumption is that ideology is a *terrain* on which political struggles are carried out. Thus the main body of this chapter was concerned with the explanation and description of statism as an ideology wielded by the dominant classes. And the last few pages have been concerned with how oppositional groupings, whether or not such groupings were of the subordinate classes, drew their resources for political struggles from the same ideological terrain as did the ruling classes.

Perhaps the best way of defining ideology is in counterposition to what ideology is not. First ideology bears certain resemblances with, yet differs importantly from, discourse. The constituent elements or units of ideology in this sense are 'ideas' while the constituent units of discourse are 'statements'. Ideologies are thus more or less systematically cohering, interarticulating networks of ideas, while discourses are more or less systematically cohering and inter-articulating networks of statements. The centrality of ideas to ideology has to do with the rootedness of ideology as a concept in the (late eighteenth- to early twentieth-century) assumptions of the philosophy of *consciousness*, while the notion of discourse is rooted in the more recent assumptions of philosophies of *language*. The other central distinction is that ideology always implies relationships of power while discourses can also exist outside of power relations.

Second, ideology is conceived in contrast to coercion. Social control can be exercised in a social formation through some combination of ideological (or discursive) and coercive resources. This combination in Germany, we saw above, gave a comparatively very large place to coercive apparatuses and a relatively minor role to the ideological. This was due, I argued, to the lateness of the development of the state in early German history. Such a retarded state development was later compensated for by the construction of an overly modern leviathan which dwarfed German civil society in its very substantiality.

Further, I argued that much of the remaining functions of social control that ideology did fulfil in Germany were fulfilled by statist ideology. Statist ideology is analytically separate from the state and is quite distinct from coercion. It is instead a set of *ideas* that glorifies the state and is captured by Gramsci in his discussion of 'statolatry'. Hence my claim that the coercive state apparatuses in Germany functioned not once but twice – first in their characteristic capacity as coercion and second as ideology. A good deal of my support for this claim was drawn from historical discussion of political institutions and political and juridical doctrines. Here the object was the exposition of a set of ideas that underlay debates in political discourse which assumed – even in the most liberal circles – the reality and desirability of a particularly salient role for the state. The discussion of political and legal philosophy, in comparison especially to the English case, also pointed to a set of ideas whose governing principle was statism.

This chapter has also dealt with a parallel set of problems regarding the relation of ideology and modernity. Above, in a loosely Foucaldian framework, I made the following observations about the relationship between the state and the social in modernity.

(1)   Prior to modernity, under absolutism, the principle of the social was subordinated to the principle of the state. It is not the state which functions to reproduce the social, but the social which functions to reproduce the state.

(2)   In the modern, which, for example, Foucault dates from the beginning of the nineteenth century, the principle of the social becomes hegemonic. And now the state functions to reproduce the power of the dominant classes in the social.

(3)   To the extent that we are now moving into a postmodern era, once again the principle of the social may well lose its hegemonic place. Now it is networks of communication and information, the images of the mediascape which challenge as a governing principle. And instead of the latter functioning to reproduce class power in the social, the social functions to reproduce the mediascape.

In this context, I argued that German exceptionalism lay in the fact that the hypertrophic development of the state with respect to the social meant that Germany probably did not move into the era of modernity until the establishment of the Weimar Republic. I suggested that if Germany had a retarded development of modernity, it also was prematurely *post*modern. That is, the social became subordinated as early as the Third Reich, as the expressive needs of the atomized German masses were, so to speak, imploded into the spectacle. But the spectacle at issue was not the 1980s' mediascape, but the Nazi state.

Now where can ideology and discourse stand in all of this? For Foucault, prior to modernity, power did not primarily operate through discourse, or, for our purposes, ideology. In his *Discipline and Punish*, the pre-modern power of the absolutist king operated directly and coercively on the body of the accused. Only in the modern, disciplinary age, did power come to act through discourse on the wrongdoer. Correspondingly, the notion of ideology was coined by de Tracy at roughly the same time as the French Revolution's heralding of the predominance of the social, and the young Marx and Engels used ideology to speak quite specifically of class domination in modern capitalist societies, in which the principle of the social is hegemonic. What I am suggesting here is that *ideology and discourse are characteristic phenomena of modernity*.

This is both bad news and good news for modernity. It is bad news to the extent that the ideas and statements of discourse and ideology tend to reproduce the power of the dominant classes. The good news is that implicit in the very notions of ideology and discourse is the assumption of the possibility of rational argumentation. Ideology is thus composed of ideas and is unthinkable outside of the rationalist and Enlightenment assumptions of the likes of de Tracy and Marx. Discourse too is composed of statements and hence propositions, which imply reasoned argument. Foucault's discourses are indeed bodies of rational knowledge, such as clinical medicine, jurisprudence and so on. Ideological statements must in this context be sustained or legitimated through some sort of reasoned argument. And not only dominant but subordinate classes are capable of using this. That is, subordinate classes and oppositional groupings can use rational argument on their own part for emancipatory purposes. If the bourgeoisie can, for instance, use reasoned notions of abstract rights to back up claims to property, then working class, anti–racist and feminist groupings can also use such notions of rights to legitimate their own emancipatory demands.

The really bad news, however, comes in postmodernity. Now it is the networks of communications and information themselves which are primarily being reproduced. Hence ideology and discourse come to be superfluous in their constitutive role, i.e. of reproducing the social and its characteristic power relations. Further, in post-modernity, the role of ideas is progressively displaced by the flatness of the image, the propositions of discourse to the 'rush' of the spectacle. Enlightenment assumptions of reasoned argument – implicit in the notion of ideology and in discursive culture in general – are simply erased in postmodernism's figural culture. It may well be true that networks of images and simulacra of postmodernism also provide a terrain that can be made use of by oppositional as well as dominant forces. But if postmodernism does mean a decline in reasoned discourse, there is surely no guarantee that even oppositional forces can use the new cultural terrain to build a better world. The pre-eminently modern assumptions of growing self-reflexivity, of social change as a *Lernprozess*, are simply not present in the flattened cultured of the image and figure. They are very much present, and indeed are part and parcel of, the very same *Weltanschauung*, as notions of ideology and discourse. Daniel Bell, in another register, once celebrated the implications for ideology of the coming of the post-industrial society. On very different grounds, we may indeed one day regret that the coming of postmodernity has heralded the decline, indeed the end, of ideology.

Bibliography

Abendroth, W. (1975), *Arbeiterklasse, Staat und Verfassung* (Frankfurt: Europaische Verlagsanstalt).
Anderson, P. (1974), *Lineages of the Absolutist State* (London: New Left Books).

Bahro, R. (1986), *Building the Green Movement* (London: GMP).
Beck, L. (1965). *Studies in the Philosophy of Kant* (Indianapolis, Ind.: Bobbs-Merrill).
Bendix, R. (1964), *Nation Building and Citizenship* (New York: Wiley).
Bendix, R. (1978), *Kings or People* (Berkeley, Calif.: University of California Press).
Blackbourn, D. and Eley, G. (1984), *The Peculiarities of German History* (Oxford: Oxford University Press).
Böckenförde, E. (1976), *Staat, Gesellschaft, Freiheit. Studien zur Staatstheorie und zum Verfassungsrecht* (Frankfurt am Main: Suhrkamp).
Bourdieu, P. (1984), *Distinction: a social critique of the judgement of taste* (London: Routledge & Kegan Paul).
Braun, R. (1975), 'Taxation, sociopolitical structure, and state-building: Great Britain and Brandenburg-Prussia', in C. Tilly (ed.), *The Formation of National States in Western Europe* (Princeton, NJ: Princeton University Press), pp. 243–327.

Cassirer, E. (1955), *The Philosophy of the Enlightenment* (Boston, Mass.: Beacon Press).
Craig, G. (1955), *The Politics of the Prussian Army, 1640–1945* (Oxford: Oxford University Press).

Dahrendorf, R. (1980), *Society and Democracy in Germany* (Westport, Conn.: Greenwood).

Eisel, S. (1967), 'Die Gefahr des Irrationelen. Wie die Grünen der ideologischen Versuchung erliegen', in M. Langner (ed.), *Die Grünen auf dem Prüfstand* (Bergisch Gladbach: Lubbe), pp. 249–82.
Evans, E. L. (1981), *The German Center Party, 1870–1933* (Carbondale, Ill.: Southern Illinois University Press).
Eyck, E. (1958), *Bismarck and the German Empire* (London: Allen & Unwin).

Finnis, J. (1980), *Natural Law and Natural Rights* (Oxford: Clarendon Press).
Fischer, W. and Lundgreen, P. (1975), 'The recruitment and training of administrative and technical personnel', in C. Tilly (ed.), *The Formation of National States in Western Europe* (Princeton, NJ: Princeton University Press), pp. 481–538.

Foucault, M. (1980), *Power/Knowledge* (Brighton: Harvester).

Gerschenkron, A. (1962), *Economic Backwardness in Historical Perspective* (Cambridge, Mass.: Belknap).
Gordon, C. (1987), 'The soul of the citizen: Max Weber and Michel Foucault on rationality and government', in S. Whimster and S. Lash (eds), *Max Weber, Rationality and Modernity* (London: Allen & Unwin), pp. 293–316.

Habermas, J. (1976), *Legitimation Crisis* (London: Heinemann).
Hamerow, T. (1966), *Restoration, Revolution, Reaction, Economics and Politics in Germany, 1815–1871* (Princeton, NJ: Princeton University Press).
Hart, H. L. A. (1961), *The Concept of Law* (Oxford: Clarendon).
Herf, J. (1984), *Reactionary Modernism* (Cambridge: Cambridge University Press).
Historikerstreit (1987), *Die Dokumentation der Kontrovers um die Gegenwärtigkeit der nationalsozialistischen Judenvernichtung* (Munich: Piper).
Hubatsch, W. (1985), 'Frederick the Great and the problem of raison d'état', in W. Hubatsch, *Studies in Medieval and Modern German History* (New York: St Martin's Press), pp. 70–92.

Kehr, E. (1977), *Economic Interest, Militarism and Foreign Policy* (Berkeley, Calif.: University of California Press).
Kennedy, E. (1987), 'Carl Schmitt and the Frankfurt School', *Telos*, no. 71, Spring, pp. 37–66.
Kirchheimer, O. and Neumann, F. (1987), *Social Democracy and the Rule of Law* (London: Allen & Unwin).
Kocka, J. (1977), 'Zur Problematik der deutschen Angestellten, 1914–1933', in H. Mommsen, D. Petzina and B. Weisbrod (eds), *Industrielles System und politische Entwicklung in der Weimarer Republik* (Düsseldorf: Droste), pp. 792–810.
Kocka, J. (1981), *Die Angestellten in der deutschen Geschichte, 1850–1980* (Gottingen: Vandenhoeck & Ruprecht).
Kocka, J. (1987), 'Bürgertum und Bürgerlichkeit als Probleme der deutschen Geschichte vom spaten 18 zum frühen 20 Jahrhundert', in J. Kocka (ed.), *Bürger und Bürgerlichkeit im 19 Jahrhundert* (Göttingen: Vandenhoeck & Ruprecht), pp. 21–63.
Krieger, L. (1957), *The German Idea of Freedom* (Chicago: University of Chicago Press).
Kroker, A. and Cook, D. (1988), *The Postmodern Scene* (London: Macmillan).

Lancaster Regionalism Group (1990), *Restructuring Class and Gender* (London: Sage).
Langner, M. (1987), 'Die Grünen im Parteisystem', in M. Langner (ed.), *Grünen auf dem Prüfstand* (Bergisch Gladbach: Lubbe), pp. 31–59.
Lash, S. (1985), 'Postmodernity and Desire', *Theory and Society*, vol. 14, pp. 1–33.
Lash, S. (1987), 'Modernity or modernism: Weber and contemporary social theory', in S. Whimster and S. Lash (eds), *Max Weber, Rationality and Modernity* (London: Allen & Unwin), pp. 355–77.
Lash, S. and Urry, J. (1987), *The End of Organized Capitalism* (Cambridge: Polity).

Lepsius, R. (1987), 'Zur Soziologie des Bürgertums und der Bürgerlichkeit', in J. Kocka (ed.), *Bürger und Bürgerlichkeit im 19 Jahrhundert* (Gottingen: Vandenhoeck & Ruprecht), pp. 79–100.

Luhmann, N. (1983), *Legitimation durch Verfahren* (Frankfurt am Main: Suhrkamp).

Lyotard, J.-F. (1984), *The Postmodern Condition* (Manchester: Manchester University Press).

Maravall, J. (1986), *Culture of the Baroque* (Manchester: Manchester University Press).

Meinecke, F. (1977), *The Age of German Liberation, 1795–1815* (Berkeley, Calif.: University of California Press).

Mommsen, W. (1984), *Max Weber and German Politics* (Chicago: University of Chicago Press).

Moore, B. (1978), *Injustice* (London: Macmillan).

Offe, C. (1984), *Contradictions of the Welfare State* (London: Hutchinson).

Offe, C. (1985), 'The divergent rationalities of administrative action', in C. Offe, *Disorganized Capitalism* (Cambridge: Polity), pp. 300–16.

Papcke, S. (1986), 'Ökologie – Politik – Macht: Uberlegung zu ihrer Vernetzung', in N. Kunz (ed.), *Ökologie und Sozialismus* (Cologne: Bund-Verlag), pp. 132–57.

Poggi, G. (1978), *Development of the Modern State* (London: Hutchinson).

Ritter, G. (1968), *Frederick the Great* (Berkeley, Calif.: University of California Press).

Rosenberg, H. (1966), *Bureaucracy, Aristocracy and Autocracy, The Prussian Experience, 1660–1815* (Boston, Mass.: Beacon Press).

Ruppert, W. (1984), *Bürgerlicher Wandel, Diem Geburt der modernen deutschen Gesellschaft im 18 Jahrhundert* (Frankfurt am Main: Fischer).

Sheehan, J. (1978), *German Liberalism in the Nineteenth Century* (Chicago: University of Chicago Press).

Spretnak, C. and Capra, F. (1986), *Green Politics* (Santa Fe, N. Mexico: Bear).

Stern, F. (1961), *The Politics of Cultural Despair* (Berkeley, Calif.: University of California Press).

Strauss, L. (1953), *Natural Right and History* (Chicago: University of Chicago Press).

Turner, S. and Factor, R. (1987), 'Decisionism and politics: Weber as constitutional theorist', in S. Whimster and S. Lash (eds), *Max Weber, Rationality and Modernity* (London: Allen & Unwin), pp. 334–54.

CHAPTER

4

Re-reading Japan: capitalism, possession and the necessity of hegemony

ANTHONY WOODIWISS

The Dominant Ideology Thesis and contemporary Marxism

I share with Abercrombie *et al.* (1980) their rejection of the dominant ideology thesis. However, I also share with Therborn (1984) his doubts concerning the accuracy of their ascription of this thesis to contemporary Marxists. More specifically, it has always seemed to me that the train of thought which was so influentially exemplified by Gramsci's concept of 'hegemony', created the possibility of a clear move away from any such thesis. A move made necessary not least by the fact that, if the thesis was correct, it would be extremely difficult to conceive of how a socialist revolution might be possible. At least as regards the issues raised in *The Dominant Ideology Thesis* and with the benefit of hindsight, it now seems that there is little that separates Abercrombie *et al.* from the aforementioned train of Marxist thought (cp. Jessop, 1982, ch. 5; Wolpe, 1980, intro.). Both camps would appear to agree with the following propositions: (1) that the relationship between capitalism as an economic structure and its political and economic conditions of existence is best understood as a relatively autonomous one; (2) that the combination of ideological and political structures and their attendant sets of relations with economic ones at the birth of capitalism exhibited wide variations from case to case; (3) that the conditions necessary for the continuing existence of capitalist economic relations were and are of a general rather than a specific kind; and (4) that because of these requirements capitalist economic relations exert a certain influence over political and ideological relations as well as vice versa.

What continue to separate the two camps, however, are their contrasting answers to the question as to whether or not the relationships between capitalism and its conditions of existence are ultimately contingent. Abercrombie *et al.* say they are, whereas the neo–Marxists say they are not. The body of this chapter comprises a discussion of the development of Japanese capitalism, in the course of which I will take the neo–Marxists' part in this argument. However, in order that this decision may be understood some further discussion of the theoretical differences between the present position and that of Abercrombie *et al.* is required.

Discourse, law and hegemony

In my view, and implicitly in Abercrombie *et al.*'s (1986, p. 181) too, one of the structural conditions necessary to capitalism's initial and continuing existence is the secure possession of the means of production by some to the exclusion of others. As Abercrombie *et al.* have correctly emphasized, the 'dull compulsions' that are the result of the unequal distribution of economic and political resources have an important part to play in the explanation of how such possession is retained, but still a part. In addition, attention has to be paid to the ideological realm, since within it are defined some of he bases upon which, and some of the mechanisms through which, any system of unequally distributed resources and powers is established and continued. These particular bases and mechanisms are those upon which and through which are defined who is entitled to the possession of what. In other words, they comprise both general justificatory discourses such as may be extracted from religious and/or secular bodies of thought (e.g. individualism) and, typically, legal discourses. Of course, Abercrombie *et al.* do not deny the pertinence of the law nor indeed the necessity of capitalist possession being legally secured. Unfortunately, like most other social scientists and even jurists, they appear to have difficulty in recognizing the social and sociological significance of the fact that the law is in part an instance of discourse and hence, by definition, an instance of the ideological too. Thus it seems to me (Woodiwiss, 1990a, intro., ch. 5), that if one says that there are certain legal conditions that are necessary for capitalism's existence then one is also saying that certain ideological conditions are necessary. It is important to note, however, that to say certain non-economic conditions are necessary for capitalism to exist does not mean that they will automatically be present every time capitalist economic relations are present. All it means is that if such conditions are not present then capitalist economic relations cannot survive.

As a historical generalization, it seems reasonable to say that, so long as those identified as the possessors in the general justificatory discourse are also those who are actually in exclusive and unchallenged possession of both the means of production and the power necessary to enforce their possession, the role of legal discourse will be a subordinate one. Where or as such conditions cease to hold (e.g. as in the transition from feudalism to capitalism in western Europe), the demand increases for the specific, state-supported tasks performed by a legal system (i.e. those of allowing and validating claims to possession and of adjudicating upon claims that are contested). What is important in the current context, however, is neither the difference between the general justificatory discourses and the legal ones nor the specifics of the changing relations between them. Rather what is important is that (*contra* Abercrombie *et al.*), regardless of whether or not the law is an aspect of it, possession has to have an ideological dimension if it is to be secure. However, this dimension need have no very specific content, even where capitalist possession is concerned. Specifically, it need not even include a legal system premised upon rights to so-called 'absolute private property'. For example, in England feudal law was made/was able to find room for capitalist private property, and the rights of title and possession so constituted were for a long time quite sufficient to secure capitalist possession of the means of production (Woodiwiss, 1987b).

Turning now to Abercrombie *et al.*'s continued refusal of the concept of hegemony, this again is a position with which I cannot agree, since, to repeat, I am persuaded that, so far from carrying the dominant ideology thesis with it, it is only the concept of hegemony which allows processes of ideological transition to be investigated with any subtlety and precision. As understood by Laclau and Mouffe (1985), the concept of hegemony enables one to understand how it is that, sometimes, the discourses of rulers may coexist with but at the same time still dominate other and opposed ones. To be more specific, when combined with the concept of discourse, that of hegemony enables one to understand how an opposed discourse is, so to speak, partially absorbed by what then becomes, if only temporarily, a superordinate one through the successful broadcasting of a set of 'equivalences' (ibid., pp. 134 ff.); for example, as is attempted every time a conservative politician says to the media audience, after disparaging a group of strikers, something like, 'We believe in high wages *too, but* the best way to obtain them is by allowing management to manage.' The result is that when such attempts are successful and when what then becomes the subordinate discourse is interrogated as to what it has to say about issues critical to the survival of capital, it is often found to be in agreement with the superordinate discourse.

In sum and in keeping with Gramsci's original usage, the term 'hegemony' should not be taken as referring to conditions where one discourse replaces others but rather to those where one discourse effects a displacement in others. The result is that the hegemonic ideology so defines the common sense of a society that to speak otherwise in the public realm is to risk not being taken seriously and therefore not being able to mobilize or in any sense depend upon the support of the non-normative resources and powers of that society. In sum, in and of itself an hegemonic ideology has certain powerful disciplinary effects, which, for example, may be sufficient under certain circumstances to make up for any absence of such effects on the part of the law.

Rereading Japan

Abercrombie *et al.* are quite correct to regard Japan as a critical case in relation to the development of our understanding of the role of ideology in the development of capitalist societies. However, I disagree with their reading of the literature concerned with Japan's development. The root of our disagreement appears to lie in the very divergent readings allowed by the ambiguity of much of this literature as it relates to the issue which separates us. This ambiguity is particularly marked in relation to the nature of Japan's dominant or, as I would prefer to call it, hegemonic ideology. Typically, the ideology is referred to as Confucian and 'groupist', which has the effect of sometimes and in some usages obscuring the hierarchical nature of the relationships which the ideology celebrates. Instead of 'groupist' Abercrombie *et al.* use the term 'collectivist', which, although they may not intend it, unfortunately only intensifies this effect, especially when it is read in the context of the recurrent debate about whether or not Japan is a capitalist society (see below, p. 104 ff). In sum, there is a danger, which in my view Abercrombie *et al.*

do not sufficiently guard against, that their confidence that the Japanese case provides clinching evidence for their thesis that capitalism has no particular ideological conditions of existence rests upon a representation of Japan which has built into it the very assumption they wish to prove.

In what follows I wish to contest any suggestion: (1) that Confucianism has been the ultimate and ever-present source of Japan's 'groupism'; and (2) that there has been or is anything remotely 'collectivist' about Japanese society, at least in so far as the term connotes an in any way egalitarian or non-capitalist set of social relations. Instead, I wish to argue for the following propositions: (1) that Confucianism was strenuously challenged by a number of other discourses which coexisted with it in late Tokugawa Japan; (2) that it never again became even a dominant ideology in its own right; (3) that the ideology which did become hegemonic after the restoration of 1868 was strongly marked by its fulfilling of a necessary role in the securing of capitalist possession; and finally, (4) that in the postwar period the latter ideology has itself been subject to a displacement which has made it a specifically capitalist discourse.

Since at least the latter part of the nineteenth century, the central theme of the successive variants of the discourse which has been hegemonic in Japan and the ultimate source therefore of the society's continuing nationalism, has been the idea that Japan is unique. As I have argued elsewhere (Woodiwiss, 1989a), the widespread acceptance of this idea inside as well as outside Japan has been as much the result of European/American 'orientalisms' as of indigenous Japanese discourses. The argument that Japan was or is essentially Confucianist simply gives a positive value to the claim that it was or is a very different kind of society from so-called 'western societies'. The claim made by Morishima (1982) and, following him, by Abercrombie *et al.* that Japan's Confucianism has always been different from other Confucianisms simply gives a positive value to the claim that Japan is unique.

This is the point at which my critique will begin, since other and subsequent scholarship has cast considerable doubt upon the claim that Confucianism exhausted or even dominated late Tokugawa ideology (e.g. Harootunian, 1970, 1988; Najita, 1987; Koschmann, 1987), as well as upon the claim that in its Japanese form Confucianism was always marked by a particular and distinctive stress on loyalty as opposed to benevolence (e.g. McMullan, 1987). Thus not only is Confucianism not especially germane to the explanation of Japanese economic development, but also the particularity which Morishima claims made/makes Japan's Confucianism unique is one which, if it ever did become especially characteristic, became so only after the commencement of the direct ideological challenges which included individualist, nativist, regionalist and even classist elements and which contributed to the disorder that eventually allowed the Meiji Restoration. Moreover, after the restoration Confucianism was largely absorbed into the more general patriarchialist, centralist and nationalist ideological formation that was latterly to become known as *tennosei* (belief in the emperor system).

Hegemony and the securing of capitalist possession

My alternative argument will be: (1) that, alongside a legal right to non-feudal title, the insistence on loyalty and obedience intrinsic to feudal patriarchalism at both the *han* and village levels, which as it happens was sometimes challenged by Japanese Confucianists (McMullan, 1987), was for a time ideologically sufficient to secure capitalist possession; (2) that it was stressed only as society changed and in particular as the workshop gave way to the factory as the typical setting wherein this possession was at issue. In making this argument I will also and necessarily cast doubt upon any claim that this ideology was or is in any way 'collectivistic'. My argument here will be that the effect, if not necessarily the initial purpose, of the pre- and postwar efforts to interpellate the citizenry as members of various strongly hierarchical but supposedly family-type groups, has been the same as it would have been had they been interpellated directly as individual citizens; i.e. it made a necessary if not a sufficient contribution to the securing of capitalist possession in the hands of the pertinent patriarchs whether they were human entrepreneurs or non-human corporate entities.

In order to establish these points, I will now outline the development of what not even Abercrombie *et al.* deny was an hegemonic ideology as it relates to capitalist possession for the two periods of Japanese history which are most critical in the light of the questions at issue between us: namely, the period before the promulgation of the Meiji Constitution and the period after the ending of the Pacific War. The first period is critical because the necessity of certain legal and extra-legal ideological conditions being met if capitalism is to exist is apparent even though capitalism was very underdeveloped and neither the embodiments of capital nor the office-holders in the emergent Meiji state had much conscious sense of what these might be (Akita, 1967; Marshall, 1967). The second period is critical because, although capitalist possession had long been legally secured, a transformed variant of the same patriarchalist discourse has continued to be hegemonic and, so far from ushering in what some claim is a new post-capitalist era, it has powerfully reinforced capitalist possession in the face of a sometimes strenuous trade union challenge which also has had the support of the law (Ayusawa, 1966; Moore, 1983; Woodiwiss, 1990b).

The creation of a capitalist economy

In the literature pertaining to the economic history of late Tokugawa and early Meiji Japan, there is general agreement that capitalist production relations existed and were of some significance within the economy. However, the analytical criteria upon which such judgements are made are seldom made explicit. And in so far as they are, they often seem to be in conflict with the descriptions that are offered of the relations concerned. More specifically, emphasis is placed on aspects of exchange rather than production: on the emergence of a money economy; on the consequent monetization of agricultural relationships; on the growth of a rural/urban artisanate; and on the growing importance of urban merchants (*shonin*) in terms of their wealth, the financial dependence of many feudal lords on them and their ownership of reclaimed land (i.e. *shinden*, or land 'unknown' to the shogunal authorities; Nakamura, 1983, p. 49). In these ways capitalism is said to have established itself.

When, however, one reads descriptions of the production relations obtaining within the productive units so circumscribed (e.g. Hirschmeier and Yui, 1981; Smith, 1959), one is struck by their similarity to those generally classified as simple commodity production. They are those, in other words, that normally would be recognized as father/family, or master/servant relations, wherein the powers intrinsic to possession are vested in the head of the 'house' or *ie* (household). The major difference seems to be that aspects of their conditions of existence radically reduced the autonomy of the 'houses' relative to feudalism, as well as, therefore, the possibility of their being transmuted into capitalist enterprises. For example, agricultural landholdings, merchant ownership of buildings and the land upon which they stood, reclaimed land, and the commodities in which they dealt, all seem to have been secure enough (see below, p. 105). However, the existence of both lordly prerogatives and variable tax-rent levels always influenced and could have been used to determine the productivity of and so to assert a possessory power over agriculture, although it appears they seldom were. Nevertheless, loans could be, and often were, forced from merchants by the *daimyo* (feudal lords), who seldom felt under any obligation to repay them. Additionally, restrictions on the free movement of labour were rigorously enforced. And finally, even the non-feudal possessory rights which did exist were legitimated by an uncompromisingly feudal ideology, which made the enjoyment of any such rights very dependent upon the goodwill of social superiors, which in the case of the merchants was virtually everyone else, including their employees, the peasantry.

All that said, there seems to be no reason to doubt that many artisans, merchants and other non-lordly property-holders nevertheless not only sustained their autonomy as simple commodity producers, but also succeeded in transforming their 'houses' and farms into capitalist enterprises, albeit generally of a very small size. What distinguished the production relations obtaining in the latter as compared to the former, of course, was that the labourers were free to leave when they pleased and therefore able to bargain over their wages and conditions. And this despite the facts that these freedoms were supported by no legal rights, contractual or otherwise, and that the dominant ideology continued to deprecate them in the strongest possible terms. (For the existence of an urban free labour market, see Wilkinson, 1965, and for that of a rural one see Smith, 1959.)

Many individual units of both kinds of enterprise were entirely dependent upon demands emanating from feudal society, and so dependent upon the wider effects of its ideological thrall that they failed to survive its disappearance. Nevertheless, simple commodity and capitalist production were the principal economic beneficiaries of the collapse/destruction of feudalism. For the first time their existence was entirely secure, if only negatively for the first four years after the restoration, given that the hitherto dominant feudal system no longer existed. These two modes of production, then, largely by default, defined the principal ways in which the production of 'traditional' commodities and that of newly introduced 'western' ones would be carried out from then on (Nakamura, 1983, pp. 104 ff.). Of the two modes of production, simple commodity production was the dominant one, since it was, almost automatically, what was left in agriculture after the disappearance of Japan's 'feudalism without manors'. It was also usually all that was financially or technologically possible in manufacturing and services. Both forms of production sustained themselves in agriculture and expanded quite markedly in manufacturing. Small capitalist production grew at the expense of simple commodity production in both sectors, and *rentier* capitalism also grew at its expense in agriculture (Moore, 1966, pp. 275 ff.). However, neither simple commodity nor capitalist producers were among the direct beneficiaries of the larger scale, state-sponsored investments in infrastructure and production, when these began to pay off towards the end of the period under review.

The newly established banks, which rapidly became the major providers of capital, preferred to invest in the even more newly established joint stock companies such as Mitsubishi or the few surviving and reconstructed large-scale merchant houses such as Mitsui. They were often related to the latter anyway through interlocks of one kind or another. It was to such well-connected companies that the state preferred to sell its own enterprises, and at knockdown prices too. In this way several of the infamous *zaibatsu* were created that were eventually to dominate the economy in the interwar period. Their presence, alongside that of the remarkably resilient small-scale production units, was to be one of the major reasons why the Japanese economy gained its particularly pronounced dualistic structure (Broadbridge, 1966).

The creation of *tennosei*

The extremely rapid construction of a very potent capitalist economy is what is best known today about the early Meiji era. What ought to be at least as widely known, but is not, is that this era also saw the equally rapid reconstruction of what might be called 'traditional Confucian patriarchalism' so that it became a much more diffuse but nevertheless extremely efficacious social ideology, centred on the *tenno* (emperor) and reverence for his office.

Today, fortunately, it is far easier than it was to obtain knowledge of the construction and diffusion of this ideology, thanks largely to the work of Carol Gluck (1985). She has looked beyond the works of ideologues and read deeply into such other texts as 'village plans, teachers' reports, statistical surveys, political speeches, diaries, memoirs, popular songs' (ibid., p. 14). Before summarizing, reordering and slightly reinterpreting Gluck's broader findings so that they fit better with the analytical framework lying behind the present chapter, it is important to emphasize, as she does, that, like the use of the term *tennosei* itself, the systematization of the ideological reality to which it refers occurred only at a later date: postwar in the case of the term and in the 1930s in that of the ideological reality. Nevertheless, as she also emphasizes, this should not lead one either to doubt the ideology's earlier presence or to underestimate its earlier effects. The formation and effectivity of *tennosei* was continuous, if not uncontested (Bix, 1986, pt 4; Irokawa, 1985, chs 1–4), from the moment of restoration onwards and indeed before. Some of its roots were in the Shinto revivalism, nativism and scholarly political theory of the late Tokugawa period, as one would expect given the centrality of the *tenno* in the emergent anti-*bakufu* (anti-shogunate) struggles (Earl, 1964; Hall, 1968a; Harootunian, 1970). Its supposedly non-ideological and originally Confucian insistence on 'loyalty' and 'filial piety' perfectly matched the non–party nature of the ongoing state-making politics and also reflected the practical significance of these values in a polity otherwise riven by personalistic factionalism.

At first the ideological relationship sought by the *tenno* and his 'advisers' (*genro*) was a direct, representational one in the sense that the monarch was the head of the national family with little in the way of an intermediary concept of the nation to qualify the literalness of the claim so made. Appropriately, soon after the restoration the court embarked upon a series of six great journeys around the country to show itself in all its pomp. Also, Shintoism, with its stress on ancestor worship, was made the established religion, although only for a few years. However, such were the changes wrought within the society in the aftermath of the restoration, such was its increasing and undeniable complexity, and so clearly were other, more narrowly economic institutions displacing the family as the core of social life, that it rapidly became apparent that the repetition of the homology of individual family/national family would no longer suffice as an interpellative mechanism. Gradually, a recognition was forced upon the *tenno* and the oligarchs that the ideological relationship they sought necessarily had to be an indirect rather than a direct one, and that the term '*tenno*-state' could signify the concept 'nation' rather than refer directly to a real family of people.

But this did not occur before strenuous efforts had been made to shape the ideological sphere according to the needs of the earlier project. Hence the stress on loyalty in the school curriculum (Passin, 1965) as well as in the ideological training of the new conscript army (Norman, 1940); hence also the obsessive tinkering with the institutional structure of the state and the incessant worrying over the various legal codes as well as the constitution then all still under construction, lest more than necessary should be given away; hence, finally, the practice of issuing pedagogic, Confucian-style Imperial Rescripts. Nor was all this activity in vain. *Tenno* Meiji retreated from public life even before the promulgation of the constitution in 1889 and increasingly spoke only in terms of nationalist generalities. The attendant shift from a representational to a significatory inter-pellative strategy (not then understood in such terms, of course) meant that the ideological field was more open than it had been before. Space thus became available for change by connotative intervention at the level of the signifieds; i.e. by offering divergent definitions of such critical signifiers as *tenno, Kokutai* (National Polity), etc. In the event little advantage was taken of this space during the Meiji era. So limited were the opportunities available for the few who wished to voice alternative conceptions of what the nation should be, and so clearly foreign were most of their sources of inspiration, that even they, for the most part, had to couch their arguments in *tennosei* terms if they wished to have any chance of gaining a hearing (Irokawa, 1985, chs 5–8).

In this way, then, the ideology became hegemonic whose principal signs and claims thereof were summarized most succinctly in the Imperial Rescript on Education that was issued in 1890, and which every child soon knew by heart:

Know ye, our subjects!

Our Imperial ancestors have founded our empire on a basis broad and everlasting and have deeply and firmly implanted virtue; our subjects, ever united in loyalty and filial piety, have from generation to generation illustrated the beauty thereof.

This is the glory of the fundamental character of our empire, and herein also lies the source of our education. Ye, our subjects, be filial to your parents, affectionate to your brothers and sisters; as husbands and wives be harmonious, as friends true; bear yourselves in modesty and modera-tion; extend your benevolence to all; pursue learning and cultivate arts, and thereby develop your intellectual faculties and perfect your moral powers; furthermore, advance the public good and promote common interests; always respect the constitution and observe the laws; should any emergency arise, offer yourselves courageously to the state; and thus guard and maintain the prosperity of our Imperial throne, coeval with heaven and earth. So shall ye not only be our good and faithful subjects, but render illustrious the best traditions of our forefathers.

The way here set forth is indeed the teaching bequeathed by our Imperial ancestors, to be observed alike by their descendants and subjects, infallible for all ages and true in all places. It is our wish to lay it to heart in all reverence, in common with you, our subjects, that we may all thus attain to the same virtue.

Law before the *Rechtsstaat*

The early Meiji state was not a *Rechtsstaat* (law-state): the judiciary had no independence, nor did it have access to a unified and coherent body of independently generated law which had to be universalistically applied to the citizenry (Henderson, 1968b, pp. 415 ff.). Nor, despite the statutory granting of private property rights in 1872, was it a straightforwardly capitalist legal system: capital's representatives possessed neither the means nor even the need to restructure the law around the primacy of the requirements of surplus-value appropriation.

In order to confirm these points and to give some substance to the explanation for the absence of any threat to capitalist possession in early Meiji Japan which they point towards, something must first be said about Tokugawa law. This is because with certain *ad hoc* alterations, it remained in force until the activation of the new and more explicitly capitalist codes in the 1890s. What is more, as is clear from Henderson's monumental work *Conciliation in Japanese Law* (1977), not only were many of the particulars of Tokugawa law repeated in the codes, but also and significantly the general law/society relation continued to take basically the same form after their promulgation; ie. one wherein, for example, property and family rights were established in state-administered registries (Stevens and Takahashi, nd, pp. 406 ff.) rather than courts, wherein the courts were anyway not as important as less formal conciliation fora, and where, finally and consequently, resort to the law was both difficult and socially deprecated. These, then, are some of the reasons why Japanese law lacked sufficient disciplinary effects to guarantee on its own the relationships it ostensibly protected and why it needed the support of a reinforcing hegemonic ideology.

Henderson has outlined the Tokugawa legal system in the following terms:

> The entirety of Tokugawa legal phenomena was a highly complex accumulation of imperial symbolism; a federalistic, doubledecked, feudal order; an elaborate status hierarchy of great constitutional import resting solidly on the rice tax; a base of rural villages regulated intramurally by diverse customary laws covering the whole range of private transactions; and a Confucianistic family system – all made plausible by the isolation policy. As a whole these features may be regarded as a constitution in the English sense, articulated by some key, piecemeal, positive law decrees (e.g. the *buke-shohatto* and isolation decrees), customary practices, and precedents, all rationalised by orthodox Tokugawa Confucianistic philosophy (*shushigaku*). Clearly considerable positive law was generated

by the shogunate (and daimyo) . . . it is necessary first to understand the shogunate's own thinking about law itself. Essentially, it was a natural law approach (*ri* as formulated in *shushigaku*). The static legal order was regarded as both natural and just, and positive law decrees were largely declaratory of these laws of nature. Even in the positive law there was little concept of made-law, for the efficacy of human endeavor to shape its environment was at the time low, and the concepts of law reflected that fact. (Henderson, 1968b, pp. 393–4)

This very definitely feudalistic legal system was pivoted around the maintenance of feudal landholding through the reinforcement of the Five Relationships (see the Rescript on Education above, p. 108) central to the neo-Confucianism that had become dominant if not hegemonic in the mid-seventeenth century. Nevertheless, as in Britain it was made/able to find room for the existence of simple commodity and even capitalist production. This it did, despite or because of the existence of positive law to the contrary, through a device known as *dappo koi*. This was a legal fiction whereby it appeared that land had been transferred in payment of a debt rather than on payment of a price (Henderson, 1974, pp. 58–9). In this way a surrogate right of title to the means of production was established which is a necessary, if not by itself a sufficient, prerequisite for the possessory freedom required where any form of 'commodity production' exists. In the Japanese case the remaining ideological prerequisites for such freedom were met by familial patriarchalism, which latterly was supported by the more diffuse patriarchalism of *tennosei*.

Most prominent among the discursive feudalistic particulars that were continued after the restoration and indeed later repeated in the new codes, were those that related to the position of the *tenno* and to family relations (i.e. those most pertinent to the enforcement of patriarchalism and its component signs of 'loyalty' and 'filial piety'). The effects of these repetitions were not confined, however, to those areas to which they most directly referred but gave a distinctive cast to legal discourse as a whole. Both the repetition of these particulars and of this result were linked through relations of mutual entailment to the continuation of the general form of the Tokugawa law/society relation in the post-restoration social formation: where there is patriarchalist right and a means of successfully enforcing it, there is certainly no discursive space and perhaps little social need for other rights and/or other means of defining, deciding and enforcing disciplinary balances, and vice versa. Thus, in so far as there was little in the way of other rights, etc., to provide a counter to patriarchalism (for the persistence of conciliatory fora, for example, see Henderson, 1977, pp. 209 ff.), there was also little to stop the latter reasserting itself. For a time it even seemed likely that ancient Chinese law would provide the model for Meiji jurists looking to the future (Chen, 1981)!

As it happens, another ancient but this time indigenous concept, *jori*, provided the means whereby traditional patriarchalism maintained itself as the Meiji era progressed and as it was absorbed by *tennosei*. This concept was so important during this period of rapid change since it referred to a source of law which could be invoked absent positive or customary law. *Jori* is often translated as 'reason', but as Takayanagi has convincingly argued (1976, pp. 175 ff.; see also Noda, 1976, pp. 222–4), it is perhaps better translated as 'common sense'. Its discursive effects may be best illustrated by quoting from a treatise by a very prominent Meiji lawyer which shows how patriarchalism maintained itself even within the very discourse of property which otherwise might have been expected to be its solvent:

> The issue of a law in 1872, which abolished the prohibition of sale of land and granted title deeds to landowners . . . and the establishment of joint-stock companies . . . mark[ed] the next step in the development of the separate property of house-members. The course of law began to recognise house-members' separate property in title-deeds . . . and the like, which they held in their own names, and afterwards in other things also, when their separate titles could be proved.
>
> In this manner individual property grew up *within the house*, that is to say, a house-member began to have his own property as an individual and not as a house-member. This change took place while the house-system was still in full vigour; and the consequence was that, the devolution of this new kind of property after the death of the owner resembled more the feudal escheat than succession. It *did not descend* to the children of the deceased, but *ascended to the house-head*. (Hozumi, 1938, pp. 172–3)

Thus the presence of patriarchalist elements within legal discourse could prevent an owner, and one empowered as such by positive law issuing from the *tenno* himself, from deciding upon the dispositions to be made of his property after his death. However, it takes little imagination to appreciate that the effects of the same presence on the freedom available to the employees of such a property-owner were even more restrictive. Especially since in their regard, besides an edict of 1872 establishing freedom of contract, neither positive nor customary law contained any liberalistic counter-signs, such as any right to freedom of association (Beer, 1984, pp. 46–53). Instead, Tokugawa prohibitions of peasant unions and collective bargaining were expressly continued (Nakamura, 1962, p. 34).

Thus, with little change of discord, traditional patriarchalism and incipient *tennosei* chimed nicely with the authoritarian structures and still familialist nature of the discourses of production in the typical small manufactories, as well as with the female nature of most of the labour force in the larger enterprises such as the textile mills (Allinson, 1975, pp. 46, 51). The net effect of all this as well as, it should be noted, the insufficiency of ideology to secure capitalist possession on its own, may both be seen in the very vigorous efforts made by mill-owners to prevent any mobility on the part of their employees (Hane, 1982; Taira, 1970, pp. 110 ff.). A partial exception to the almost totalitarian constraint on the freedoms of labourers may be found in the conditions obtaining in some of the larger enterprises, such as the shipyards and iron works (Gordon, 1985, ch. 1). Here the majority of unskilled workers were subject to the patriarchal discipline imposed by the labour sub-contractors (*oyakata*) who hired them and thus their relations replicated the highly repressive *oyabun* (parent)/*kobun* (child) relationships of the feudal period (for the conditions in Mitsui's Takashima mines, see Taira, 1970, p. 106). However, the small number of skilled workers, whether certificated or self-taught, often enjoyed considerable freedom to come and go as they pleased and to bargain, albeit individualistically, over their wages and conditions (Gordon, 1985).

The continued presence of patriarchalist discourses in post-restoration law and society, then, is what explains both why early Meiji law did not spontaneously evolve into a species of properly capitalist law and why this did not matter much. Title was secure but not only or most importantly on the basis of the primacy of property right. Similarly, possession was also secure but not primarily or most importantly on the basis of freedom of contract. In sum, in what was in effect the economic absence of capitalist law, capitalist possession was nevertheless secured thanks to the hegemony of the old and new patriarchalisms. (In the 1930s, of course, the hegemony of a militaristic patriarchalism enunciated by the state sometimes appeared to be a threat to capitalist possession but that is another story.)

Against the contingency thesis

The general lesson which seems to me to emerge from a consideration of how capitalist possession was secured in early Meiji Japan is that there is an element of necessity in the initial relation between capitalism and its ideological conditions of existence, in addition to the latterly developing 'functional interdependence' allowed by Abercrombie *et al*. Thus in the context of the present argument the most significant difference which remains between the type of neo-Marxism represented by the present text and Abercrombie *et al*.'s position is that, whilst a wide variety of ideological conditions may have accompanied the birth of capitalism, they were not just any conditions, since minimally they had to be pertinent to the securing of capitalist possession of the means of production.

Ideology after *tennosei*

The sole condition insisted upon by the Japanese government as it negotiated surrender terms with the Allies was 'preservation of the national *Kokutai*'. This it achieved when a place was allowed to the *tenno* in the new constitution. For most commentators this was a case of a battle won but another war lost. The Occupation reforms and the democratization which they set in train are generally supposed to have caused 'the prewar concept of *Kokutai* [to have] crumbled away altogether' (Gluck, 1985, p. 284). Here, however, a contrary position will be advanced. Namely, that the economically critical elements of *tennosei* were not so much destroyed as displaced and partially transformed. Specifically, it will be argued that the central role as the embodiment of Japan's uniqueness, hitherto played by the *tenno*, was taken by that of the *ie*. Thus the hegemonic ideology was sociologized as well as secularized by the somewhat ambiguous transfer of sovereignty from the *tenno* to the people (Quigley and Turner, 1956).

From the point of view of those still interpellated by a very literal reading of *tennosei*, such as the conservatives of the immediate postwar period, the ambiguities in the transfer of sovereignty had much to recommend them in what for them were desperate days, somewhat akin, in anthropological terms, to those faced by messianic cults 'when prophecy fails' (Cohn, 1957). They granted some legitimacy to the arrangements fate had imposed and, in the words of the *tenno*'s surrender broadcast, enabled the irreconcilables to 'endure the unendurable' – the important, almost the only, point was that the *tenno*-line remained unbroken, just as it had during the Shogunate. From the points of view of those not so interpellated – the majority it would appear (Gluck, 1985, p. 286) – who either by conviction or out of necessity wished to take or to be seen to take the new democratism seriously, the uniqueness of their society, which only the most committed of communists and socialists doubted, gradually came to be seen as lying in their way of life.

Respect for the *tenno* was of course an aspect, and an important one, of this way of life, but increasingly the *tenno* became, as stated in the new constitution, its 'symbol' rather than its essence. Thus the society appears to have experienced what might be called a 'Durkheimian revelation' concerning the relation between the sacred and the social, except that for Durkheim the discovery that in worshipping its gods a society was in fact worshipping itself destroyed the basis of religious belief. In postwar Japan this does not seem to have been the result. The veneration once reserved for the ancestral spirits and the *tenno* was in large part transferred to such institutions as the *ie* or, more substantively, to the institutions and especially the *kaisha* (large companies) which supposedly embodied the *ie* essence. Indeed, it was the repetition of a certain reverence towards such institutions in everyday conversation which first suggested to me that what one is confronted with in the changing ideological structure of postwar Japan is an instance of a complex displacement rather than of a simple transformation – a displacement whereby the discursively dominant sign, *ie*, is one which used to be subordinate (i.e. as an aspect of the society's 'beautiful customs' – a favourite prewar euphemism for hierarchy). Whereas in *tennosei* proper the *tenno* gave the society its 'beautiful customs', in its transmuted postwar form the 'beautiful customs' gave society its '*tenno*'. (The texts which best exemplify the process whereby this displacement took place in constitutional/legal discourse are those contained in the reports of the proceedings of the Commission on the Constitution which met between 1958 and 1964; see Maki, 1980.)

Thus far I have referred to the hegemonic postwar ideology only as a secularized and sociologized form of *tennosei* because I wanted to stress the continuities involved. From now on, in order to be able to acknowledge the differences which have followed from what was certainly a radical even if not a revolutionary discursive reordering, I propose to use the term '*Kigyoushugi*' (enterprisism or belief in the company system) to refer to it. The attraction of the term is that in identifying the Japanese company as the principal object of the currently hegemonic discourse it acknowledges both the occurrence of the displacement just discussed and the exemplary role of the *kigyō* or *kaisha* in the postwar reconstruction of Japanese institutions more generally. This said, it is necessary for me to emphasize that, in opting to use the term *Kigyōshugi*, I am not saying that the company is the sole source of themes in the hegemonic discourse, but only that it is the dominant source of such themes and therefore of the interpellative means whereby the Japanese people are attached, and attach themselves, to their society. For example, all of the signifiers that feature in the discourse which is hegemonic in the United States (i.e. 'self-reliance', 'responsible unionism', 'opportunity', 'loyalty' and 'modernity', see Woodiwiss, 1990, ch. 7) also feature in that of Japan, as indeed to a lesser degree do their more social–democratic Western European equivalents. However, what they signify both individually and collectively is very different, thanks largely to the discursive omnipresence of 'the group' in the form of the signifier 'company' or its non-business equivalents and their very particular Japanese significations. The core of what these significations are is what must now be explicated.

The belief that there is something unique about Japan's social arrangements and that this is crystallized in a supposed trans-institutional *ie* form of organization is one which appears to be gaining ground in Japanese academia. Indeed the academy is one of the principal sites where '*Kigyoushugi*' is currently reproduced. However, it is not the only or even the most important of such sites, since the academics and the less scholarly contributors to the hugely popular *Nihonjinron* (theories of Japaneseness) literature (see Dale, 1988) have made their contributions as a result of reflecting upon what appears to be going on at other sites. Nor, of course, are the non-academics whom the ideology additionally interpellates necessarily aware of believing in anything called a 'trans-institutional *ie* form of organization'. Rather they are so interpellated by working and living in 'industrial enterprises, government organisations, educational institutions, intellectual groups, religious communities, political parties, village communities, individual households and so on' (Nakane, 1970, p. i), each of whose structures is constructed, or so the academics argue, on the basis of what Nakane has termed 'the vertical principle' and Murakami (1984, p. 309) 'homo-functional hierarchy'. Nakane (1970, p. 44) elaborates as follows:

> The relationship between two individuals of upper and lower status is the basis of the structural principle of Japanese society. This important relationship is expressed in the traditional terms *oyabun* and *kobun*. *Oyabun* means the person with the status of *oya* (parent) and *kobun* means the status of *ko* (child) . . . The essential elements in the relationship are that the *kobun* receives benefits or help from his *oyabun*, such as assistance in securing employment or promotion, and advice on the occasion of important decision-making. The *kobun*, in turn, is ready to offer his service whenever the *oyabun* requires them.

Murakami (1987, pp. 35–6) is somewhat less metaphorical and defines two variants of the structure, which are supposedly exhaustive of virtually all significant institutional life in Japan. He suggests that the first may be found most often within single institutions, whereas, until recently at least, the second may be found most often where otherwise separate institutions are combined, as in *Keiretsuka* (the financial/industrial groupings that have replaced the *zaibatsu*) and *shitauke* (main contractor/subcontractor groups):

1   The *ie* genotype is the tight version of the indigenous organisational principle and is defined as a group having the following characteristics:

   a   Collective goal: eternal continuation and expansion of the group, which is often symbolised by stem succession to group leadership.

   b   Membership qualification: 'kintractship,' that is, no member should leave the group once he or she joins it.

   c   Hierarchy-homogeneity balance: all members are organised in a hierarchy aiming at some functional goal, and various complementary measures further their homogeneity.

   d   Autonomy: the group encompasses all functions necessary to its perpetuation.

2   The *mura* variant, the loose version of the indigenous organisational principle, is defined as a group with the following characteristics:

   a   Collective goal: very long term continuation and expansion of the group.

   b   Membership qualification: every member should stay with the group as long as it continues.

   c   Homogeneity-hierarchy balance: all members are considered to be homogenous and therefore treated equally, but they implicitly share a sense of ranking that reflects, by and large, functional capability.

   d   Multifunctionality: the group achieves and reconciles diverse interrelated functions.

The *terminus ad quem* of this line of argument as it relates to economic institutions has recently been stated with particular clarity by Kuwahara (1989, p. 10):

The Japanese enterprise . . . should be called a 'business community maintained by labour and management, rather than a 'capitalist enterprise'.

What cannot be doubted, as all public pronouncements by Japanese institutions, all studies and any experience of working in them attest, is that a great deal of effort is put into making it appear that the harmony (*wa*) expected of *ie* or *mura*-type institutions does in fact characterize them. What, equally, can only be doubted is the claim made by such as Nakane, Murakami and official spokespeople that these efforts are wholly successful and that, therefore, contemporary Japanese institutions are entirely free of the structural tensions, especially between labour and capital, which most schools of sociology, excluding structural-functionalism, regard as intrinsic to capitalism. As it happens, there are many signs of structural-functionalism in the texts written by such authors (e.g. they are explicit in Nakane's talk of 'shared values' and throughout the quotation from Murakami given above). However, they do not base their claims upon a commitment to any particular school of sociology, let alone one so quintessentially American as structural-functionalism. Instead they argue that they are based simply on observation. However, observation is never as theoretically or as ideologically innocent as they appear to think, and in their case it was and remains powerfully affected by a prior commitment to the uniqueness assumption.

Kigyoushugi and the denial of class

The normal range of forms of capitalist class relations may be discerned without difficulty in Japanese enterprises. However, as in most if not quite all other advanced capitalist societies, strenuous efforts have been and still are made by those positioned wholly or in part by capital to deny that the inequalities between them and those less fortunately positioned are intrinsic to the capitalist mode of production. What is different about the Japanese case, thanks to the pervasiveness of *Kigyoushugi*, is that the discourse which carries this denial is of a piece with and indeed is central to that which carries the national identity. This has the result that accepting one's position in one's *kaisha* is made to appear as equivalent to accepting one's position in society and vice versa. The two levels of discourse reinforce one another and thus represent a formidable source of resistance to the influence of alternative discourses such as those intrinsic to trade unionism or socialism, which are anyway defined by *Kigyoushugi* as alien.

In smaller companies, as on the farms, the pertinent protective discourse of class denial remains the traditional patriachalist one whose critical elements are the ideas of *ie*, employer responsibility and employee loyalty (Bennett and Ishino, 1963). In the years since the ending of the war, it may be safely assumed that this discourse has lost some of its disciplinary effectivity as job mobility has increased amongst smaller companies, as the skills required within them have been enlarged and enhanced (Koike, 1988, ch. 5), as wage levels have approached those in the larger companies (Friedman, 1988, ch. 4), as state-provided welfare facilities of all kinds have been improved (Maruo, 1986), as women and minorities have slowly become more assertive (Cook and Hayashi, 1980) and, finally, as sources of capital for new small businesses apart from parents, in-laws and ambitious/ grateful employers have become available (Friedman, 1988, ch. 5; Patrick and Rohlen, 1987). Of course, the discourse of patriarchalism may still be heard in the smaller workplaces and its applicability within them is still asserted by journalistic as well as academic commentators. It may also be assumed, although somewhat less safely, that its place at the centre of workplace discourse has been taken by the much more diffuse and abstract *Kigyoushugi* variant, which is broadcast by such commentators, and which gives a particular cast to the always subordinate, more straightforwardly calculative economistic discourse, which Japanese working people share with their equivalents in other advanced capitalist societies. Sometimes this global patriarchalism is supported by the Buddhism of *Sokagakkai*, and about as often it is challenged by trade unionism, socialism, or communism (Curtis, 1988, pp. 24–30).

In larger companies the pertinent protective discourse of class denial is far more elaborate than in the smaller ones, as has been made clear in a wide variety of studies (e.g. Allinson, 1975; Abegglen and Stalk, 1985; Clark, 1979; Dore, 1973; Gordon, 1985; Hirschmeier and Yui, 1981; Koike, 1988; Levine, 1958; Inagami, 1988). Although *Kigyoushugi* scholars like Nakane and Murakami very consciously use originally feudal terms like *oyabun, kobun* and *mura*, to refer to the social relations to be found in large Japanese enterprises, in fact most of the features which distinguish them from their smaller counterparts and indeed from their overseas equivalents are the products of postwar developments. Large Japanese companies are extremely hierarchical and proudly acknowledge themselves to be so. However, in two senses they are also often claimed and claim themselves to be classless: first, in the sense that promotion within them depends upon seniority and merit rather than family background or inherited position; second, in the sense that the company is an organic whole and hence not marked by class antagonisms like 'western' companies.

Concerning promotion, the vast majority of new members of the larger Japanese companies join straight from either school or university and are assigned to white- or blue-collar career tracks according to their level of education and their gender. Although there are some opportunities for jumping tracks for shopfloor workers, new entrants generally progress as cohorts along those to which they were initially assigned, according to seniority and, increasingly, to merit. However, because the hierarchy which they are ascending eventually becomes markedly pyramidal in shape, the proportion of the cohort rising to its topmost levels is rather low. Those who fail to make the rank of managing director or higher and thus to join the managing committee (*jomukai*) are generally satisfied and indeed considered satisfactory if, within fourteen years, they make the rank of *kacho* (section chief) or become one of the *tantomin* (people in charge of something), which are regarded as the middle-management career grades. Thus the blue-collar/white-collar divide remains an important determinant of 'life-chances' (Vogel, 1963). However, as befits organizations which aspire to be what Murakami has termed 'homo-functional', strenuous efforts are made to counter any explicit antagonisms between capital and labour, let alone any that might create the possibility of solidarities between blue- and white-collar employees.

Many companies espouse 'company philosophies', which explicitly deny the existence of even the possibility of such antagonisms and, because they often take the form of a statement of the founding patriarch's personal philosophy, they tend to acquire a quasi-sacred status; for example, consider Matsushita Konosuke's oft-repeated 'little lecture':

> Don't think I run this company [Matsushita Electric]. Each of you has a part to play in its management. We need the ideas, skill, and knowledge of everyone to make a reservoir of wisdom for more efficient operations, better product and service quality, and effective management. We have a good future if we can work that way. (Matsushita, 1984, p. 52)

In the same way that there are great similarities between these company philosophies, so there are great similarities in the ways in which they are put into practice, pronounced enough indeed that they are commonly referred to collectively as 'the Japanese Employment System'. In addition, as is consistent with their role in *Kigyoushugi* discourse, these techniques of class denial are often referred to with traditional terms. For example, among the most common of these techniques is the practice of pre-meeting lobbying, which is greatly dignified by having the term *nemawashi* (the root-binding necessary when moving a tree) used to refer to it. Again, the more specifically

Japanese practice of circulating and gaining support for suggestions originating in the lower ranks before they are submitted to superiors is similarly dignified by using the term *ringi-sho*, which is an ancient term of art in Japanese politics. Finally, the terms used to refer to the different components of wages and salaries – *nenko* (seniority), *shokuno* (ability) and *bonus* – all continue to connote the prewar patriarchalist/paternalistic management and payment system in which they originated as discretionary payments (Gordon, 1985), despite the fact that nowadays, at least where unions are present, they are generally subject to negotiation.

In Japan as elsewhere, the term 'trade union' of course evokes an antithetical discourse to that of patriarchalism. However, for reasons which are in part fortuitous, the consequences of the presence of this sign in the workplace are not as disruptive of the dominance of the discourses of class-denial as might at first be imagined. Quite accidentally and indeed largely because of the factory occupations of the 1940s, the enterprise has been the prime focus of union activities since the ending of the Pacific War. Quite accidentally also, Japan's postwar labour law allows all employees below the rank of section chief (*kacho*) to be members of the same union. Finally, and again quite accidentally, the same law allows and even supports the possibility of dual unionism.

Not so accidentally, the possibilities inherent in this combination of circumstances were eventually grasped by employers as they contended with the often militant and industrially oriented unions of the 1950s. As a result employers sometimes took advantage of strike situations by encouraging the formation of second, more moderate, more enterprise oriented and often white-collar-led unions, and then settling with them on favourable terms (Cole, 1971; Gordon, 1985, ch. 10; Shimodaira, 1985; Totsuka, 1984). Very often this had disastrous consequences for the unions which initiated the strikes as well as an inhibiting effect upon other unions. Again not so accidentally and as permitted by law, companies are free to and usually do provide favoured unions with offices and all the other equipment and facilities they require in order to perform their role – e.g. automatic dues check-off, the union shop (i.e. a post-entry closed shop) and time-off for conducting union business. In a society where knowledge of the purpose and effects of such pre-giving is part of its day-to-day fabric, the significance of such a set of gestures is very clear. Moreover, the possibility that the expectations of union behaviour thus encouraged might be disappointed is minimized by the unions' participation in consultative committees, by the enlistment of their support for after-hours quality circle activity and by, wherever possible, the exclusion of outsiders, whether from employers' associations or from the trade union federations, from collective bargaining sessions.

Finally, all of the relations between the two sides are conducted in the context of such implicit denials of class difference as are represented by the requirements that all employees, regardless of rank, wear a uniform (if not always the same one), sometimes eat in the same canteen and sometimes attend the same social activities, as well as in the context of shared dependencies upon the company for health, welfare, housing and lifetime employment. In sum, at every point at which the unions might have assumed or asserted a difference, the embodiments of capital have already said '*kaisha*' and so established a set of equivalences with a remarkable degree of depth and strong pacificatory consequences.

All that said, the discourses and techniques of class denial cannot obscure the following: (1) that joint consultation committees have very little say in and certainly do not allow for negotiations in such critical areas as strategic policy, organizational change, the introduction of new technology, hiring policies, employee transfers, health and safety, training, welfare and finally even cultural and sports policies (Inagami, 1988, p. 25, table 6); and (2) that collective bargaining is substantially affected by the norms established during the *shunto* (unified Spring Labour Offensive) (Takanashi *et al.*, 1989). In other words, the exigencies arising from capitalist class relations continue to have a determinative effect upon the relations possible between the embodiments of capital and labour as well as upon the outcomes of the negotiations between them. Despite their relative freedom from shareholder control, Japanese managers cannot give up more than a very restricted *quantum* of their rights and powers of possession and control – strikingly, and provided one discounts the quite widespread but typically gestural worker-shareholding schemes, the rights and powers of title are seldom if ever mentioned whether in the context of union-management discussions or in academic/journalistic commentary. Similarly, contrary to the stereotype, working people in Japan as anywhere else depend upon the support of their fellow employees and trade unionists in order to win wages and conditions that are better than those that the company might otherwise grant (Levine, 1982, pp. 49 ff.).

In the end, then, it is the persistence of these class-structural effects which falsifies Murakami's picture of the *kaisha* as a 'homo-functional hierarchy' as well as all other representations of it as some sort of post-capitalist, communitarian organization comparable to 'western employee-managed companies' where all or most of the equity is held by the labour force (Dore, 1987; Kuwahara, 1988). My guess is that this is a judgement which will become more generally shared as the Japanese Employment System becomes frayed at the edges in response to the changing economic environment whose challenges are summarized in such phrases as 'the strong yen' and 'the hollowing out of Japanese industry'; as, to be more specific, 'half-a-lifetime-employment' becomes more frequent, as enterprise unions lose their effectiveness (Tabata, 1989), as the proportion of temporary and part-time employees in large companies increases and, relatedly, as organizing opportunities for minority and/or general unions increase (Aoki, 1987; Japan Institute of Labour, 1983, 1988; Kamata, 1983; Kawanishi, 1986; Osawa, 1988; Shimada, 1980, 1988).

It might also be that the growing sense of economic grievance engendered by and reflected in these and other developments (e.g. the introduction of a new consumption tax) may have been powerfully reinforced by the scandals which have recently beset the Liberal Democratic Party. All in all, what with these developments, the uniting of all of the non-communist unions in a new organization (*Shin Rengo*) and the Socialist Party's grasping of at least some of the levers of state power, the world is possibly about to hear about a rather different Japan as compared to that which has recently been the source of so many one-sided lessons. In which case, the employee's proud talk of 'his/her company' might be about to take on a more explicitly proprietorial air which hitherto has been tuned out by those who have been the keenest for us to learn from Japan.

Conclusion

Although Japan may not be of the same phenotype as other advanced capitalist societies, it is most definitely of the same genotype, irrespective of the aspect – economic, political, or ideological – at which one looks. And this is because in Japan, as anywhere else capitalist relations of production exist, certain conditions, including certain ideological ones, have to be met if capitalism is to exist. The difference between the Japanese case and its American and European equivalents is that both because of the persistence of certain structural continuities and because of certain historical accidents, those ideo-logically identified as the possessors of property in the means of production have seldom been seriously challenged as regards either actual possession or the power to enforce their right to it. In sum, the various pseudo-collectivist and patriarchalist discourses which have been successively hegemonic, and which have helped capitalist possession to survive any challenges it has so far faced, have never been seriously threatened.

The result is that, to a degree unparalleled in other advanced capitalist societies, everyday life and especially work life is lived, formally at least, in the same terms as those present in official discourse. The degree of hegemony so attained may appear remarkable but, ironically, it is also somewhat fragile, since it still coexists in an apparently symbiotic relationship with a pervasive, personalistic factionalism. The latter appears to be endemic within Japanese institutions, to dominate the less formal side of life within them and sometimes to threaten their very existence. No matter how strong it may superficially appear, a single signifying thread is still just a single thread. The consequences of its breaking are impossible to predict except that, as in the past, they are probably still likely to involve a degree of social disorganization and explosive outpourings of highly personalized anger which are seldom matched elsewhere. The question 'why?' is one which both those who would derive 'lessons' from Japan and those who have to listen to them would do well to ask themselves.

Bibliography

Abegglen, J. and Stalk, G. (1985), *Kaisha: The Japanese Corporation* (New York: Basic Books).

Abel, R. L. (ed.) (1982), *The Politics of Informal Justice* (New York: Academic Press).

Abercrombie, N., Hill, S. and Turner, B. (1980), *The Dominant Ideology Thesis* (London: Allen & Unwin).

Abercrombie, N., Hill, S. and Turner, B. (1986), *Sovereign Individuals of Capitalism* (London: Allen & Unwin).

Akita, G. (1967), *Foundations of Constitutional Government in Modern Japan, 1868–1900* (Cambridge, Mass.: Harvard University Press).

Allen, G. C. (1946), *A Short Economic History of Modern Japan, 1867–1937* (London: Allen & Unwin).

Allen, G. C. (1965), *Japan's Economic Expansion* (Oxford: Oxford University Press).

Allinson, G. D. (1975), *Japanese Urbanism* (Berkeley, Calif.: University of California Press).

Aoki, S. (1987), 'A case study of new-type trades unions', mimeo, Department of Sociology, Meiji Gakuin University.

Ayusawa, I. (1966), *A History of Labour in Modern Japan* (Honolulu, Hawaii: East West Center Press).

Beer, L. W. (1984), *Freedom of Expression in Japan* (Tokyo: Kodansha International).

Bennett, J. and Ishino, I. (1963), *Paternalism in the Japanese Economy* (Minneapolis, Minn.: University of Minnesota Press).

Bix, H. (1986), *Peasant Protest in Japan, 1590–1884* (New Haven, Conn.: Yale University Press).

Broadbridge, S. (1966), *Industrial Dualism in Japan* (London: Frank Cass).

Brown, D. M. (1955), *Nationalism in Japan* (Berkeley, Calif.: University of California Press).

Burks, A. (1966), *The Government of Japan* (London: Methuen).

Chen, P. (1981), *The Formation of the Early Meiji Legal Order* (Oxford: Oxford University Press).

Clark, R. (1979), *The Japanese Company* (New Haven, Conn.: Yale University Press).

Cohn, N. (1957), *The Pursuit of the Millennium* (London: Faber).

Cole, R. (1971), *Japanese Blue Collar: The Changing Tradition* (Berkeley, Calif.: University of California Press).

Cook, A. and Hayashi, H. (1980), *Working Women in Japan: Discrimination, Resistance and Reform* (Ithaca, NY: Cornell University Press).

Curtis, G. (1988), *The Japanese Way of Politics* (New York: Columbia University Press).

Dale, P. (1986), *The Myth of Japanese Uniqueness* (London: Routledge).

Dore, R. (1959), *Land Reform in Japan* (London: Oxford University Press).

Dore, R. (1973), *British Factory, Japanese Factory* (London: Allen & Unwin).

Dore, R. (1986), *Flexible Rigidities: Industrial Policy and Structural Adjustment in the Japanese Economy, 1970–80* (London: Athlone Press).

Dore, R. (1987), *Taking Japan Seriously* (London: Athlone Press).

Dower, J. (ed.) (1975), *The Origins of the Modern Japanese State: Selected Writings of E. H. Norman* (New York: Pantheon).

Earl, D. M. (1964), *Emperor and Nation in Japan* (Seattle: University of Washington).

Friedman, D. (1988), *The Misunderstood Miracle* (Ithaca, NY: Cornell University Press).

Garon, S. (1987), *The State and Labour in Modern Japan* (Berkeley, Calif.: University of California Press).

Gluck, C. (1985), *Japan's Modern Myths: Ideology in the Late Meiji Period* (Princeton, NJ: Princeton University Press).

Gordon, A. (1985), *The Evolution of Labour Relations in Japan* (Cambridge, Mass.: Harvard University Press).

Hackett, R. (1968), 'Political modernisation and the Meiji *genro*', in Ward (1968), *Political Development in Modern Japan*, pp. 65–98 (Princeton: Princeton University Press).

Halberstam, D. (1986), *The Reckoning* (New York: Bantam).

Haley, J. O. (1978), 'The myth of the reluctant litigant', *Journal of Japanese Studies*, vol. 4, no. 2.

Haley, J. O. (1982a), 'Sheathing the sword of justice in Japan: an essay on law without sanctions', *Journal of Japanese Studies*, vol. 8, no. 2, pp. 265–83.

Haley, J. O. (1982b), 'The politics of informal justice: the Japanese experience', pp. 125–48, in R. L. Abel (1982).

Hall, J. W. (1968a), 'A modern monarch for modern Japan', in Ward (1968).

Hall, J. W. (1968b), *Studies in the Institutional History of Early Modern Japan* (Princeton, NJ: Princeton University Press).

Hall, J. W. (1985), 'Reflections on Murakami Yasuke's "Ie society as a civilisation" ', *Journal of Japanese Studies*, vol. 11, no. 1, pp. 48–56.

Halliday, J. (1976), *A Political History of Japanese Capitalism* (New York: Pantheon).

Hane, M. (1982), *Peasants, Rebels and Outcasts: The Underside of Modern Japan* (New York: Pantheon).

Harootunian, H. (1970), *Toward Restoration* (Berkeley, Calif.: University of California Press).

Harootunian, H. (1982), in T. Najita (ed.), *Conflict in Modern Japanese History: the Neglected Tradition* (Princeton, NJ: Princeton University Press).

Harootunian, H. (1988), *Things Seen and Unseen: Discourse and Ideology in Tokugawa Nativism* (Chicago: University of Chicago Press).

Henderson, D. F. (ed.) (1968a), *The Constitution of Japan: Its First Twenty Years* (Seattle, Wash.: University of Washington Press).

Henderson, D. F. (1968b), 'Law and political modernisation in Japan', in Ward (ed.) (1968), *Political Development in Modern Japan*, pp. 387–456 (Princeton: Princeton University Press).

Henderson, D. F. (1974), ' "Contracts" in Tokugawa Japan', *Journal of Japanese Studies*, vol. 1, no. 1, pp. 51–90.

Henderson, D. F. (1977), *Conciliation in Japanese Law*, 2 vols (Seattle, Wash.: University of Washington Press).

Henderson, D. F. and Haley, J. (eds) (1978), 'Law and legal process in Japan', mimeo, University of Washington.

Hirschmeier, J. and Yui, T. (1981), *The Development of Japanese Business* (London: Allen & Unwin).

Hozumi, N. (1938), *Ancestor Worship and Japanese Law* (Tokyo: Hokuseido Press).

Inagami, T. (1988), *Japanese Workplace Industrial Relations* (Tokyo: Japan Institute of Labour).

Irokawa, D. (1985), *The Culture of the Meiji Period* (Princeton, NJ: Princeton University Press).

Ishii, R. (ed.) (1968), *Japanese Legislation in the Meiji Era* (Tokyo: Kasai).

Ishii, R. (1980), *A History of Political Institutions in Japan* (Tokyo: University of Tokyo Press).

Japan Institute of Labour (1983), *Highlights in Japanese Industrial Relations*, Vol. 1 (Tokyo).

Japan Institute of Labour (1988), *Highlights in Japanese Industrial Relations*, Vol. 2 (Tokyo).

Jessop, B. (1982), *The Capitalist State* (Oxford: Martin Robertson).

Johnson, C. (1982), *MITI and the Japanese Miracle . . .* (Stanford, Calif.: Stanford University Press).

Kamata, S. (1983), *Japan in the Passing Lane* (London: Allen & Unwin).
Kawanishi, H. (1986), 'The reality of enterprise unionism', in G. McCormack and Y. Sugimoto (eds) (1986), pp. 138–56, *Democracy in Contemporary Japan* (Sydney: Hale & Iremonger).
Koike, K. (1988), *Understanding Industrial Relations in Modern Japan* (Basingstoke: Macmillan).
Koschmann, J. V. (1987), *The Mito Ideology . . . 1790–1864* (Berkeley, Calif.: University of California Press).
Koshiro, K. (1984), 'The reality of dualistic labor market in Japan: scarcity of good employment opportunities and industrial relations', *East Asia*, vol. 2, p. 33 ff.
Kuwahara, Y. (1988), 'Industrial relations and human resource management in Japan', in Y. Kuwahara, G. Bamber and R. Lansbury (eds) (1988), *Industrial Relations in Advanced Countries: Factors of Maturity and Change* (Tokyo: Japan Institute of Labour).
Kuwahara, Y., Bamber, G. and Lansbury, R. (1988), *Industrial Relations in Advanced Countries: Factors of Maturity and Change* (Tokyo: Japan Institute of Labour).
Kuwahara, Y. (1989), *Industrial Relations System in Japan: A New Interpretation* (Tokyo: Japan Institute of Labour).

Laclau, E. and Mouffe, C. (1985), *Hegemony and Socialist Strategy* (London: Verso).
Lehmann, J. P. (1982), *The Roots of Modern Japan* (London: Macmillan).
Levine, S. (1958), *Industrial Relations in Postwar Japan* (Urbana, Ill.: University of Illinois Press).
Levine, S. (1982), 'Japanese industrial relations: an external view', in Y. Sugimoto, H. Shimada and S. Levine (1982), p. 39, *Industrial Relations in Japan* (Melbourne: Japanese Studies Centre).

Maki, J. (trans. and ed.) (1980), *Japan's Commission on the Constitution: The Final Report* (Seattle, Wash.: University of Washington Press).
Marshall, B. (1967), *Capitalism and Nationalism in Prewar Japan* (Stanford, Calif.: Stanford University Press).
Maruo, M. (1986), 'The development of the welfare mix', in R. Rose and R. Shiratori (1986), *The Welfare State East and West* (New York: Oxford University Press).
Matsushita, K. (1984), *Not for Bread Alone: A Business Ethos, A Management Ethic* (Kyoto: PHP Institute Inc.).
McCormack, G. and Sugimoto, Y. (eds) (1986), *Democracy in Contemporary Japan* (Sydney: Hale & Iremonger).
McLaren, W. W. (1914), 'Japanese government documents', *Transactions of the Asiatic Society of Japan*, vol. XLII, no. 1, p. 1.
McLaren, W. W. (1965), *A Political History of Japan During the Meiji Era* (London: Frank Cass).
McMullan, I. J. (1987), 'Rulers or fathers? A casuistical problem in early modern Japanese thought', *Past and Present*, vol. 116, pp. 56 ff.
Mehren, A. T. van (ed.) (1963), *Law in Japan* (Cambridge, Mass.: Harvard University Press).
Mitchell, R. H. (1976), *Thought Control in Prewar Japan* (Ithaca, NY: Cornell University Press).

Moore, B. (1966), *Social Origins of Dictatorship and Democracy* (Harmondsworth: Penguin).

Moore, J. (1983), *Japanese Workers and the Struggle for Power* (Madison, Wisc.: University of Wisconsin Press).

Morishima, M. (1982), *Why has Japan 'Succeeded'?* (Cambridge: Cambridge University Press).

Murakami, Y. (1984), 'Ie society as a pattern of civilisation', *Journal of Japanese Studies*, vol. 10, no. 1, pp. 279–364.

Murakami, Y. (1985), '. . . response to criticism', *Journal of Japanese Studies*, vol. 11, no. 2, pp. 401–21.

Murakami, Y. (1987), 'The Japanese model of political economy', in K. Yamamura and Y. Yasuba (1987), *The Political Economy of Japan: The Domestic Transformation* (Stanford, Calif.: Stanford University Press).

Najita, T. (1974), *The Intellectual Origins of Modern Japanese Politics* (Chicago: University of Chicago Press).

Najita, T. (1987), *Visions of Virtue in Tokugawa Japan* (Chicago: University of Chicago Press).

Najita, T. and Korshmann, J. V. (eds) (1982), *Conflict in Modern Japanese History: the Neglected Tradition* (Princeton, NJ: Princeton University Press).

Nakamura, H. (1960), *The Ways of Thinking of Eastern Peoples* (Tokyo: Unesco).

Nakamura, K. (1962), *The Formation of Modern Japan: As Viewed from Legal History* (Tokyo: Centre for East Asian Cultural Studies).

Nakamura, T. (1983), *Economic Growth in Prewar Japan* (New Haven, Conn.: Yale University Press).

Nakane, C. (1975), *Japanese Society* (Harmondsworth: Penguin).

Nitta, M. (1988), 'Structural changes and enterprise-based unionism in Japan', in Y. Kuwahara, G. Bamber and R. Lansbury (eds) (1988), *Industrial Relations in Advanced Countries: Factors of Maturity and Change* (Tokyo: Japan Institute of Labour, Mimeo).

Noda, Y. (1976), *Introduction to Japanese Law* (Tokyo: University of Tokyo Press).

Norman, E. H. (1940), *Japan's Emergence as a Modern State* (New York: Institute of Pacific Relations).

Osawa, M. (1988), 'Structural transformation and industrial relations in the Japanese labour market', in Y. Kuwahara, G. Bamber and R. Lansbury (eds) (1988), *Industrial Relations in Advanced Countries: Factors of Maturity and Change* (Tokyo: Japan Institute of Labour, Mimeo).

Passin, H. (1965), *Society and Education in Japan*, Teachers' College and East Asian Institute, Columbia University, 1965.

Patrick, H. (ed.) (1976), *Japanese Industrialisation and Its Social Consequences* (Berkeley, Calif.: University of California Press).

Patrick, H. and Rosovsky, H. (eds) (1976), *Asia's New Giant: How the Japanese Economy Works* (Washington, DC: Brookings Institution).

Patrick, H. and Rohlen, T. (1987), 'Small-scale family enterprises', in K. Yamamura and Y. Yasuba (1987), pp. 331–84, *The Political Economy of Japan: The Domestic Transformation* (Stanford, Calif.: Stanford University Press).

Pittau, J. (1967), *Political Thought in Early Japan, 1868–1889* (Cambridge, Mass.: Harvard University Press).

Quigley, H. and Turner, J. (1956), *The New Japan* (Minneapolis, Minn.: University of Minnesota Press).

Rohlen, T. (1974), *For Harmony and Strength: Japanese White Collar Organisation* (Berkeley, Calif.: University of California Press).
Rose, R. and Shiratori, R. (1986), *The Welfare State: East and West* (New York: Oxford University Press).

Said, E. (1979), *Orientalism* (New York: Vintage).
Scalapino, R. A. (1983), *The Early Japanese Labour Movement* (Berkeley, Calif.: Institute of East Asian Studies).
Sheldon, C. D. (1958), *The Rise of the Merchant Class in Tokugawa Japan* (New York: Russel & Russel).
Shimada, H. (1980), *The Japanese Employment System* (Tokyo: Japan Institute of Labour).
Shimada, H. (1988), 'New challenges to contemporary industrial relations in Japan . . .', in Y. Kuwahara, G. Bamber and R. Lansbury (eds) (1988), *Industrial Relations in Advanced Countries: Factors of Maturity and Change* (Tokyo: Japan Institute of Labour Mimeo).
Shimodaira, H. (1985), 'Notes on some general features of the Japanese union movement', mimeo, Faculty of Economics, Shinshu University.
Silberman, B. and Harootunian, H. (eds) (1974), *Japan in Crisis: Essays on Taisho Democracy* (Princeton, NJ: Princeton University Press).
Smith, T. C. (1959), *The Agrarian Origins of Modern Japan* (Stanford, Calif.: Stanford University Press).
Stevens, C. R. and Takahashi, K. (eds) (no date), 'Materials on Japanese law', mimeo, Columbia University Law School.
Storry, R. (1960), *A History of Modern Japan* (Harmondsworth: Penguin).
Sugeno, K. (1988), 'Japanese industrial relations system and a paradigm of labour-management law', in Y. Kuwahara, G. Bamber and R. Lansbury (eds) (1988), *Industrial Relations in Advanced Countries: Factors of Maturity and Change* (Tokyo: Japan Institute of Labour Mimeo).
Sugimoto, Y., Shimada, H. and Levine, S. (1982), *Industrial Relations in Japan* (Melbourne: Japanese Studies Centre).

Tabata, H. (1989), 'Changes in plant-level trade union organisations: a case study of the automobile industry', *Annals of the Institute of Social Science*, no. 31, pp. 57–87.
Taira, K. (1970), *Economic Development and the Labour Market in Japan* (New York: Columbia University Press).
Takanashi, A. *et al.* (1989), *Shunto Wage Offensive: Historical Overview and Prospects* (Tokyo: Japan Institute of Labour).
Takayanagi, K. (1963), 'A century of innovation: developments in Japanese law', in Tanaka (1963).
Takayanagi, K. (1976), 'A century of innovation: the development of Japanese law, 1868–1961', in Tanaka (ed.) (1976).
Tanaka, H. (ed.) (1976), *The Japanese Legal System* (Tokyo: University of Tokyo Press).

Therborn, G. (1984), 'New questions of subjectivity', *New Left Review*, 143, p. 97.

Toshitani, N. (1976), Japan's modern legal system: its formation and structure', *Annals of the Institute of Social Science*, 17, p. 1 ff.

Totsuka, H. (1984), 'Rationalisation and the Japanese trade unions', *Bulletin of the Socialist Research Centre*, no. 7.

Toyoda, T. (1969), *A History of Pre-Meiji Commerce in Japan* (Tokyo: Japan Cultural Society).

Tsunoda, R. (ed.), *Sources of the Japanese Tradition* (New York: Columbia University Press).

Vogel, E. (1963), *Japan's New Middle Class* (Berkeley, Calif.: University of California Press).

Ward, R. E. (1957), 'The origins of the present Japanese constitution', in H. Tanaka (ed.) (1976), pp. 642–52, *The Japanese Legal System* (Tokyo: University of Tokyo Press).

Ward, R. E. (ed.) (1968), *Political Development in Modern Japan* (Princeton: Princeton University Press).

Wilkinson, T. O. (1965), *The Urbanisation of Japanese Labour, 1868–1955* (Amherst, Mass.: University of Massachusetts Press).

Wolpe, H. (ed.) (1980), *The Articulation of Modes of Production* (London: Routledge).

Woodiwiss, A. (1987a), 'The discourses of production (pt 1): law, industrial relations and the theory of ideology', *Economy and Society*, vol. 16, no. 3, pp. 275–326.

Woodiwiss, A. (1987b), 'The discourses of production (pt 2): the contract of employment and the emergence of democratic capitalist law in Britain and the United States', *Economy and Society*, vol. 16, no. 4, pp. 441–525.

Woodiwiss, A. (1989a), 'Paradox Lost (and with it Japan's uniqueness)', *Pacific Review*, vol. 2, no. 1, pp. 38–43.

Woodiwiss, A. (1989b), *Rights v. Conspiracy: A Sociological Essay on the History of American Labour Law in the United States* (New York/Hamburg/London: Berg).

Woodiwiss, A. (1990a), *Social Theory After Post-Modernism: Rethinking Law, Production and Class* (London: Zwan/Pluto).

Woodiwiss, A. (1990b), *From Repression to Reluctant Recognition: Law, Unions and Society in Japan* (forthcoming).

Woronoff, J. (1983), *Japan's Wasted Workers* (Tokyo: Lotus Press).

Yamamura, K. and Yasuba, Y. (1987), *The Political Economy of Japan: The Domestic Transformation* (Stanford, Calif.: Stanford University Press).

CHAPTER

— 5 —

Argentina: Dominant ideology or dominant cleavage?

EPHRAIM J. NIMNI

Introduction: a description of the impasse

The Argentine Republic is a land of paradoxes: it is an agrarian country with a small peasantry, a large middle class, a low birth rate, a substantial manufacturing sector and a highly unionized working class. It is a country which had complex forms of urban life before any meaningful industrial development. In more than one way, Argentina appears to be an oddity in the 'underdeveloped' world. Its capital city, Buenos Aires, was long ago considered one of 'the most interesting, dynamic and attractive cities of the Americas' (Ross and McGann, 1982, p. xv), whose intellectual and cultural sophistication was paralleled only by the most important European capitals. As Crawley states, Buenos Aires 'play-acts at being a city that really belongs somewhere in the northern hemisphere and, although it "somehow" drifted to the South Atlantic, it is still attached to the parental body by an imaginary umbilical cord' (1984, p. 5).

The social reality of contemporary Argentina is bedevilled by a perplexing paradox: the most fertile, urbanized and literate nation-state in Latin America has a history of political instability, violence, bloody repression and dictatorships, coupled with periodical cycles of hyper-inflation, unemployment and a crippling foreign debt. In the half century 1930–80, twenty-one years were lived under military rule (Di Tella, 1983, p. 198). Since the Second World War, Argentina

has experienced five civilian governments and five military interventions and has had, in all, ten appointed and seven elected
presidents, of whom only one – Juan Perón, 1946–52 – has, so far,
finished his full constitutional term. A second president – Raul
Alfonsin – resigned in 1989, five months before completing his full
constitutional term.

This chapter will argue that this paradoxical configuration of the
Argentinian state and society clearly indicates that, throughout its
turbulent history, Argentina has never managed to develop a
comprehensive and inclusive dominant ideology. Lacking the
incorporating mechanisms of a stable hegemonic bloc, the prevailing
characteristic of Argentina's political culture has been an endemic
political cleavage, which is immediately translated into the ideological positions of the dominant classes and principal political
protagonists. The political history of Argentina shows that, all too
often, opposing political forces develop totalizing and Manichaean
discourses, which result in crusades for the exclusion and/or
obliteration of real or imaginary opponents.

While this lack of institutional and political integration was initially
the result of the patterns of land tenure and clientalist networks
emanating from prevailing forms of the Castilian early settlement of
the River Plate basin, the problem was then compounded tenfold by
a class system and an internal power structure which have reflected
Argentina's chronic dependency on the volatility of international
agricultural and meat markets. This chapter will argue that the
structural linkage of these last two factors has been the single most
important cause for the contemporary stagnation of Argentinian
society – and its concomitant inability to constitute stable forms of
dominant discourses and institutionalized government.

Impasse degree zero: the landed oligarchy and the Europeanized political elite

It is impossible to exaggerate the importance of agrarian production in
the Argentinian economy. Agrarian exports constitute the almost
exclusive source of export revenue for the Argentinian economy.
During the decade 1963–73, 85 per cent of all Argentinian exports
originated in agrarian production. This is not untypical of other
periods of Argentinian history (Sidicaro, 1982, p. 61; Cardoso and
Falleto, 1973, p. 59).

The strategic role of the agrarian oligarchy initially emerged as the result of patterns of land settlement and farming methods utilized in the central plains. Extensive farming was made possible by the fertility and temperate climate of the *pampas* (vast grassy treeless plains of central Argentina) and resulted in the development of large ranches called *estancias* which required a relatively small number of *peones* (waged landless peasants). This situation caused the *pampas* (and by implication, Argentina), to be in the unusual situation of having a dominant agricultural economy without a numerically and politically significant peasant population. While this farming pattern existed since the early days of Spanish settlement, it was consolidated towards the second half of the nineteenth century, following the process of economic development and political institutionalization which took place during that period. At this time, agrarian expansion simply meant decimating or expelling the Aboriginal tribes towards Patagonia. Almost from the start, the fertile lands of the *pampas* were concentrated in the hands of a few large landlords – the core of the landed oligarchy. Following a centuries-old Castilian tradition, land taken from the Aboriginal tribes was distributed to the victorious soldiers in accordance with rank. But in the conditions of nineteenth-century Argentinian capitalism, only a small part of the conquered land was kept by the victorious soldiers; the rest was rapidly sold in the open market, where the price of the fertile lands of the *pampas* was sky-high. The end result of decades of land speculation was that, by 1912, the country had a population of slightly below 8 million, and a mere 1,843 families owned little less than one-sixth of the entire national territory (Crawley, 1984, pp. 9, 34–5; Rock, 1986, p. 154).

The political consolidation of the Argentinian national state occurred during the period 1852–81, and culminated with the city of Buenos Aires becoming the nation-state's capital. During the 1880s, an enlightened elite, known as *la generación del ochenta* (the generation of the eighties), 'drunk with a Spencerian notion of progress' (Crawley, 1984, p. 8), took upon itself the task of moulding Argentinian society within the canons of the liberal European tradition. The government of the period introduced laws creating a system of lay and compulsory primary education, a state registry and civil marriage. While this legislation undermined the position of the Church, the government fell short of legislating a total separation between the state and the Catholic Church (Levene, 1960, p. 243). It also introduced a restricted franchise.

But, above all, it was the socioeconomic changes which resulted partly from the 'Europeanizing' ideology of the generation of the eighties and partly from the technological developments of the period, which pushed Argentina into the social configuration that was to characterize its society in the twentieth century. Three related actions account for this pattern of change – the development of refrigerated transportation of meat to the European continent, mass immigration, mainly from southern Europe, and the construction of a British-owned railway network.

The project of the liberal elite was deceptively simple – to develop in South America a culturally European enclave, the economy of which would supply food to Europe. In return, Argentina would receive industrial products. The ideal partner for this venture was the British Empire. It has the industrial goods to sell to a consumer-hungry Argentina, while Argentina had the food to sell to a United Kingdom hungry for food (Levene, 1960, p. 238; Pendle, 1963, p. 56).

Even if subsequent events proved that the deal choked Argentina's potential for industrial development, the partnership apparently worked for a time. The development of an effective system of marine refrigeration in the 1870s gave economic viability to the project of the liberal elite. The refrigeration of meat reduced the cost of transportation to the European consumer and led to the development of a highly profitable network for the commercialization of Argentinian meats, and dramatically enhanced the position of the landed oligarchy in the Argentinian economy. At the same time, the liberal elite encouraged massive European immigration, attracting migrants with stories of the riches of the Argentinian countryside. Between 1871 and 1914 some 5.9 million immigrants arrived in Argentina and between 1830 and 1950 Argentina absorbed some 10 per cent of all European migrants to the American continent. In 1895, the foreign-born population in the most highly populated Argentinian province, Buenos Aires, was 30.8 per cent, while in the province of Santa Fe it was 41.9 per cent. In 1895 the population of the country was 3.9 million. By 1914 the number rose to 7.8 million. One-third of the population was foreign-born and 80 per cent of the population was either foreign-born or descended from immigrants who arrived after 1850 (Rock, 1986, pp. 141–2, 165–6).

In the minds of the Europeanized elite, the purpose of fostering massive European immigration was to form communities of small landowners, applying European farming skills to the 'most fertile soil in the world' (Crawley, 1984, p. 9). This vision was destined to certain failure for two main reasons. First, the land distributed to the soldiers participating in the conquest of the wilderness rapidly found its way to the big landowners and speculators. Second, traditional 'patrician' families had benefited from the 'law of emphyteusis', an ancient

Roman law widely used in the early years of the Argentine Republic. In essence, this law granted to early settlers and their decendants long-term access to and exclusive use of land which was, in principle, state property. Since the state was unable (or unwilling) to exercise any form of control over lands claimed in this way, the land was open to exploitation by private individuals, and it constituted the stepping-stone for the development of large *estancias* (Rock, 1986, p. 99).

Most immigrants found that they lacked purchasing power, or the ability to access a credit system which was almost entirely based on land mortgages. While it was relatively simple for a landowner to obtain credit to purchase land or agricultural equipment using previously held land as collateral, it was almost impossible for most landless and penniless immigrants to do so. In this situation, most immigrants were forced into share-cropping or tenancy of land owned by the agrarian oligarchy, or simply confined to the role of *peones*. The tenant farmers and share-croppers acted as pasture improvers for the big *estancias* by developing cyclical yields of alfalfa. After a few years, lands cultivated in this way were taken back by the big landowners. The immigrants therefore began slowly to drift into the cities. According to Crawley (1984, p. 9), by 1895 only one-third of foreign-born residents were engaged in agriculture.

The third element which consolidated the economic domination of the agrarian oligarchy was the establishment by British companies of railway networks, to secure fast and cheap transportation of agricultural produce to the ports and livestock to the *frigoríficos* (combined slaughter houses and meat-packing plants) which began to mushroom in the vicinity of the main ports. The railway networks not only reached far-away corners of the *pampas*, but went as far as the sugar-cane plantations of Tucuman province and the vine-producing areas at the foothills of the Andes in the provinces of Mendoza and San Luis. Around the turn of the century, railroad investment accounted for the majority of the then considerable British investment in the Argentine economy (Crawley, 1984, p. 8).

The unevenness of socioeconomic change resulted in a weak and politically powerless rural middle class and a disproportionately large urban middle class. The distorting effect of the immense economic power of large landowners was, as Rouquie (1978, p. 34) argues, an important factor in preventing the formation of a coherent and integrated national society. The refusal of this oligarchy to share access to the agro-exporter economy poses severe limitations on the formulation of an inclusive political project for the formation of dominant ideology. This is perhaps the single most important difference between Argentina and similar white settler societies in temperate climates such as Australia and Canada. While in the British dominions the state apparatus intervened to support a more equal access to 'frontier' land, in the Argentinian case millions of hectares were concentrated in the hands of a tiny sector, and the state was much too weak to antagonize this agrarian oligarchy, despite the liberal and reformist intentions of the political elite (O'Donnell, 1979, pp. 122–3). The domination of the agrarian oligarchy prevented the political leadership from establishing a meaningful hegemonic bloc, an 'expansive hegemony', or even an incorporating dominant ideology. Under these circumstances, the coherence of the liberal discourse sustained by the Europeanized ruling elite began to crack. The liberal discourse was perceived by urban middle- and working-class sectors to be incongruent with the agrarian oligarchy's uncompromising control over the economy and the restrictive democratic practices of the ruling elite. This challenge to the agrarian oligarchy and the Europeanized political elite resulted in a request for the extension of democratic rights and took the concrete form of a 'radical' and 'intransigent' demand for universal male suffrage.

The chain of reactive impasses: from the Unión Cívica Radical to the infamous decade

The liberal elitist political project was an alliance between an enlightened and modernizing political elite on the one hand, and an agrarian ruling class symbiotically linked to British commercial interests on the other, both requiring a 'modernizing' project to legitimize their positions as natural rulers of their respective fields of action – the economy and the state. The liberal elitist project, however, did not become a dominant discourse or the site of a hegemonic project. It did not offer sufficient concessions, nor did it attempt to accommodate the desire for political participation of the emerging urban middle and working classes. These sectors were equally alienated from the main source of Argentina's wealth by the restrictive practices of the oligarchy.

Under these conditions, a popular backlash against the 'democracy of the fat cows' was only a matter of time. In 1891 the Unión Cívica Radical (UCR) was formed, the first national political party organization to be constituted in Argentina with the aim of achieving state power through democratic elections (Rouquie, 1978, p. 54). This represented a bid by sectors of the urban middle class for a more egalitarian access to political power and economic wealth. In the same period, a more militant, working-class radicalism appeared. This was substantially different from the UCR's reformist version. The first stage was the emergence of trade unions. The second saw political organizations of a socialist and anarchist persuasion.

Working-class radicalism had an unexpected impact on the Argentinian political system. It gave impetus to the process of electoral reform. Some far-sighted members of the Europeanized political elite saw in the emergence of working-class radicalism a prolegomenon to the mass socialist agitation of *fin-de-siècle* European society and feared that an alienated middle class could join forces with the workers to topple the system. In the situation of rapid economic growth with large trade surpluses experienced by Argentina during the first decade of the twentieth century, these 'enlightened conservatives' reasoned that if electoral reform were introduced, the redistributive capacity of the agrarian oligarchy would foot the bill for the necessary concessions to incorporate the contented middle classes into the power bloc. This project would also have the effect of neutralizing the UCR without dramatically changing the nature of the country's political and economic leadership. Such a strategy had the added advantage that electoral reform could also incorporate some 'moderate' sectors of the working class into the political process, repeating the experience of reformist social democratic politics in Europe. Consequently, this reformist movement among the conservative elite attempted for the first time in Argentinian politics to create a 'dominant discourse' and an incorporating political bloc, based on the discourse of liberal-participatory democracy.

In 1910 Roque Sáenz Peña was inaugurated as president. Following the electoral practice of the period, he was the nominee of the outgoing president and a member of the dominant elite. He was also an 'enlightened conservative', who believed in the necessity for electoral reform, and two years after his election the Law of Electoral Reform was sanctioned by both houses. The new electoral law, since then known as the Sáenz Peña Law, provided for universal and compulsory male suffrage (the enfranchisement of women was not even discussed), secret ballots and a strict system for the registration of voters (Pendle, 1963, pp. 68–9; Crawley, 1984, p. 34; Rock, 1986, pp. 189–90).

The passing of the Sáenz Peña law represented a turning-point in Argentinian politics. The enlightened conservative project of constituting a stable hegemonic group under the leadership of the traditional political elite dramatically backfired. The traditional political elite was unable to overcome regional and personal differences and remained politically divided. A fraction of the agrarian oligarchy began to vacillate in its support for the traditional elite and switched allegiances to the UCR, frightened by the 'spectre of communism' which it believed to be behind urban working-class agitation. In the ensuing deadlock, the initiative in the attempt to develop a broad coalition of forces with the view of developing a hegemonic project, passed over to the embittered opponents of the traditional elite, the UCR under the populist and charismatic leadership of Hipolito Yrigoyen.

This episode was the first expression of one of the underlying problems which have prevented the formation of a successful dominant ideology in Argentina's political system: the manifest inability of both the agrarian oligarchy and the traditional political elite to constitute a solid conservative party (in the style of Australia's 'Country Party'). Instead, the politically weak, but economically strong, coalition of agrarian oligarchy and conservative elite, endeavoured to veto politics of political opponents whom it could neither neutralize nor incorporate into its dominant project. In this situation, the reactive recourse to coercive and authoritarian solutions appears as the way out of the impasse.

A characteristic which distinguishes Argentinian society from the rest of Latin America (with the exception of Uruguay), is its disproportionately large urban middle class, a phenomenon that reflects the narrowness of the productive base of the Argentinian economy. The middle class of Buenos Aires was (and is) the largest group of its kind in Latin America and it had an overwhelmingly immigrant background. The lower stratum of the middle class consisted usually of self-employed traders, shopkeepers and petty manufacturers. The upper stratum of the middle class was usually employed in the liberal professions and the public service. Within this stratum, salaried and non-entrepreneurial sectors dominated (Rock, 1986, p. 175).

This upper middle-class stratum generally received a broad humanistic education in the *colegios nacionales* (secondary institutions that replicated the curricula of the French *lycée* or the central European *Gymnasium*), or were university graduates. Given the immigrants' limited access to land ownership, the principal avenue for upward mobility was through formal education, a path which was further legitimized by the discourse of the Europeanized political elite. Under these conditions formal education became a status symbol among the immigrant community, and many immigrant families underwent great sacrifices to give a complete and formal education to their children. In occupational terms, the upper stratum of the middle class was composed of 'first generation Argentines', mostly sons (but also a few daughters) of the predominantly immigrant lower middle class (O'Donnell, 1979, p. 124; Crawley, 1984, p. 18; Rock, 1986, p. 175). It was these 'first generation Argentines' who felt most acutely a sense of relative political deprivation *vis-à-vis* the economic and political elites, and therefore became the logical constituency of the programme for electoral reform of the UCR.

Yrigoyen's UCR was the first party to win an election under the new electoral law. The novelty that brought the UCR government to power was that it exploited a fissure in the coalition of landed oligarchy and political elite, by organizing a broad coalition of dissatisfied minority fractions of the landed oligarchy with the newly enfranchised middle classes and some sections of the working class. An ambiguous discourse of 'radical' and 'intransigent' implementa- tion of representative democracy and decent government (*la causa* – the cause), coupled with a Manichaean identification of all the country's evils in the corrupted practices of the old regime (*el régimen*), was the shaky ideological basis for the formation of a dominant discourse designed to mobilize large and diverse sectors of Argentinian society.

Laclau (1977, pp. 182–3) suggests that the radical discourse represented a pronounced shift from the non-democratic liberalism of the conservative elite to a liberal discourse which accepted the full consequences of representative democracy. But at the same time, it stretched the boundaries of the liberal-democratic discourse to its conceptual limits: it opened the way for a broad political participation of subordinated sectors, without having the strength to tackle the developmental constraints imposed by the predominance of the agro-exporter economy. Large sections of the traditional conservative elite regarded Yrigoyen's popular appeal as an unwarranted intromission of the mob (*la chusma*) into the centre of power of the political arena. The left and the working class were also suspicious of Yrigoyen's legalistic reformism, believing that he was a mere surrogate (*testaferro*) of large commercial interests aiming to demobilize a militant working class with a largely cosmetic reformist project. Given that Argentina did not have during this period an independent industrial bourgeoisie which could have become the support base for the UCR's liberal democratic project, Yrigoyen was deprived of a stable base to develop an incorporating dominant discourse, and he increasingly resorted to the charisma of his personal appeal to maintain momentum for his reforms and the support of the middle classes.

The 1853 constitution disallows a successive presidential re-election and, when Yrigoyen's term of office came to an end in 1922, the successful UCR candidate was Marcelo T. de Alvear, a member of one of the wealthiest land-owning families and a founding member of the UCR. The Alvear administration proved to be more conservative than the previous one, a situation which created strong tensions in the UCR but appeased the scattered conservative forces and pleased the agrarian oligarchy and foreign business. With the increased demand for Argentinian produce in the international markets, the redistributive capacity of the agrarian oligarchy was considerably augmented, a situation which in Crawley's words was like 'pouring a balm on the social tensions of preceding years' (1984, p. 42).

However, Alvear's policy of building bridges towards the con-servatives and of 'rationalizing' the huge bureaucratic apparatus created by the Yrigoyen administration infuriated a large section of the rank and file of the UCR. In a country where the agrarian sector required few skilled workers, and with an underdeveloped industrial sector and an overdeveloped middle class, the commercial sector and an inflated civil service were the only employment outlets for the increasing number of secondary school graduates. When the Alvear administration engaged in large-scale dismissals in the civil service, the president rapidly lost support among the party faithful. A major characteristic of the Alvear administration was its reluctance to industrialize, in line with the nineteenth-century ideological dicta that local industry was 'inefficient and wasteful'; to support 'artificial' Argentinian industries was tantamount to inducing 'chronic inefficiencies' and would generate social tensions (Rock, 1986, p. 207). This ideological 'complex of inferiority' was well in tune with the economic aims of the agrarian oligarchy and faithfully represented the dominant discourse of the period. But it was a divisive argument which was increasingly questioned by large sections of the working and middle classes. It was destined to collapse during the tensions generated by the world economic crash of the 1930s, to which Argentina's agrarian export-oriented economy was overexposed.

The conservatives were stunned by the return of Yrigoyen to the presidency of the republic in 1928. They began to plot his overthrow almost from the moment that he was sworn in. The anti-Yrigoyen camp was this time a powerful force to reckon with, including the traditional oligarchy and the conservative forces, the supporters of

Alvear, and large sections of the army. Failing to defeat Yrigoyen by electoral means, the opposition deposed him in a military coup, the first example of what was to become the continuous intervention of the armed forces in the political life of the country. The coup initiated a period of conservative restoration known in Argentinian history as *La década infame* (The infamous decade). While the military called for elections a year after the coup, the UCR was ineligible to participate, and the elections were rigged, leading to the restoration of the alliance which ruled the country before 1916. The conservatives, in turn, repeatedly rigged elections to keep themselves in power. During this period (1930–43), most of the reforms initiated by the radical administrations were abandoned.

The period 1916–30 is best described as an exercise in informal power-sharing between the traditional elites and the urban middle classes (Rock, 1986, p. 215). However, this informal power-sharing neither was a proper political alliance, nor did it constitute the basis for the formation of a dominant discourse or power bloc. This informal power-sharing nevertheless functioned, despite the cleavages between the main participants (the middle class, the agrarian oligarchy and the conservative elite), because of the cyclical expansion of the economy. Economic expansion enhanced the redistributive capacity of the agrarian oligarchy, inhibiting its tendency to engage in veto politics. However, this enhanced redistributive capacity neither was sufficient to co-opt the working class, nor did it create a communality of political goals between the middle class and the conservative elite.

The monopolies of the agrarian producers and their alliances with foreign interests, and the concomitant weakness of the middle class to lead the way to industrialization and the subsequent diversification of the Argentinian economy, resulted in the chronic cleavages which were to divide the Argentinian society during the first three decades of the twentieth century. This delicate balance of forces was finally upset by the economic collapse of the 1930s.

In the aftermath, the United Kingdom government reviewed its trade policies towards Argentina. At the Ottawa Conference of 1932, it decided to retreat behind the boundaries of its white imperial offspring, giving preferential treatment to Australian and Canadian meat and cereals. This agreement was tantamount to a virtual 'expulsion' of Argentina from the informal (economic) British Empire and deeply shocked the agrarian oligarchy (Horowicz, 1985, p. 29). But rather than attempting to reduce Argentina's vulnerability to the British agricultural market by diversifying exports and industrializing the economy, the conservative government was determined to maintain at all costs the economic supremacy of the agrarian oligarchy by enhancing further Argentina's dependency on exports of meat and grain to Britain (Rouquie, 1978, p. 237).

This is the background to the vilified treaty signed in 1933, between Walter Runciman, president of the British Board of Trade, and the son of the 'conqueror of the wilderness', Argentinian Vice-President Julio A. Roca Jnr. The Roca–Runciman treaty gave British capital a ruinous preferential treatment in the importation of coal and manufactured goods, as well as an advantageous rate of exchange for the repatriation of profits. It also included some humiliating clauses, such as the cancellation of licences for the Buenos Aires bus service (the *colectivos*) because it was in direct competition with the Anglo-Argentine Tramway Company. All of these concessions were made in exchange for a British undertaking not to reduce imports of Argentinian meat (Gillespie, 1982, p. 4; Pendle, 1963, pp. 77–8; Rock, 1986, pp. 224–5).

The impact of the Roca–Runciman treaty on the political mythology of Argentinian nationalism was similar to the impact of the Versailles treaty on the political mythology of the Weimar Republic. In the nationalist discourse, terms such as *entreguismo* (from the Spanish verb *'entregar'*, to hand over, to surrender), and *cipayaje* (from the term 'sepoy', denoting subservience to foreign interests), identified the actions of local collaborators with a rapacious enemy poised to ruin the country economically. The fact that the treaty was signed in 1933 – the year in which Hitler became Chancellor – added a new and sinister dimension to Argentina's humiliation, since the signing of the treaty pushed an influential group of right-wing, nostalgic nationalists among the aristocracy into the arms of fascism. Nietzschean concepts such as 'superman' were used in the nationalist discourse to exalt the alleged 'macho' virtues of the founding fathers (*Los Próceres*) of the Argentinian nation, and the works of the French right-wing writer Charles Maurras became widely read in literary circles. Clericalist terms such as *La Hispanidad*, coined by the Spanish falangist ideologue José Antonio Primo de Rivera, and its more localized version, the concept of *La Argentinidad*, began to denote in the right-wing nationalist discourse those alleged metaphysical attributes of legendary pastoral Argentina, which were corrupted by both *entreguismo* and the 'judeo-bolshevik conspiracy'.

This discourse, with its emphasis on tradition, ultramontane Catholicism, distrust of parliamentary democracy and exaltation of discipline found its way to an institution which was structurally well poised to assimilate its authoritarian characteristics – the armed forces. As Rock (1986, p. 228) argues, the idea that Argentina was a nation graced by nature and by God, with a 'manifest destiny' of power and greatness – an idea which had its origins in the positivist tradition of the 1880s – lingered into the 1930s, becoming the foundation for the close association between nationalism and the armed forces.

The most 'credible' impasse: Peronism

In spite of the developmental constraints imposed by the Roca–Runciman treaty, Argentinian industry began to develop at a modest but steady pace by means of import substitution. This process was dramatically accelerated by the outbreak of the Second World War, reaching its peak in 1943, when the value of industrial output surpassed that of agriculture (Rock, 1986, p. 232). This change prepared the ground for the entry of organized labour into the political arena and had a profound impact on the configuration of Argentina's state and society.

The industrial growth which began in the mid-1930s was the result of a number of causes, in part connected with the world market and in part with the growth of Argentina's domestic economy. First, after the Roca–Runciman treaty, most non-British industrial products were subjected to heavy duties; and the relatively high cost of British textiles encouraged the development of a local textile industry. Second, in order to circumvent protectionist legislation, a number of foreign (mainly North American) corporations decided to produce light industrial goods in Argentina. Third, the steady growth in urban population encouraged the development of an indigenous light service industry, particularly in the area around the city of Buenos Aires. But, above all, what triggered the accelerated industrial development of the early 1940s was, as usual, an external factor – the outbreak of the war in Europe and the unavailability of British industrial products. Rock (1986, pp. 234–5) provides staggering figures: in 1930, domestic manufacturers provided less than 9 per cent of the country's total consumption of textiles, while in 1943 their share rose to 82 per cent. Between 1935 and 1946 the number of workers employed in the textile industry grew from 83,000 to 194,000 and in the food and drink sector from 111,000 to 235,000. Nevertheless, industrial development was mainly confined to light and consumer goods industries.

During this era of growing industrialization, Argentinian society changed significantly, as a new industrial working class, more numerous and with a different social background, began to find its place in the Argentinian jigsaw. A different pattern of urban migration was established. International immigration was not forthcoming, because of protective restrictions enacted during the depression years and because of the disruption caused by the war. The net result was a massive internal migration from the country to the main cities, especially to the conurbations on the southern periphery of Buenos Aires. Rural unemployment during the war period pushed many rural workers out of the countryside, while the growth in manufacturing industry attracted them to Buenos Aires. These new urban workers were substantially different from the hitherto anarchist and socialist-leaning foreign–born working class, and were alienated from traditional working-class politics (Pendle, 1963, p. 77).

The changes experienced by Argentinian society during the period led to the formation of an industrial bourgeoisie, which rapidly found support in the nationalists' rhetoric, and was relatively independent from the agrarian oligarchy. The turning-point was the year 1943, when the volume of industrial production surpassed the volume of production of the agrarian sector (Carpani, 1973, p. 80). Industrialists sought to increase their influence over the conservative government, which was invariably biased towards the agrarian oligarchy. In their demand for more favourable conditions for industrialization, they had the support of the nationalists and their influential friends, the armed forces, who saw industrialization as the path towards world power. Fascist roads to industrialization, tried in Europe in the 1930s, were considered useful models for an industrializing Argentina. The Catholic Church, under the influence of the events of the Spanish Civil War, gave its blessing to the 'crusaders' of the anti–democratic movement. In this situation, a powerful new discourse began to challenge the liberal elitism of the traditional conservative alliance, and the banal democratic discourse of the UCR (O'Donnell, 1979, p. 127).

The conservative governments continued with their corrupt political practices, oblivious to change. But under these new conditions the conservative elite and the agrarian oligarchy could no longer count on the support of the armed forces. In June 1943 a military coup ousted the conservative government which the same armed forces, albeit with a different political complexion, had brought to power a decade earlier. The immediate reason for the coup was the imminent corrupt election of a pro–British oligarch and sugar baron to the presidency of the republic and his alleged desire to break Argentina's neutrality by declaring war against the Axis forces. The more structural reasons resulted from the profound social change experienced by Argentinian society. The agrarian oligarchy and the conservative elite were increasingly isolated from the middle classes, the army and the working class, which was, in turn, alienated from socialist and anarchist organizations. A new industrial bourgeoisie was bidding for the dominant position in the economic arena. The UCR supported the coup. Civil society, for the first time, had mustered enough strength to mount an effective challenge to conservative and oligarchical domination. There was, however, an important sector which was left outside the coalition – the working class. This was soon to be corrected.

The coup of 1943 was instigated by a group of middle- and low-ranking army officers, organized in a highly secretive lodge, only known by its acronym GOU. This shadowy pro-Axis organization – with an alleged project for the domination of South America and a corporatist programme for political and economic organization – subsequently became the dominant force behind the military government. The *éminence grise* of the GOU was an unknown colonel whose name was later to send shock waves through the Argentinian political arena – Juan Domingo Perón.

The most significant aspect of the military administration was Perón's control of the national labour department, which he redefined as the Secretariat for Labour and Welfare. From this position the colonel astutely understood the alienated position of the urban working class and attracted its loyalty by improving the workers' lot with highly publicized concessions to workers' demands (pay, vacations, accident compensation, annual bonuses, housing, etc.), while carefully isolating communist and socialist trade unionists from their rank and file. During this period, an incongruous spectacle evolved: a government of anti-communist zealots and ultramontane Catholics supported workers' demands by squeezing concessions from the capitalists (Rock, 1986, p. 258). In late 1944, the employers' organization Union Industrial Argentina (UIA) broke with Perón over year-end bonuses (*aguinaldos*) that he had decreed, accusing him of being a fascist demagogue.

Opposition to the military government came from a broad spectrum of political forces – the UCR, the conservatives, the oligarchy, large sections of the left, large sections of the middle classes – all opposed to different aspects of government policies. Most were opposed to the lack of civil liberties, some to the ultramontane drift in education and some to the high government expenditure on manufacturing and the military (Rock, 1986, pp. 253, 258).

The events which followed were a decisive turning-point. The United States government, anxious to enhance its influence in Argentina, began to advocate the overthrow of the military dictatorship, caricaturing Perón as a hard-line fascist. At this point the armed forces were divided. Opponents of Perón's policies appeared to have the upper hand and forced a reluctant president to dismiss and imprison Perón. The Argentinian working class was bent upon shattering the imperialist dreams of the State Department. In the days following Perón's imprisonment, in an island off the coast of Buenos Aires, his closest friends and supporters, led by his fiancée Maria Eva Duarte, began to canvass support. On 17 October 1945, the workers, the poor and the underprivileged (in short the 'popular masses'), took to the streets of Buenos Aires demanding the return of Perón. After the police's refusal to disperse the marchers, the demonstration gathered momentum, concentrating hundreds of thousands of workers in front of Government House. When confronted with this show of strength, the military opposition to Perón fell apart, and Perón was reinstated with a clear promise for a free election five months later. Perón's supporters organized a new party that later took the name of its leader, the Peronist Party. In one of the cleanest elections in Argentina's history, the Peronists won the support of 54 per cent of the electorate.

The first Peronist government was characterized by a policy of income distribution in favour of industry and the popular sector and the enactment of comprehensive labour and welfare legislation, putting Argentina on a par with West European welfare states. During Perón's period in office, the standard of living of urban and rural workers rose significantly, labour rights were effectively protected, workers felt that they had gained some influence in the political arena and the electoral law was reformed to enfranchise women. The share of wages in national income rose from 38 to 46 per cent, and in the same period 500,000 new homes were built, putting the per capita rate of construction among the highest in the world (O'Donnell, 1979, pp. 128–9; Rock, 1986, p. 263). The cornerstone of the Peronist economic policy was the expansion of the domestic market coupled with a marked increase in industrial production. This policy tied in well both with the interests of industrialists and of the popular sectors, since the expansion of the internal market necessarily meant increasing the purchasing capacity of workers. Income redistribution, the growth of light industry and an increase of consumption were the structurally linked aspects of economic development. This policy, however, accentuated one of the chronic difficulties of industrial growth in Argentina: the inability to direct resources to the development of heavy industry.

Most agrarian exports were channelled through an institution for the promotion of trade, best known by its Spanish acronym, IAPI. This institution had a monopoly over the export of agrarian produce, buying meat and cereals from the producers at a standard price and selling abroad at a profit, and then using the price differential to finance both industrial projects and income distribution. But despite all his anti-oligarchical rhetoric, Perón fell short of enacting a programme of land reform which would have given the *coup de grâce* to the debilitated, but not yet defeated, landed oligarchy. This is something that the Peronists learned to regret, since it became one of the main causes of the downfall of the Peronist administration.

Peronism can be seen as a comprehensive attempt to develop a stable hegemonic bloc and a dominant ideology in Argentina. To achieve this aim, Peronism attempted to develop a 'counter-hegemonic' project, both to eliminate the political and economic impasse which resulted from the agrarian oligarchy's (and its foreign supporters') veto power over the country's development, and to secure a policy of income redistribution which the Peronists considered to be in tune with the needs of an industrial welfare state. Both aims were to be achieved by mobilizing the popular masses and the incipient industrial bourgeoisie against the oligarchy and its overseas supporters, through a discourse of an industrializing, popular-corporatist and authoritarian nationalism.

The corporatist discourse of Peronism was aimed at creating the ideological basis for class collaboration and national-state integration through the doctrine of the 'organized community'. While there is some fascist influence in the political project outlined above, it would be misleading to call Peronism a form of fascism, since Peronism did not adhere to the totalitarian (in the sense of *Der totale Staat*) form of state organization. On the other hand, it would also be misleading to call the Peronist project socialist (in the Marxist sense) because it advanced class collaboration and respect for certain forms of private property of the means of production. This should not be taken to mean that there are no fascist, Marxist, or even liberal readings of Peronism. In fact, as Laclau argues, Peronism constructed a *sui generis* popular-democratic subject. But the specificity of Peronism lies in its working-class base (Laclau, 1977, p. 190).

An important factor in Peronism's capacity for popular mobilization was its ability to construct a powerful symbolic language, which both condensed and constructed the identity and aspirations of the popular sectors of Argentinian society. For example, the term *descamisados* (shirtless) was initially a pejorative label used by a fashionable middle class to refer to the inelegant dress of the workers. In Peronist political discourse the negative connotation of the term was transformed into an oppositional category through which the poor and the underprivileged were made 'conscious' of both their common political predicament and their relative deprivation *vis-à-vis* the wealthy sections of society. Once the identity of the *masas descamisadas* (shirtless masses) was constructed in this way, it became a powerful vehicle for political mobilization.

Another important symbol of the Peronist movement was the myth of Maria Eva Duarte, Perón's second wife. Evita, as she was affectionately known, campaigned vigorously for the rights of women and the dispossessed, initiating the process of electoral reform which enfranchised women. She also used her considerable political and rhetorical skills to support the work of the Peronist movement in the trade unions. Her iconic image converted the gender prejudices of a Latin Catholic society into political assets for the Peronist movement. Charity work located Evita in one of the poles of the Latin feminine stereotype, that of a dignified madonna, best exemplified in her titles *La abanderada de los trabajadores* (the flag-bearer of the workers) and *La jefa espiritual de la nacion* (the [female] spiritual chief of the nation). Her image was at once 'the glittering ceremonial showpiece' and 'the feminist crusader who instigated the destruction of the oligarchy and privilege', all of this cunningly condensed in the slogan *Perón cumple, Evita dignifica* (Perón fulfils, Evita dignifies) (Rock, 1986, p. 288).

For the conservative opposition she represented the other pole of the feminine stereotype, the dissolute prostitute who cunningly uses her beauty, charm and sexual favours to achieve power and riches. But, above all, what directed the venomous attacks of the oligarchy and the conservatives against Maria Eva Duarte was a powerful and revolutionary Cinderella effect. In the myth of 'Evita', the oligarchy and high society's monopoly on status and social achievement was subverted by the humble and the despised (Crawley, 1984, p. 117). In 1952 Maria Eva Duarte died of leukaemia, compounding the mythical effect of her influential existence.

The beginning of the end of the Peronist administration was the result, again, of an event unconnected with the Argentinian domestic situation. In 1948 the United States administration decided that Marshall Plan aid could not be used to purchase Argentinian meat and grain, but should be used instead to supply Europe from United

States, Canadian and Australian reserves. A decline in international prices compounded the problem. Before 1949, IAPI was in a position to dictate terms of trade with European customers. But after 1949 this position was reversed. In 1950, to maintain the level of export income of the previous five years, Argentina had to increase production by 30 per cent, an impossible task due to the increase in domestic consumption and the trade restrictions imposed by the Marshall Plan. The agrarian oligarchy responded to the crisis by reducing meat production, a step calculated to damage the Peronist administration. By 1951 Argentina consumed 86 per cent of all the meat it produced, and even the reduced export quotas were not met (Rock, 1986, pp. 296–7).

Again, as so often happened in Argentinian politics, the political consequences of an export crisis were soon to be felt. During its first period in office, the Peronist administration tolerated a bitter but localized opposition because its redistributive policies assured the support of a large section of the population. Following the export crisis, the government's redistributive capacity was drastically curtailed, and the Peronist movement resorted both to an increased political mobilization with propaganda which assumed theatrical proportions, and to a clamp-down on left and right opposition. The massive trade union confederation (CGT) was organized through a 'vertical' chain of command and opposition leaders were imprisoned or exiled.

Ominously, Perón's relations with the Catholic Church began to sour. His use of Catholic symbols to enhance the rhetorical value of *Justicialismo* – the vague and convoluted Peronist doctrine – offended the Catholic hierarchy and, furthermore, the Church was not inclined to lose its autonomy and considerable privileges under the corporatist order of 'the organized community'. The middle class was never over-enthusiastic about Perón's populism and was alienated even further by the theatrical and authoritarian postures of the regime. The left regarded Peronism as a form of authoritarian demagoguery, a regime committed to 'paying bribes' to the working class and distracting the workers from 'real' revolutionary tasks. The Peronist hatred of the oligarchy was reciprocated tenfold and eventually the armed forces began to distance themselves from the regime. Finally, Perón was overthrown by a military coup in 1955, three years after he had been re-elected to the presidency (following a controversial constitutional reform).

The continuous impasse: military dictatorships

Peronism represented the following paradox: the most viable attempt to constitute a stable power bloc and dominant discourse in Argentina's contemporary history was, at the same time, the most divisive political discourse in contemporary Argentina. The Peronist doctrine of 'social harmony', 'reconciliation of classes', the 'third position' – which was meant to avoid 'the divisiveness of communism and capitalism' – was pursued with zeal and determination, but it resulted in a bitterly divided society. The defeat of Peronism was, in more than one way, a symptomatic repetition of the impasse which has characterized Argentina's twentieth-century political development – dependence on international food markets, defective industrialization, an obstructionist landed oligarchy, a large but relatively powerless middle class, and, after Perón, a highly organized but ineffectual working class.

Following the overthrow of Perón, the country was pushed by the military dictators and the revengeful desires of the oligarchy through a period of 'de-Peronization', which meant carefully erasing most references to what the conservative press called *el régimen depuesto* (the deposed regime), and *el tirano profugo* (the fugitive tyrant). The terms 'Perón' or 'Peronism' were hardly used. The powerful trade union confederation (CGT) was ruled by a military government appointee; it had its assets confiscated and was prevented from any significant trade union activity. Electoral attempts to restore a semblance of parliamentary democracy were conducted with the implicit proscription of Peronism, the largest political force in the country. One president – Arturo Frondizi – was elected with the tactical support of the Peronist vote, but later reneged on an agreement with the Peronists, and was eventually overthrown by another military coup. The recurrence of military coups in Argentina appeared to be a way out of a political deadlock, but they in fact changed nothing and perpetuated the deadlock. After the overthrow of an ageing UCR president in 1966, the armed forces began a self-styled 'Argentinian revolution', aimed at sustaining power for a long period so as radically to transform Argentina's political scene.

Following the Brazilian example, the leader of the coup, General Ongania, attempted to create a modernizing autocracy for which popular support was irrelevant. With an iron fist, the military curbed opposition forces and paralysed the Peronist trade unions. Military repression established a peace of sorts. During this period multinational corporations invested heavily in the car industry. But the dreams of autocratic modernization were shattered by the *Cordobazo*, a radical workers' and students' uprising in the city of Córdoba, the base for the largest car plants in the country. This uprising was the beginning of a more radicalized form of resistance to the military government.

The Peronist movement over this period grew into a poly-morphous mass (Rock, 1986, p. 359), with competing interpretations from left, right and centre, all claiming to be 'true' Peronists. The trade union bureaucracy on the whole remained within the orthodox Peronist camp, while it divided between those who wanted to maintain the 'vertical' chain of command from the leader, and those who wanted a 'Peronism without Perón'. Perón showed his remarkable political skill by remaining aloof from internal disputes and using the policy of 'divide and rule' to maintain his position of head of the movement, supporting different factions at different times, and showing no permanent commitment to any. In this way, the charisma of Perón and his steadfast support from the working class were the only elements which kept the Peronist movement united.

Faced with the growing radicalization of the working class and of the youth wing of the Peronist movement and the menacing activities of the urban guerrilla organizations, the military government decided to seek a pact with Perón, rehabilitating his name and allowing him to return to Argentina. This was yet another attempt to constitute a dominant discourse which could stabilize the volatility of Argentinian politics. The army and the dominant political elite realized, albeit too late, that the reformism of the traditional Peronist movement was not a significant challenge to the structure of Argentinian capitalism and that a pact with Perón could deliver the support of the working class without making significant concessions. Perón was subsequently elected president with an overwhelming majority in 1973.

The programme of the new Peronist government was similar to that of 1946. The main political objectives were income redistribution in favour of labour, subsidized industrialization through the resurrection of IAPI, state control over the banking system, etc. (Rock, 1986, p. 361). But the political climate was dramatically different from that of 1946. A radicalized Peronist left saw in Perón's return and the military collapse a clear indication that the revolution was 'just around the corner'. It pressed for more radical measures, which threatened the 'verticalist' structure of the Peronist movement and visibly annoyed the leader. The backbone of the Peronist movement was its trade union movement, and the undemocratic practices of Peronism produced a powerful and corrupt leadership (the 'trade union bureaucracy'), which was considered by the left and the *Montoneros* movement to be a treacherous superimposition to curb the militancy of class-conscious workers. Perón understood, however, that with all its faults, the trade union bureaucracy was both relatively popular with the rank and file because it made gains for members on bread-and-butter issues, and an essential transmission belt of the 'verticalist' structure of the Peronist movement. Perón was unwilling to compromise in order to unite the movement and declared war upon 'terrorist' and 'subversive Marxist groups' which had 'infiltrated' the Peronist movement (Gillespie, 1982, p. 144).

With the international economy in recession after 1973, the purchase of Argentinian foodstuffs declined with adverse effects on the domestic economy. After Perón's death, with the inflation rate at 566 per cent, with the Peronist movement paralysed by in-fighting, with a government that suffered an almost complete lack of credibility because of its astonishing incompetence and corruption, the military ousted the third Peronist administration in March 1976, to the relief of the majority of the population. This was the very administration which had won office three years earlier in the biggest landslide in Argentina's electoral history. What followed was, without doubt, the blackest period in Argentina's troubled contemporary history.

The attempt to build a stable hegemonic bloc within the dominant discourse of Peronism was an unmitigated fiasco. By the time of the coup, the country was bitterly divided and economically paralysed. Peronism in the early 1950s offered a feasible hegemonic project, but the radical transformations it suffered in the 1960s and 1970s made it into a mirror image of the deep divisions affecting the Argentinian society as a whole. The ensuing paralysis made visible its fundamental weaknesses and it lost all credibility as a hegemonic project. Impasse and deadlock were, again, the name of the game.

Before attempting to comprehend what the lawyer Eduardo Luis Duhalde (1983) called 'The terrorist Argentinian state', it is important to understand the scope of Argentinian left-wing terrorism and urban guerrilla activity, and the challenge it presented to the dominant capitalist system. The two main guerrilla organizations were the pro-Peronist *Montoneros* and the neo-Trotskyist ERP (Spanish acronym for 'Revolutionary People's Army'). Apologists of the military dictatorship and the urban guerrilla movements claim that the urban guerrillas were close to a breakthrough which would have led them to political power, a claim that is greatly exaggerated. With all its weaknesses, Argentina has a complex and fairly developed civil society. There are no 'Winter Palaces'; and to dominate the complex economic and political life of the country, it is necessary to have broad support across different sectors of society – a situation which the guerrilla organizations were never close to achieving. Even at the peak of the popularity of the *Montoneros* in 1973, Perón himself estimated the strength of his left-wing vote to be at the most 10 per cent of his 7 million votes (Gillespie, 1982, p. 207). Moreover, even in the doubtful case that any of the guerrilla organizations could have achieved massive popular support, they were never in a position to challenge the military might of an army of close to 100,000 men. The Argentinian armed forces have almost zero capacity to fight external wars – the Falkland-Malvinas war is eloquent proof of this – because during the last sixty years, they had excelled in their commitment to police internal dissent.

The military government which came into power in 1976 did not enjoy popular support, but was greeted with signs of relief by the vast majority of the population after the spectacular collapse of the Peronist administration. It called its administration 'the process for national reorganization', and so the government began to be known as *El Proceso* (the process), a suitably Kafkaesque title for the mindless bureaucratic violence which it was about to unleash. The 'process' was organized in two fronts, a holy 'dirty war' against 'subversion', a term which was given a broad and all-inclusive meaning, and a stern monetary policy designed to destroy all forms of state subsidies to urban sectors including civilian industry, in order to allow for the expansion of the agrarian sector. In short, the economic rule of the agrarian oligarchy returned with a vengeance.

This war against 'subversion' acquired truly Dantesque dimensions. The term was not only applied to urban guerrilla organizations, which were in decline by that time, but it implied all forms of cultural, intellectual and aesthetic expressions of pluralism and liberal ideas. This reached its highest expression in the paranoiac doctrine of 'national security'. This doctrine had its origins in the counter-insurgency theories developed in the 'School of Inter-American Defense', a CIA institution for the 'education' of military officers from Latin America located in the United States-controlled Panama Canal zone. Under Argentinian conditions the original theory was considerably expanded and enriched to encompass notions of 'total war' and systematic destruction of the 'subversive enemy'. Argentina, according to this doctrine, was targeted for destruction by 'international subversion' – a vague term which refrained from accusing the Soviet Union because of its good commercial relations with

Argentina – but pointed an accusing finger to Cuba and sometimes Libya. There was 'ideological subversion' which was advocated by large sections of the press, the arts and persons from disciplines such as psychology and sociology. 'Economic subversion' was detectable in policies 'which destroyed the national economy'. Not only was the whole network of Argentina's civil society 'infiltrated' by 'subversives', but also the White House, the European press and the Catholic Church (Rock, 1986, pp. 366–72; Crawley, 1984, p. 421).

This paranoiac ideology was put into action to create 'the terrorist Argentinian state'. A vast network of secret detention centres emerged. Thousands of people 'disappeared', abducted by anonymous kidnappers driving cars with no number plates. People were dragged away from homes, offices, etc., never to be found. Towards the 1980s, the guerrilla movement was destroyed, the 'dirty war' subsided and a substantial number of Argentinian middle-class intellectuals opted for exile. Huge industrial conglomerates were absorbed by military industry, while large sections of private industry were ruined. The government began to encourage massive foreign investment which maintained the currency artificially high, procuring large returns to financial speculators at home and abroad. A new financial sector closely connected with the agrarian oligarchy began to emerge, making large fortunes in dealings with foreign investors – all at the cost of vastly increasing the indebtedness of the Argentinian treasury.

The attempt to recapture the Malvinas islands (the Falklands) was a populist adventure designed to unite an increasingly discontented Argentina behind the military dictatorship. But the result of the military fiasco was the final collapse of *El Proceso*. Presidential elections were called in October 1983 and the candidate of the left of centre fraction of the UCR, Raul Alfonsin, defeated electorally the Peronists for the first time in their history. Within two years, the main leaders of *El Proceso* were behind bars serving long custodial sentences, imposed in the strictest compliance with the constitutional role of an independent judiciary. The armed forces were one of the most hated sections of Argentinian society.

El Proceso was a clear attempt at an oligarchical restoration in collusion with one of the most brutal and barbaric forces which emerged out of Argentinian nationalism. There was no attempt here to develop a dominant ideology, the expectation was that naked brute force would lead the country out of the impasse. The aims of the process failed in both accounts; the oligarchical restoration brought the country to the verge of economic collapse and the barbarities of the armed forces failed to restructure Argentinian society. True, the guerrilla movement was obliterated, but the causes which had led to its emergence remained intact. Peronism and the working class were badly beaten but not defeated. The UCR staged a come-back in the figure of an honest man, Raul Alfonsin, whose main intention was to restore constitutional democracy and the rule of law – a mammoth task in a polarized Argentina. The radical administration was relatively successful in this task. However, it failed abysmally in its economic policies. Indeed, the unprecedented – even by Argentina's chaotic standards – economic collapse of 1989 rendered the country ungovernable and forced President Alfonsin to resign in disgrace shortly after the presidential elections, and five months before completing his term of office. The newly elected Peronist president, Carlos Menem, immediately embarked on a policy of widespread privatization and elimination of subsidies that reneges on traditional Peronist economic doctrines. The new administration is also seeking a pact with conservative forces and an appeasement of the military, but without a resolution to the urgent economic problems, the administration would not succeed in its bid for a 'reconciliation of the Argentines'. In the meantime, what ex-President Alfonsin called 'praetorian messianism' is badly beaten but not defeated.

Conclusion

Studies of the dominant ideology attempt to portray inclusionary systems in which the strategic location of the dominant strata permit the formation of stable hegemonic blocs. According to Gramsci (*Selections from the Prison Notebooks*, 1971, p. 57), a social class must exercise 'intellectual and moral leadership' as a precondition for the exercise of stable governmental power. This is done by providing leadership and winning over allied strata, and neutralizing political opponents. In an influential discussion of the concept of hegemony, Chantal Mouffe (1979, p. 184) argues that the originality of the Gramscian analysis resides in the understanding of hegemony as the formation of a higher synthesis, so that all its elements fuse in a new 'collective will' which becomes the new protagonist for political action. Hegemony is then not simply an instrumental alliance between classes or strata that maintain a separate corporate identity, but the negotiated fusion of participant groups under a new set of ideological symbols (collective will). According to this interpretation of Gramsci, 'a class does not take state power, it becomes state' (Laclau and Mouffe, 1985, p. 69).

A crucial limitation of the original Gramscian concept of hegemony is – as Laclau and Mouffe amply demonstrate – that class domination is not a contingent result of the process of hegemonic construction, but, on the contrary, an ontological foundation ultimately based on the epistemological principles of historical materialism. In this context, political hegemony becomes a mere zero-sum game between classes, since the failure of the working class can only be followed by the reconstitution of bourgeois hegemony.

The discussion of the Argentinian case points towards the complementary opposite of this analytical scheme. The perpetual institutional stalemate that results from the failure of various classes or strata to constitute a stable hegemonic block, frustrates the formation of an incorporating dominant discourse and results in a continuous ideological cleavage. Argentina's historical heritage is a system of oligarchical domination that originates in the patterns of Spanish settlement in the River Plate basin. This oligarchical class needs to control closely a versatile but inefficient industrial and financial system in order to maintain the monopoly of its narrow productive base. In this situation the Argentinian oligarchy is incapable of granting the necessary concessions for the formation of a stable dominant discourse and hegemonic bloc without, at the same time, seriously compromising the control of the agro-exporter sector over the rest of the economy.

This explains the absence of an agrarian-conservative party. Conversely, the Argentinian industrial bourgeoisie has the capacity to inhibit the political rule of the agro-exporter sector, but it is too dependent on agro-exporter revenues to initiate its own hegemonic project. The large urban middle class has, on the basis of its sheer numbers, the capacity to inhibit oligarchical domination, but it is largely dependent on the redistributive capacity of the state, which in the long run depends on the size of the agro-exporter revenue. The existence of an endemic social and political cleavage did not deter atempts to develop a dominant hegemonic discourse. The Peronist movement attempted to develop such a project through the discourse of an industrializing, popular-corporatist and authoritarian national-ism. The Peronist government was in essence an attempt to incorporate an organized working class into a project of state-directed capitalist and corporatist industrial development, which could have effectively challenged the predominance of the oligarchy.

But the dramatic fall in agro-exporter revenues which resulted partly from a sudden increase in internal consumption and a sharp fall in the international demand for Argentine meat and grain, gave the oligarchy the necessary force to frustrate this project. Paradoxically, the political practice of Peronism – the most important attempt in Argentina's history to create an incorporating dominant discourse – resulted in the most serious and lasting political cleavage faced by twentieth-century Argentina – the Peronist versus the anti-Peronist confrontation. The ensuing factional impasse is then perpetuated both by the armed forces in their role of 'praetorian arbitrators' and by an uncompromising, militant and Manichaean nationalism which results from ultramontane peninsular Catholic values. This political impasse deepens even further Argentina's dependency on a capricious international agrarian market, and over-exposes its economy to the penetration of foreign capital. This, in a nutshell, is the specificity of the dominant cleavage which underlines the Argentinian paradox.

Bibliography

Cardoso, Fernando Henrique and Faletto Enzo (1973), *Dependencia y dessarollo en America Latina* (Buenos Aires: Siglo XXI editores).

Carpani, Ricardo (1973), *Nacionalismo, peronismo y socialismo nacional* (Cordoba, Argentina: Editorial centro de estudios politicos).

Crawley, Eduardo (1984), *A House Divided* (London: Hurst).

Di Tella, Guido (1983), *Argentina under Peron* (New York: St Martin's Press).

Duhalde, Eduardo Luis (1983), *El estado terrorista argentino* (Buenos Aires: Ediciones El Caballito).

Gillespie, Richard (1982), *Soldiers of Peron* (London: Oxford University Press).

Gramsci, Antonio (1971), *Selections from the Prison Notebooks*, ed. and trans. by Quintin Hoare and Geoffrey Nowell-Smith (London: Lawrence & Wishart).

Horowicz, Alejandro (1985), *Los cuatro peronismos* (Buenos Aires: Editorial Legasa).

Laclau, Ernesto (1977), 'Towards a theory of populism', in *Politics and Ideology in Marxist Theory*, pp. 143–98 (London: New Left Books).

Laclau, Ernesto and Mouffe, Chantal (1985), *Hegemony and Socialist Strategy* (London: Verso).

Levene, Gustavo G. (1960), *La Argentina se hizo asi* (Buenos Aires: Libreria Hachette).

Mouffe, Chantal (1979), 'Hegemony and ideology in Gramsci', in C. Mouffe (ed.), *Gramsci and Marxist Theory*, pp. 168–204 (London: Routledge & Kegan Paul).

O'Donnell, Guillermo (1979), *Modernization and Bureaucratic-Authoritarianism* (Berkeley: Institute of International Studies, University of California).

Pendle, George (1963), *Argentina* (London: Oxford University Press).

Rock, David (1986), *Argentina, 1516–1982* (London: I. B. Taurus and Co. Ltd.).

Ross, Stanley R. and McGann, Thomas F. (1982), *Buenos Aires: 400 Years* (Austin: University of Texas Press).

Rouquie, Alain (1978), *Pouvoir Militaire et Société Politique en République Argentine* (Paris: Presses de la fondation nationale des sciences politiques).

Rouquie, Alain (1982), 'Hegemonia Militar, Estado y Dominación Social', in Alain Rouquie (ed.), *Argentina Hoy*, Buenos Aires, Siglo XXI Editores, 1982, pp. 11–50.

Sebreli, Juan Jose (1983), *Los deseos imaginarios de peronismo* (Buenos Aires: Editorial Lagasa).

Sidicaro, Ricardo (1982), 'Poder y Crisis de la Gran Burguesia Agraria Argentina', in Alain Rouquie (ed.), *Argentina Hoy*, pp. 51–104 (Buenos Aires: Siglo XXI Editores).

CHAPTER

— 6 —

Australia: the debate about hegemonic culture

BRYAN S. TURNER

Introduction

In this chapter I shall argue that, while there are many pervasive and general ideological themes within Australian culture, there is not a dominant, or even a common ideology. It is not possible to show that contemporary Australian capitalism requires a particular ideological legitimation, or that its dominant classes are organized around a single integrative ideology, or that subordinate groups are successfully incorporated by a general ideological system, or finally that alternative analyses and criticisms of Australian society are precluded by the presence of an all-pervasive dominant discourse. In presenting this account of contemporary Australia, my position runs somewhat counter to the critical or neo-Marxist elements within contemporary Australian social science which, following the work of commentators like R. W. Connell (1977), have claimed that Australia is indeed characterized by both a ruling class and a ruling culture.

These critical interpretations of contemporary Australian politics and society were dominant in sociology in the 1970s and early 1980s; however, there are currently indications that this neo-Marxist tradition within the perspective of Antonio Gramsci is itself coming under critical scrutiny. For example, Keith Windshuttle in his study of the media (1984) rejected the principal assumptions of what he called 'theories of ideological control' on the grounds that, if the working class is completely incorporated by the ideology transmitted through the media, then the possibilities of significant political change are remote. A strong commitment to a dominant ideology perspective leads necessarily to political fatalism, because it precludes the possibility of progressive change. The dominance of Gramsci's theory of hegemony within Australian radical social science can be seen in retrospect as an effect of the crisis brought about by the Vietnam War and by the dismissal of the Whitlam government in 1975. These events divided the social sciences into sharply conflicting ideological camps, so that radical thinkers became politically committed to the notion of a dominant ideology as an explanation of the alleged political apathy of the Australian electorate. The subordinate position of Australia within the world economy has also promoted a radical social science tradition which perceives the Australian working class as pawns within a global capitalist hegemony.

In this analysis of contemporary Australian politics, it will be argued that the coherence of the society depends primarily upon economic and political processes rather than upon culture or ideology. The incorporation of the Australian working class in the postwar period was an effect of postwar reconstructionist politics, social reformism and the relative success of the economy within the world economic system. However, the precarious situation of the Australian economy in the 1980s as a producer of primary com-modities has been highlighted by the global economic downturn which started in 1973, bringing into question the political consensus which has characterized much of Australian life in the second half of the twentieth century (Lloyd, 1987). Whether the consensus between the major parties within the political system can be maintained appears to be highly uncertain, given the high rates of inflation, industrial decline, rising unemployment, high interest rates and overseas indebtedness which currently characterize the Australian economy. It is clear that in order to understand the special features of Australian culture and politics, we need to see Australia as a relatively dependent society within a world economic system. In addition, to understand the debate which has surrounded the character of ideology in Australia, we must briefly consider the history and social structure of Australia as a white settler society (Denoon, 1983). In this introduction therefore, I shall focus on the peculiarities in the development of Australia as a society and in the formation of its state.

The peculiarities of the Australians

The central peculiarity of Australian society historically was that the state preceded the existence of civil society, whereas in European political history it is the state which emerged out of a civil society increasingly divided by social class. Within the framework of Marxist political economy, the state is seen as the historical development of a society already existing and divided by economic class interests. The main characteristic of colonial Australia was the dominance of the state over social, political and religious life. More simply, Australia has the historical peculiarity of being created by a form of state violence, that is, the imposition of unfree labour in the form of convicts as a method of land settlement and colonization. The dominance of the state in Australian society is a clear example of both a colonial and a post-colonial social formation. Whereas most European societies were formed by the transition from feudalism to capitalism, Australia emerged as a consequence of the transition from convict settlement to agrarian pastoralism within the world economy.

Between 1788 and 1821, New South Wales became a major outlet for convicts from Britain. During the Napoleonic Wars, the number of convicts arriving in Australia was relatively small, but after 1815 the rate of transportation increased partly as a result of the growth in criminal convictions in Britain (Fletcher, 1976). With the loss of the American colonies, Australia became the principal terminus of convict transportation. More importantly, the Australian settlements were seen to be important experimental locations for the new penitentiary system developed under a Benthamite ideology of prison reform. The new penitentiaries which had been originally developed in Britain spread throughout the colonial settlement of dominion capitalism providing a uniform architectural surveillance for criminal populations (Evans, 1982). We can argue that Australia was the first society to provide the location for a complete experimental testing of the system of panopticism. The state was to become the principal institution of surveillance and discipline of a civilian population composed largely of convicted criminals (Foucault, 1977). This peculiar starting-point for a white settler society created a legacy of Benthamite utilitarianism which shaped Australia over the next two centuries.

We need to analyse this significant development of convict settlement in a more precise fashion. As a result of convict settlement, there developed two strands of political thought on the nature of the state. The first viewed the state as an institution central to the penitential control of convicts; the second regarded the state as an institution which maintained a supply of cheap labour power (Brugger and Jaensch, 1985). In turn, these two political perspectives on the state can be seen as reflections of two sets of attitudes towards convicts, namely the emancipist and the exclusivist. The emancipist position gave rise to the notion that the state had a moral duty in the transformation of its civil society and the creation of a nation of ethically upright citizens. The second view of convict settlement regarded the state as a necessary instrument for the production and maintenance of an effective market for the production of cheap commodities for the world market. These two contradictory views of the state have survived into contemporary Australian politics, long after the disappearance of convict settlement, which was terminated in Van Diemen's Land in 1853. With the discovery of gold in the early 1850s, there was in any case a significant boost to white settlement in Australia in search of gold-fields in Victoria.

Within the Australian context, the peculiarities of settlement ruled out *laissez-faire* politics as a practice and as an ideology which could characterize the state and its relationship to the economy. Various forms of utilitarian and liberal thought in Australia had to take into account the fact of the state's penetration of the social system and the economy. We can see this institutional centrality of the state in the emergence of a pastoralist ruling class and an agrarian working class. The settlement of emancipated convicts on the land and the requirements of the public sector had in the early days of colonialism stimulated the emergence of a petty-commodity-producing sector which through farming began to emerge as a distinct agricultural class providing the state with necessary supplies. In addition, there emerged a group of officer-traders who began to monopolize the import-export business. In short, a private market emerged alongside the creation of a convict settlement. Despite the growth of a private economy, the state continued to be a major supplier of the means of production, particularly land grants and convict labour (McMichael, 1980). With the decline of convict supplies to the labour market, the expansion of the frontier depended significantly on squatting. In order to regulate the settlement of the land and the labour supply, the British state adopted the principles of Edward G. Wakefield, whereby the state sought to concentrate agrarian society into a sharp division between landowners and proletarians as a result of artificially maintaining the price of land. In commenting upon Wakefield's principles of systematic colonization, Karl Marx noted in *Capital* that the aim of these artificial land prices was to transform the peasant into a wage labourer; these arrangements attempted to preclude the emergence of a class of independent peasant settlers. The problems of settlement in Australia proved to Marx that the exploitation of labour was necessary to transform money into capital. However, in a letter to Kautsky (12 September 1882), Engels expected that Australia would quite quickly become independent.

As Australia was drawn into the world economy through the production of wool, there developed a powerful pastoral class of wool producers linked to urban centres by merchant capital and to the world markets through the London banking system. Against this pastoralist class, there developed a strong democratic populist movement of small squatters, small property owners, gold-field workers and the labouring classes. These egalitarian notions were summarized under the slogan 'Every man a vote, a rifle, and a farm'. This 'popular arcadian view of Australia' nevertheless had a clearly petty bourgeois dimension (McMichael, 1984, p. 209). While the conflicts associated with the Eureka and Barcaldine protests are often portrayed in the national mythology as revolutionary incidents against state control, they were in fact the 'defensive manoeuvre' of 'dispossessed small-holders' (McQueen, 1970, p. 179). One consequence of gold-mining was the development of urban capital and new markets which favoured the development of an urban bourgeoisie, somewhat in opposition to the pastoralist class.

These divisions between the conservative pastoralist class whose wealth depended upon land and sheep production, and an emerging urban industrial class, centred on the large cities, were also reflected in an ideological division between the ethic of social service and the ethic of hard work and profitability. The ideology of the pastoral gentry was based upon the notion of a moral ascendancy which distinguished the pastoralists from the ex-convict population by claims to moral value and inherited cultural superiority. The values of moral ascendancy emphasized the importance of social service and culture over and against both the degenerate convict and the money-grasping urban entrepreneur (Connell and Irving, 1980). This ideology was also associated with the pastoralist's assumption that the only objective for the state, apart from preserving social order, was that of providing cheap labour. The conservatism of the pastoralist group was reflected not only in its theory of moral ascendancy but also in its nationalism and racism, which assumed the natural superiority of white settlement over Aboriginal inhabitants; the pastoralists also approved, however implicitly, of assisted passage for white migrants, in order to prevent the dominance of the Asian coolie, especially in the gold-mines and cane-cutting areas of Australia (McQueen, 1970). By contrast, the ideology of the urban capitalist class emphasized social progress, hard work, saving and the virtues of private property; this was an ideology for social mobility, not of inherited cultural and economic capital. There was also a religious dimension to this bourgeois culture which has been described as 'a vigorous artisan radicalism' (Connell and Irving, 1980, p. 64).

Australia was a white colonial settler society with a Westminster system of government and a population primarily of English descent, but Australia also had the peculiar feature of convict settlement and state management, as definitive factors in its history and social structure. Australia also had a frontier. A number of writers have suggested that the frontier experience of Australian settlement played an important part in shaping national ideology and popular culture. The frontier thesis in the American context was developed by Frederick Jackson Turner, who in *The Frontier in American History* claimed that the frontier environment promoted an ideology of self-reliance, rugged individualism and egalitarianism. In attempting to provide an account of Australian nationalism, Russell Ward in *The Australian Legend* (1980) argued that the frontier experience in the Australian context did not lead so much to individualism as to a collective sharing of problems and an emphasis on egalitarianism which were responses to the harsh environment during colonial settlement. Both legislation and aridity ruled out the isolation and autonomy of the small man in a society where the state, not the individual, settled the land.

However, the frontier experience in Australia, combined with the conflict over shearers in the pastoral sector, produced a culture which emphasized egalitarianism, anti-authoritarianism, anti-intellectualism and male chauvinism. That is, the populist tradition in the Australian bush gave rise to a cultural stereotype (the ocker) which celebrated mateship, masculine virtues and physical strength, as an oppositional position to hierarchy, authority and state control (Oxley, 1979). While these attitudes were generated through the colonial frontier experience, the egalitarian dimension to ocker culture still survives in marginal, depressed, working-class groups, where male mateship provides the basis for much local organization (Oxley, 1974). As we shall see, these values had an important part to play in the culture which followed from Australia's military experiences in two world wars.

What emerges from the study of male culture in Australia is the picture of a bifurcated society not so much along class lines, but in terms of 'us' and 'them'. On the one hand, there is the ocker tradition which represents an oppositional male culture linking the modern working class through the shearers of the late nineteenth century to the early degenerate convicts of the settlement period; this male culture emphasizes strength, egalitarianism and anti-authoritarianism. This culture has found its global celebration in the great box-office success of *Crocodile Dundee* (Morris, 1988). In opposition to this tradition, there is the urban culture of the bourgeois class with its emphasis on the ethic of respectability, and the pastoralist class which embodies the establishment values of responsibility. The existence of an ocker culture in the Australian tradition also serves to define and reinforce a profound gender division in the market-place, the state and the home. The result has been a profoundly sexist culture which from colonial days has regarded women either as 'Damned Whores' or as 'God's Police'; that is, women have been regarded either as morally corrupt and dangerous, or as the guardians and reproducers of the moral world (Summers, 1975). The experience of female subordination is a crucial feature of the home and the workplace (Williams, 1981).

The traditional suspicion that women were untrustworthy as guardians of the nation has been closely associated with an alliance between the Church and the family from colonial times. From the early days of settlement, the state regarded the clergy as useful in the enforcement of social order through their regulation of the family and sexual life (Mol, 1985). Church and state were united in the aim of a moral transformation of the convict population, but the Church was essentially a weak and underdeveloped institution within the colony. While it was taken for granted that Anglicanism would become the dominant religious institution, the traditional structure of the Church of England was not wholly suitable to the social and geographical environment of Australia. Given the remoteness of the rural population, it was often difficult for the Church to have much impact on the new settlers.

In many respects, Australia is a secular society in which the Church's institutional apparatus is weak; census figures on religious adherence and religious practice show that organized Christianity is the practice of a minority of the Australian population. While approximately three-quarters of the population in 1981 identified themselves as Christians, only 22 per cent of Australians in 1981 claimed to have been to church within the previous week (Black and Glasner, 1983). However, it is more interesting to entertain the possibility of a civil religion in Australia having functions comparable to civil religions in North America (Turner, 1987).

The Australian civil religion can be said to have the following components: male chauvinism, militarism and a nostalgic conception of the bush. Australian art in the nineteenth century (through the famous Heidelberg circle) created a powerfully romantic and nostalgic record of the taming of the bush, culminating in a fine landscape tradition which still adorns the living-rooms of most Australian homes. The national mythology of Australia generates male heroes who, after a noble period of struggle, typically come to a forlorn defeat. Characteristic of this genre is the history of Ned Kelly, an anti-hero, somewhat in the mould of an Irish Robin Hood. Manning Clark (1985) has drawn attention to the fact that in popular culture the English explorers were regarded as a cultural elite, and that there has been an emphasis on 'dinkum' Aussie heroes who were bushrangers embodying the full sentiments of male ocker values. The Aussie hero of the bush tends to be individualistic, anomic, in opposition to English political regulation and a figure representing the common people. In addition, the Gallipoli disaster, which is celebrated monumentally through endless wartime memorials in rural Australia, further reproduces this combination of male strength and national defeat through which Australians experienced a certain redemption. The fall of Singapore, the making of the Burma railway and the campaign against Japanese occupation of the Pacific have become potent symbols of patriotism; they also help to explain the social prominence of the Returned Servicemen's League in local life. Again Australia's greatest secular ritual, the Anzac Day celebrations, reaffirms and celebrates the values of Australian patriotism, male strength, grit and anti-authoritarianism. Indeed the Anzac Day is central to Australian civil culture;

> Australian patriotic sentiment was captured instead by the story of Anzac, by belief that the achievements of the Australian soldier at war showed what being an Australian meant. Pride in being an Australian expressed in Anzac Day marches centred on Australia, not the Empire or the Monarch, but not on a republican Australia either. Anzac Day brought Australians together regardless of class, religion or politics because it reminded people not of a history glorifying Protestantism and the Empire or the struggle for socialism but of a history of Australians united on the battle field. (Firth and Hoorn, 1979, p. 21)

However, Anzac Day is very much a popular ritual which recognizes the division between people and state, and Anzac celebrations have to be contrasted with more official, state-sponsored celebrations such as Australia Day (Kapferer, 1988, p. 169). Finally, these civic values are in contemporary Australia reproduced and fought out in male-dominated sports, especially in Australian Rules Football. These sports attempt to combine mateship, virtue through strength and hostility to female values (Bryson, 1983; Carroll, 1986).

In this discussion, I have attempted to trace some elements of both official and popular ideology from the period of colonial settlement to the emergence of an industrial economic base. We have seen that various elements of the dominant and subordinate cultures intersect, producing a patriotic and populist culture with distinctive male values. I have attempted in addition to locate some of the peculiar features of Australian society in its history and social structure. Australia, like many other colonial and post-colonial societies, possesses a rural mythology and a nostalgic vision of the pure values of early settlement society and rural culture. The visual impact of the bush plays an important part, not only in the folk tradition, Australian ballads and folklore, but also in contemporary film, advertising and life-styles. While there is this emphasis on bush values and culture, it should be remembered that Australia, which has a land mass of almost 3 million square miles (roughly equivalent to the United States of America), has a population of some 15 million people (roughly equivalent to the Netherlands). Furthermore, this population is largely concentrated in the capital cities which, for climatic and transport reasons, are located along the coastal plains (Mullins, 1988). By the early 1980s, partly as a consequence of increased postwar migration, only 14 per cent of the Australian population lived in rural areas, while 64 per cent lived in highly congested metropolitan centres. The mythology of mateship and the bush contrasts strongly with the empirical fact that Australia is one of the most urban societies within the developed world and, given the low level of land prices, one of the most suburban societies in the southern hemisphere. Therefore, Australia may be conceptualized as a society constituted by metropolitan centres, within a federal political structure, where, because of the enormous distances between these centres, there is extreme isolation of these metropolitan cultures, local elites and structures.

Dimensions of the ideological system

It has already been suggested that Australian culture, rather than being a coherent and integrated cultural system, is by contrast characterized by its fragmentation, diversity and ideological pluralism. Even the apparent unity of the legal system and its ideology masks considerable internal division and fragmentation (Tomasic, 1988). As we will see, these thematic divisions within the civil culture have been accentuated by postwar migration and by the emergence of multiculturalism as a state ideology. While there is ideological division, it is also possible to detect a number of unifying themes, especially within the political tradition on which a number of writers have commented; these themes centre on the issue of individualism, liberalism and civil rights against the background of significant state regulation and control, which has been typically legitimized in terms of various forms of utilitarianism. Indeed, Hugh Collins (1985, p. 148) has defined Australia as a 'Benthamite society' in which the crucial dimensions of the dominant ideology are utilitarianism, legalism and positivism. This characterization of Australian political culture is one which is widely shared in the literature. For example, Brugger and Jaensch (1985) describe Australian ideology in terms of a utilitarian tradition based upon the legacy of Bentham and the tradition of social liberalism which flourished under conditions of decentralized federation and local state politics. Many of these components of the liberal tradition have been derived from an earlier study by Tim Rowse of *Australian Liberalism and National Character* (1978). Thus, while Hugh Collins's account of the political ideology of Australia (1985) is not essentially new, it does provide a particularly useful sketch of the principal components of the Australian official ideology.

The Benthamite combination of rationalism and utilitarianism may, according to Collins, have flourished in Australia precisely because the state assumed a strongly interventionist and instrumentalist role in the new colonies. More importantly,

> each of the six Australian colonies was centred upon an administrative capital from which governors disposed of land, supervised economic development, and gradually shared power with representative institutions. Furthermore, unlike their reformist cousins in England, nineteenth century Australian democrats did not have to contend against the traditionalist strengths of established church, military services, and landed aristocracy. (Collins, 1985, p. 151)

The centrality of the state in the day-to-day management of social life has been preserved in contemporary Australia where, at many social levels, state intervention is taken for granted as a necessary feature of public life and social policy (Butlin, Barnard and Pincus, 1982). The importance of state intervention under the general ideology of Benthamite utilitarian management is especially prominent in the control of industrial relations in the Australian economy. In Australia, industrial disputes, conflicts and wage settlements take place within the legal framework of a national structure of compulsory arbitration under state regulation. The three major components of the industrial relations system (employers, trade unions and government) follow their industrial and economic claims before a judicial institution within a completely regulated context. For Collins, this is a particularly strong indication of the legalism which regulates everyday contacts in the market-place and in the civil society as a whole. We should note, however, that, during the late 1980s under the Hawke government, Treasurer Paul Keating attempted to introduce a vigorous policy of economic de-regulation. Neo-conservative economic philosophy has been applied with some degree of enthusiasm by a Labor government (Sawer, 1982). It is not clear what the long-term consequences of these policies will be, but the over-frequent use of the word 'crisis' may not help to clarify this situation.

Although Australia is a highly regulated and centrally administered society, almost all observers of Australian ideology and culture draw attention to the oppositional components of both populism and the socialist traditions. In addition, this is normally connected with the male culture of mateship which, as we have seen, is strongly egalitarian, but also racist and sexist. This egalitarian tradition was enshrined in the lyrics of Henry Lawson ('But the curse of class distinctions from our shoulders shall be held – an' the sense of human kinship revolutionised the world'). According to Brugger and Jaensch (1985, pp. 88 ff.), populism emphasizes egalitarianism, the virtues of the common man against the parasitical institutions of the public sphere, the notion that Australian society might be transformed by an act of moral redemption, and finally it regards the problems of Australian society as primarily the consequences of external forces; therefore egalitarian populism has been primarily isolationist. While populism had its social roots in the bush and the country town, Australian populism eventually split into a left-wing movement, which identified with the itinerant agricultural worker, and a right-wing populist movement, which championed the rights of the small farmer against urban influences and city finance. While right-wing populism found eventually its political expression in the Country Party, left-wing populism was associated with the freedom of the bush, which produced a nostalgic commitment to rural life and found its romantic expression in the ballads of Banjo Patterson.

The theme of hegemony in Australian sociology

The notion that Australia is an egalitarian society with a democratic ethos became widespread in historical interpretations of the emergence of modern Australia from its colonial roots. The notion in the popular culture that Australia is 'The Lucky Country' found its intellectual expression in historical accounts of Australia which rejected the notion that economic class had been an important feature in the evolution of the colony. Writers like Donald Horne (1967, 1985) rejected the notion that the political system in Australia in any significant fashion reflected the underlying class structure; in addition Horne denied that there was such a thing as a 'ruling class', regarding the native bourgeoisie as an ineffectual, small and parasitic class depending for its existence on the role of transnational corporations. The theme of egalitarianism also dominated the historical analysis of K. Hancock whose *Australia* (1930) was to prove particularly influential. Against the received wisdom that Australia is essentially an egalitarian society, the radical sociological tradition emphasized by contrast the importance of class in the history and structure of Australian capitalism. The argument that Australia is dominated by a ruling class was presented forcefully by R. W. Connell (1977, 1979, 1983). In addition, much empirical research sought to understand the construction and maintenance of a class system in which ruling elites were particularly significant (Higley, Deacon and Smart, 1979; Western, 1983; Wild, 1978).

In rejecting the pluralist account of power and the myth of egalitarianism, Australian social scientists often gave particular prominence to the presence of a united, integrated and effective ruling class, drawing its wealth both from local resources and also from the linkage of the Australian economy into the global capitalist system. Australian social scientists, importing the ideas of Nicos Poulantzas and Louis Althusser, saw the Australian social structure in terms of distinctive and coherent classes, although these class divisions were often masked by a general ideology of egalitarianism (Playford, 1972). An influential movement towards a political economy of Australian capitalism developed in the late 1970s and early 1980s which was associated in particular with the work of E. L. Wheelwright and Ken Buckley (Catley and McFarlane, 1981; Crough, Wheelwright and Wilshire, 1980; Wheelwright and Buckley, 1975).

While this radical movement in the social sciences was in part a response to the tradition of historical analysis associated with writers like Keith Hancock, Donald Horne and Manning Clark, we can also in retrospect understand this movement as the outcome of a political conjuncture formed by the crisis of the Vietnam War, the confrontational politics of the Queensland government and the dismissal of the Whitlam government. The result was a somewhat enthusiastic appropriation of the theory of hegemony as developed in the work of Antonio Gramsci. There were a number of variants of the hegemonic argument (Chamberlain, 1983) from a total to a quasi-hegemonic theory. The theory of cultural hegemony became influential in the study of Australia's mass media (McQueen, 1977; Wheelwright and Buckley, 1987), in the study of the news (Windshuttle and Windshuttle, 1981), in the school system and classroom (Connell, Ashenden, Kessler and Dowsett, 1982), in the policies of multiculturalism (Lepervanche, 1984) and above all in patriarchy (Bryson, 1984). The picture created by these sociological studies was frequently one of total hegemonic incorporation and dominance.

This hegemonic culture was maintained and transmitted through the institutions of civil society, particularly the family and the school. However, within Australian social science, a particular emphasis was given to the importance of the mass media in Australia as a purveyor of dominant values and practices. One reason for this concentration on the mass media is the centralization and concentration of control and ownership within the Australian mass media industry. While there was some conflict between the principles of commercialism in the private sector and national interest in the public sector (Mundy, 1982), the concentration of ownership and the dependence on profits from advertising have ensured that broadcasting in Australia completely serves the interests of a capitalist ruling class according to the main consensus within Australian sociology of the media. The television audience in Australia is clearly substantial and provides the possibility of significant cultural penetration. For example, 96 per cent of all households in Australia have a television set, there are eighty-seven national television stations and fifty commercial stations, on average the Australian child spends twenty-one hours a week watching television and approximately 40 per cent of regular commercial television viewers spend more than three hours a day watching television (Kippax and Murray, 1979). Within this context the concentration of ownership is indeed significant. The Annan Report of 1977 on the future of broadcasting in the United Kingdom noted that Australia had one of the most monopolistic newspaper systems in the world. For example, in 1923 there were twenty-six capital city newspapers owned by twenty-one separate proprietors, but by 1976 this had declined to eighteen newspapers owned by three major proprietors (Edgar, 1980). In the Australian media system three groups, namely News Limited (Murdoch), John Fairfax and Sons, and Consolidated Press Holdings (Packer) enjoy a commanding position within the system. This concentration is seen to provide the economic basis for political and cultural hegemony. At various periods in contemporary Australian history, the concentration of ownership within the commercial sector has also been associated with a profound Americanization of Australian political and cultural attitudes (White, 1983).

Advertising in the commercial sector of the media has been associated with the spread and legitimation of individualistic values, consumerism and patriarchal attitudes towards women and the family. Since the commercial media exist basically to construct and manufacture audiences, they are of particular economic importance as media for the advertisement of commodities. The ideological content of media communication therefore has to be more or less acceptable to the leading economic interests which lie behind the media industry. Within this framework, therefore, the dominant ideology of any given society will be that set of beliefs, practices and institutions which serve and reflect the dominant economic interests so that the consciousness of subjects is shaped and determined by these basic values of the economic order.

Although the system of ownership and control may not produce an entirely uniform or monolithic ideology, in the long term the expectation is that there will be a correspondence between dominant economic interests and the ideological content within the mass media. For example, Bonney and Wilson (1983) in *Australia's Commercial Media* argue that, while there may be contradictions between economics and ideology, the media will shape human consciousness in ways which are largely compatible with capitalist interests. For example, they note the way in which the mass media shape and package individualism and femininity. In news broadcasts, there is a strong emphasis on individualism, because the news is seen to be the effects of individual actions and individual interests. Similarly, individualism in advertising assumes the natural features of individualism and competition as basic to human character. In various indirect ways, individualism as a value in the media renders the world intelligible as the struggle of individuals over scarce resources. The consequence of this individualism is to disguise or submerge the importance of structural factors in history and society, thereby placing the moral evaluation of events on to the individual rather than on the system as a whole. They also suggest that individualism is particularly significant within the Australian context where it is associated with competitive sports and thereby with the national character. However, it is in the political sphere that cultural individualism is important in defining political reality. For example,

> it [individualism] both exploits and fosters the notion that governments, and particularly leaders of government, control events. In doing so, it plays down the effects on any nation state, particularly second and third world states, of the operations of international capital, or transnational corporations. It plays up the importance of a party-political meeting room and plays down the importance of the board room of corporations. It plays up the importance of ministers, and plays down the importance of departmental bureaucracies. (Bonny and Wilson, 1983, p. 305)

Individualism within this explanatory framework is not a false consciousness; rather individualism shapes our experience of the world in such a way that it picks out events, topics and themes which illustrate the importance of the individual. The consequence is to bracket off consideration of underlying social processes and structures which shape and determine historical processes. Individualism has been frequently identified by radical critics of Australian capitalism as the central component of the national ideological system. Such criticisms fail, however, to identify different forms of individualism, some of which may be incompatible with capitalism (Turner, 1988). Furthermore, these descriptive statements concerning individualism have not shown that there are necessary relationships between a capitalist economy and individualism. As Daniel Bell has shown (1976; 1980), hedonistic individualism may clash with the requirements of bureaucratic control in capitalist production. Furthermore, analysis of the media in these terms has also failed to acknowledge the political consequences of consumer lobby groups, special interest groups and local concerns on the shaping of national policy (Lane, 1988).

In conclusion, while there is no consensus among radical sociologists, analysis of ideology has claimed that both egalitarianism, especially in its popular manifestations, and individualism are strong components of the national ideological system (Kapferer, 1988). Furthermore, it is argued that these two themes have the consequence of legitimating a society which is in fact hierarchical, unequal and highly administered. Finally, the distribution or transmission of these ideological messages depends heavily upon the mass media where the concentration of ownership has produced a monopolistic situation within the commercial sector. The media represent and articulate dominant values which are reflections of these underlying economic structures.

Towards an alternative perspective

Sociological analysis of ideology in Australia appears to suffer from many of the problems which face any sociology of the dominant ideology. For example, there is a general tendency to confuse the generality of ideological beliefs with some notion of dominance, which is given no theoretical rigour or empirical location. It is important to distinguish, furthermore, between the presence of an ideology and its effects, since we cannot assume that the growth and development of an ideological system correspond clearly with its impact and effects on a community. In addition, where too much emphasis is given to political incorporation and social harmony, there is inadequate theoretical space for the analysis and explanation of political opposition, change and conflict within a society. Radical Marxist versions of ideology come to have the same features and limitations as functionalist theories of culture (Holton and Turner, 1986, pp. 179 ff.). However, in the case of Australia the use of Gramsci's theory of hegemony appears to be particularly inappropriate. It is important to keep in mind that Gramsci developed a theory of hegemony to explain the intellectual leadership of the Roman Catholic Church at the level of the popular masses within a society in which the centralized state was underdeveloped and where the nation-state was divided into a rich industrial north and an underdeveloped peasant south. While Australia has none of these characteristics, sociologists and political scientists in generating a critique of Australian capitalism have relied heavily on this Gramscian tradition.

Another weakness of most sociological accounts of ideology and culture in Australia is the absence of any clear or decisive evidence for the existence of a hegemonic culture, other than the absence of a revolutionary political tradition. While in the Canadian case (to take a dominion capitalist society with social and historical features similar to Australia), social scientists have been able to draw upon a wealth of empirical material (Brym, 1986; Landford, 1986), Australian social scientists are often hampered by the lack of systematic, long-term empirical research on ideology and culture. Existing research on political and social attitudes (Chamberlain, 1983) suggests that there is no dominant ideology and that the class which owns and manages capitalism is most likely to exhibit adherence to beliefs about the sanctity of private property and the legitimacy of unequal forms of wealth. However, the analysis and publication of the National Social Science Survey on social and political attitudes across Australia will eventually contribute significantly to our understanding of the character and effects of ideologies within the political system and more generally within contemporary society. Of course, for some radical social scientists the positivism which underlies quantitative sociology is itself a complex manifestation of basic ideological assumptions and therefore quantitative data from survey analysis cannot provide an appropriate insight into ideology. If this position is adopted, it then becomes rather difficult to know what data, if any, would serve as counter-evidence to the presence of a dominant ideology.

Leaving to one side these epistemological and theoretical issues, the existing historical and sociological evidence does not clearly indicate the presence of a national culture, let alone a national ideology. Australia is in fact a culturally diverse social system with considerable features of localism and separate state cultures, which arise partly from the postwar pattern of migration and partly from the geopolitics of the Australian continent. There are strong regional pressures of both cultural autonomy and political independence (for example, the Northern Territories and Queensland) which contribute to the fragmentation and pluralism of the national culture.

While it is possible to identify egalitarianism and individualism as features of the dominant ideology, it is also the case that there is considerable fragmentation around a patriotic or nationalist dimension and an individualistic-liberal dimension. These divisions are further overlaid by subcultural traditions and minority cultures which have not been assimilated into the national culture and which may well flourish as independent traditions under a state policy of multiculturalism. While some Marxist critics see multiculturalism itself as an incorporating ideology, Australia is clearly divided in terms of language, ethnicity and cultural tradition. There is furthermore a profound and enduring division between white communities and Aboriginals, such that Aboriginals in a sense belong to a separate national system.

In attempting to understand the coherence of contemporary Australia, we should turn away from ideological issues towards the economic and political processes which have both made and fragmented the Australian working class. Australian sociologists have typically focused upon the inequalities of Australia, drawing attention in particular to class inequality, gender differences and the separation of Aboriginal and white societies. In Australia in the early 1970s, the top 1 per cent of the population owned approximately 22 per cent of all personal wealth, whereas the top 5 per cent owned approximately 90 per cent of personal wealth (Raskall, 1978). The inheritance of wealth and the transmission of cultural capital played a significant part in income and wealth inequalities (Broom *et al.*, 1980). However, by focusing on income and wealth inequality, sociologists all too frequently neglect the *relative* wealth of the Australian worker within an international framework and have often ignored the real achievements of welfare and political reformism in the postwar period. Australia like many other welfare democracies experienced an important epoch of postwar reconstructionism. The reformist governments of Chifley and Playford established the administrative framework for general prosperity which, while unequally distributed, did result in significant improvements in life-style and personal welfare. For example, between 1960 and 1980, life expectancy at birth increased from 71 to 74 years, the infant mortality rate fell from twenty to eleven deaths per 1,000 live births, and the percentage of 20- to 24-year-olds enrolled in higher education increased from 13 to 26 per cent.

While income inequality has been a major feature of postwar Australia and while there have been significant economic crises of low investment and industrial stagnation, the postwar period was one of significant economic and social improvement which had important redistributive consequences. This period was one of continuing state intervention and regulation, despite the liberal economic policies adopted by conservative governments. For example, under the Liberal government of R. G. Menzies (1949–66) Australia experienced a postwar reconstruction which some authors have characterized as 'the Menzies Millennium'. During the 'long boom', Menzies, while favouring conservative policies in public, adopted a pragmatic political style which was compatible with both greater state inter-vention and *laissez-faire* ideology. One striking indication of the economic changes of this period is that, whereas wool exports had in 1950 represented 65 per cent of Australia's export earnings, this was down to 12 per cent by 1970. Manufacturing industry developed under a system of protectionism, depending upon tariffs and import restrictions. In this period, there were significant increases in consumption levels especially with the development of a new communication system based upon television, the educational system was reformed, and the population doubled to around 13 million people. This boom period was dependent upon a global postwar economic revival and massive foreign capital investments, transforming Australia from a British to an American dependency in the world economy. By the end of the 1980s, however, interest rates were at 18 per cent and the trade imbalance had reached record levels.

In the debate upon wealth and equality in Australia, the issue of home-ownership has been particularly prominent. Here again, government intervention in housing was primarily a feature of the postwar system and assumed two forms, namely the facilitation of home-ownership and the provision of low-cost rental housing (Butlin, Barnard and Pincus, 1982). The consequences of these policies and the commitment to a home-owning democracy were significant. Between 1947 and 1971, the housing stock in Australia doubled from just under 2 million to 4 million dwellings. Approximately 33 per cent of these additional dwellings were built for government authorities or for purchasers whose loans were created out of Commonwealth funding. Up until the 1940s, the home-ownership rate in Australia had been approximately 52 per cent, but by 1954 this had increased to 63 per cent; by 1966 the home-ownership rate had reached 72 per cent.

It has been argued that, whereas in America the American dream had focused on the liberation of the workers from industrial capitalists, the great Australian dream refers to the prospect of home-ownership as an escape from the financial exploitation of landlords (Kemeny, 1983). Home-ownership clearly has very contradictory features. While individual home-ownership ties the owner into a system of economic relations which make the home-owner highly dependent upon capitalist financial markets, there are important benefits which may accrue from home-ownership. For the working-class home-owner, in periods of inflation the benefit of home-ownership is fairly clear, namely that the home is a significant hedge against such inflationary pressures. Home-ownership is also one way by which the middle classes can accrue significant personal wealth. By contrast, the public provision of housing creates a dependence not on the market but on the state; the political controls which follow from such forms of public ownership are obvious in societies like Singapore.

Home-ownership very directly illustrates the nature of the cash nexus in capitalism, which is both negative and positive. The negative feature of the cash nexus is that it makes the individual dependent upon economic relations in a situation where the worker is relatively defenceless against the threat of unemployment and poverty.

However, radical critics of capitalism often fail to outline the positive features of the cash nexus, namely personal consumption which in the case of home-ownership creates a political independence from the market and the state. The period of the long boom during the Menzies government brought about significant material and social advantages for the Australian working class in a context of expanding citizenship rights. The stability of capitalism can be explained by reference to the positive and negative features of economic processes and it is not necessary to look exclusively towards ideological manipulation in order to understand the political stability of capitalism during both recession and boom. It is quite wrong to explain the reproduction of capitalism largely by reference to cultural hegemony (Connell, 1980). The reproduction of capitalism depends far more profoundly on these negative and positive features of the cash nexus; in the years of economic expansion in the postwar period, the absence of a radical working-class movement is at least in part a consequence of expanded capacity for consumption.

The stability or otherwise of contemporary Australia therefore hinges upon the involvement of the Australian economy within the world economic system. The problem for Australia is precisely its dependence on external economic circumstances, which during the economic downturn of the 1980s put serious constraints upon the capacity of Australian governments to bring about significant social change. By the late 1980s, Australia was constrained economically by crippling overseas indebtedness which produced an inflation rate of 10 per cent and constrained the capacity of trade unions to press for wage increases, increased investment and rising employment. The accord which was negotiated by the Hawke government between employers and trade unionists was initially regarded as a method of wage restraint (Clegg, Boreham and Dow, 1986), since corporatism has normally been regarded by left-wing critics as a capitalist strategy to secure social harmony as the framework for constraining wages. However, in retrospect the accord may well be regarded as the only strategy available to a Labor government in a context of world economic recession. However, the Australian Bureau of Statistics figures in 1989 showed a decline in union membership of 9 per cent during the previous six years. The erosion of unionization in the working class will bring about important changes in the nature of working-class representation.

In conclusion, one consequence of my argument is that it is inappropriate to impose sociological models derived from the social history of Europe on to the Australian social structure, which has a history wholly unlike the European capitalist experience. It is more appropriate and instructive to develop a comparative strategy which would consider white colonial settler societies within the southern hemisphere within a paradigm generated from those colonial experiences rather than from the feudal and capitalist history of northern Europe. In this respect, the appropriate comparisons are probably between Argentina and Australia (Duncan and Fogarty, 1984). The Australian working class is constrained and regulated, not by the hegemonic culture of a ruling class, but by a set of objective economic relations which in their positive form have provided relatively high standards of living, while in their negative shape they tie the worker into exploitative and regulating economic circumstances. In a period of global recession, these external economic constraints limit the capacity of governments to bring about social reform and limit the capacity of working-class organizations to achieve significant economic benefits from the capitalist system of production. The consequence is a political and social stalemate. It is the cash nexus which in the last instance constrains the worker into conformity, with or without the presence of a hegemonic culture.

Bibliography

Bell, D. (1976), *The Cultural Contradictions of Capitalism* (London: Heinemann).

Bell, D. (1980), *The Winding Passage, Essays and Sociological Journeys, 1960–1980* (New York: Basic Books).

Black, A. and Glasner, P. (eds) (1983), *Practices and Belief, Studies in the Sociology of Australian Religion* (Sydney: Allen & Unwin).

Bonney, B. and Wilson, H. (1983), *Australia's Commercial Media* (Melbourne: Macmillan).

Broom, L., Jones, F. L., MacDonnell, P. and Williams, T. (1980), *The Inheritance of Inequality* (London: Routledge & Kegan Paul).

Brugger, B. and Jaensch, D. (1985), *Australian Politics, Theory and Practice* (Sydney: Allen & Unwin).

Brym, R. J. (1986), 'Incorporation versus power models of working class radicalism with special reference to North America', *Canadian Journal of Sociology*, vol. II, no. 3, pp. 227–52.

Bryson, L. (1983), 'Sport and the oppression of women', *Australian and New Zealand Journal of Sociology*, vol. 19, no. 3, pp. 413–26.

Bryson, L. (1984), 'The Australian patriarchal family', in S. Encel and L. Bryson (eds), *Australian Society* (Melbourne: Longman Cheshire), pp. 113–69.

Butlin, N. G., Barnard, A. and Pincus, J. J. (1982), *Government and Capitalism, Public and Private Choice in Twentieth Century Australia* (Sydney: Allen & Unwin).

Carroll, J. (1986), 'Sport: virtue and grace', *Theory, Culture & Society*, vol. 3, no. 1, pp. 91–8.

Catley, R. and McFarlane, B. (1981), *Australian Capitalism in Boom and Depression* (Chippendale: APCOL).

Chamberlain, C. (1983), *Class Consciousness in Australia* (Sydney: Allen & Unwin).

Clark, M. (1985), 'Heroes', *Daedalus*, vol. 114, no. 1, pp. 57–84.

Clegg, S., Boreham, P. and Dow, G. (1986), *Class, Politics and the Economy* (London: Routledge & Kegan Paul).

Collins, H. (1985), 'Political ideology in Australia: the distinctiveness of a Benthamite society', *Daedalus*, vol. 114, no. 1, pp. 147–70.

Connell, R. W. (1977), *Ruling Class, Ruling Culture* (Cambridge: Cambridge University Press).

Connell, R. W. (1979), 'Images of Australia', in J. Summers, D. Woodward and A. Parkin (eds), *Government Politics and Power in Australia* (Bedford Park: Flinders University of South Australia), pp. 243–59.

Connell, R. W. (1980), 'The transition to socialism', in Greg Crough, Ted Wheelwright and Ted Wilshire (eds), *Australia and World Capitalism* (Ringwood: Penguin), pp. 289–302.

Connell, R. W. (1983), *Which Way is Up?* (Sydney: Allen & Unwin).

Connell, R. W., Ashenden, D. J., Kessler, S. and Dowsett, G. W. (1982), *Making the Difference, Schools Families and Social Division* (Sydney: Allen & Unwin).

Connell, R. W. and Irving, T. H. (1980), *Class Structure in Australian History, Documents Narrative and Argument* (Melbourne: Longman Cheshire).

Crough, G., Wheelwright, T. and Wilshire, T. (1980), *Australia and World Capitalism* (Ringwood: Penguin).

Denoon, D. (1983), *Settler Capitalism, The Dynamics of Dependent Development in the Southern Hemisphere* (Oxford: Clarendon Press).

Duncan, T. and Fogarty, J. (1984), *Australia and Argentina, on Parallel Paths* (Carlton: Melbourne University Press).

Edgar, D. (1980), *Introduction to Australian Society* (Sydney: Prentice Hall).

Evans, R. (1982), *The Fabrication of Virtue, English Prison Architecture 1750–1840* (Cambridge: Cambridge University Press).

Firth, S. and Hoorn, J. (1979), 'From empire day to cracker night', in P. Spearritt and D. Walker (eds), *Australian Popular Culture* (Sydney: Allen & Unwin), pp. 17–38.

Fletcher, B. (1976), *Colonial Australia before 1850* (Melbourne: Nelson).

Foucault, M. (1977), *Discipline and Punish, The Birth of the Prison* (London: Tavistock).

Hancock, K. (1930), *Australia* (Sydney: Australasian Publishing Company).

Higley, J., Deacon, D. and Smart, D. (1979), *Elites in Australia* (London: Routledge & Kegan Paul).

Holton, R. J. and Turner, B. S. (1986), *Talcott Parsons on Economy and Society* (London: Routledge & Kegan Paul).

Horne, D. (1967), *The Lucky Country, Australia in the Sixties* (Ringwood: Penguin).

Horne, D. (1985), 'Who rules Australia?' *Daedalus*, vol. 114, no. 1, pp. 171–96.

Kapferer, B. (1988), *Legends of People, Myths of State, violence, intolerance and political culture in Sri Lanka and Australia* (Washington, DC and London: Smithsonian Institution Press).

Kemeny, J. (1983), *The Great Australian Nightmare* (Melbourne: Georgian House).

Kippax, S. and Murray, J. P. (1979), *Small Screen, Big Business* (Sydney: Angus & Robertson).

Landford, T. (1986), 'Workers' subordinate values', *Canadian Journal of Sociology*, vol. II, no. 3, pp. 269–92.

Lane, K. (1988), 'Broadcasting, democracy and localism, a study of broadcasting policy in Australia from the 1920s to the 1980s', unpublished dissertation, University of Adelaide, South Australia.

Lepervanche, M. de (1984), 'Immigrants and ethnic groups', in S. Encel and L. Bryson (eds), *Australian Society* (Melbourne: Longman Cheshire), pp. 170–228.

Lloyd, C. (1987), 'Capitalist beginnings in Australia: a review', *Arena*, no. 81, pp. 35–55.

McMichael, P. (1980), 'Settlers and primitive accumulation: foundations of capitalism in Australia', *Review*, vol. 4, no. 2, pp. 207–334.

McMichael, P. (1984), *Settlers and the Agrarian Question, Foundations of Capitalism in Colonial Australia* (Melbourne: Widescope).

McQueen, H. (1970), *A New Britannia* (Ringwood: Penguin).

McQueen, H. (1977), *Australia's Media Monopolies* (Melbourne: Widescope).

Mol, H. (1985), *The Faith of Australians* (Sydney: Allen & Unwin).

Morris, M. (1988), 'Tooth and claw: tales of survival and *Crocodile Dundee*', in A. Ross (ed.), *Universal Abandon? The Politics of Postmodernism* (Minneapolis, Minn.: University of Minnesota Press), pp. 105–27.

Mullins, P. (1988), 'Is Australian urbanisation different?', in J. M. Najman and J. S. Western (eds), *A Sociology of Australian Society* (Melbourne: Macmillan), pp. 517–41.

Mundy, G. (1982), 'Origins of broadcasting in the U.S., U.K. and Australia', *Australian and New Zealand Journal of Sociology*, vol. 18, no. 3, pp. 279–301.

Oxley, H. G. (1974), *Mateship in Local Organisation* (St Lucia: University of Queensland Press).

Oxley, H. G. (1979), 'Ockerism: the cultural rabbit', in P. Spearritt and D. Walker (eds), *Australian Popular Culture* (Sydney: Allen & Unwin), pp. 190–209.

Playford, J. (1972), 'Who rules Australia?', in J. Playford and B. Kirsners (eds), *Australian Capitalism* (Ringwood: Penguin), pp. 108–55.

Raskall, P. (1978), 'Who's got what in Australia: the distribution of wealth', *Journal of Australian Political Economy*, no. 2, pp. 3–16.

Rowse, T. (1978), *Australian Liberalism and National Character* (Melbourne: Kibble Books).

Sawer, M. (ed.) (1982), *Australia and the New Right* (Sydney: Allen & Unwin).

Summers, A. (1975), *Damned Whores and God's Police, The Colonisation of Women in Australia* (Ringwood: Penguin).

Tomasic, R. (1988), 'Ideology and coherence in the Australian legal order', in J. M. Najman and J. S. Western (eds), *A Sociology of Australian Society* (Melbourne: Macmillan), pp. 124–61.

Turner, B. S. (1987), 'Religion, state and civil society: nation building in Australia', in T. Robbins and R. Robertson (eds), *Church State Relations, Tensions and Transitions* (New Brunswick and Oxford: Transaction Books), pp. 233–52.

Turner, B. S. (1988), 'Individualism, capitalism and the dominant culture: a note on the debate', *Australian and New Zealand Journal of Sociology*, vol. 24, no. 1, pp. 47–64.

Ward, R. (1980), *The Australian Legend* (Melbourne: Oxford University Press).

Western, J. S. (1983), *Social Inequality in Australian Society* (Melbourne: Macmillan).

Wheelwright, E. L. and Buckley, K. (eds) (1975), *Essays in the Political Economy of Australian Capitalism*, Vol. 1 (Brookvale: Australia and New Zealand Book Company).

Wheelwright, T. and Buckley, K. (eds) (1988), *Communications and the Media in Australia* (Sydney: Allen & Unwin).

White, R. (1983), 'A backwater awash: the Australian experience of Americanisation', *Theory, Culture & Society*, vol. 1, no. 3, pp. 108–22.

Wild, R. A. (1978), *Social Stratification in Australia* (Sydney: Allen & Unwin).

Williams, C. R. (1981), *Open Cut, The Working Class in an Australian Mining Town* (Sydney: Allen & Unwin).

Windshuttle, K. (1984), *The Media, A New Analysis of the Press, Television, Radio and Advertising in Australia* (Ringwood: Penguin).

Windshuttle, K. and Windshuttle, E. (1981), *Fixing the News, Critical Perspectives on the Australian Mass Media* (Sydney: Cassell).

7

Japan and the USA: the interpenetration of national identities and the debate about orientalism

ROLAND ROBERTSON

Modern societies live partly through caricatures of themselves.

(Tom Nairn, 1988, p. 202)

America is the original version of modernity . . . [It] ducks the question of origins . . . [It] lives in perpetual simulation, in a perpetual present of signs. It has no ancestral territory . . . America has no identity problem. In the future, power will belong to those people with no origins and no authenticity who know how to exploit that situation to the full. Look at Japan, which to a certain extent has pulled off this trick better than the US itself, managing, in what seems to [Europeans] an unintelligible paradox, to transform the power of territoriality and feudalism into that of deterritoriality and weightlessness. Japan is already a satellite of the planet Earth. But America was already in its day a satellite of the planet Europe. Whether we like it or not, the future has shifted towards artificial satellites.

(Jean Baudrillard, 1988, p. 76)

I am concerned in this discussion with the empirical relationships between Japan and the USA and with the theoretical significance of the interpenetration of two forms of national identity construction. I am thus not directly engaged in an exercise in comparative sociology, for much of the relationship between these two societies has involved comparison *on the part of relevant leaders and collective actors*. In other words, I am more interested in the ways in which comparison has been undertaken as an aspect of identity construction itself than in producing my own 'objective' comparison of Japanese and American national identities; although *the intra-societal bases upon which such quotidian comparison has been accomplished* will receive some attention. The global perspective has been neglected in much contemporary thinking on ideology and culture, which has largely confined itself within the boundaries of national societies, at the cost of understanding the international dimension of the formation of national identities that I discuss in this chapter.

I begin with a fairly conventional overview of the history of the Japan–USA relationship since the mid-nineteenth century – drawing attention, however, to the complexity and depth of this globally salient site of inter-national interaction. Second, I attempt to locate the relationship within the context of the recent discussion of orientalism, arguing that not merely is the Japan–USA connection more relevant to that debate than has been recognized but that the latter brings the theme of *occidentalism* into focus. Third, I discuss briefly the limitations of social theory with respect to the analysis of international and global matters and address some issues involved in the comprehension of the bases upon which national identity construction proceeds – in a specific reference to the Japan–USA case.

The significance of the relationship

The relationship between Japan and the United States of America has undoubtedly been of tremendous importance in the shaping of the contemporary world order and of twentieth-century life generally. And there is much to suggest that the significance of that relationship will increase rather than diminish in the twenty-first century. In spite of America having been an extension of European civilization prior to the achievement of its independence as the USA towards the end of the eighteenth century and its having close contacts with and gaining the vast majority of its immigrants after independence from Europe, the fact is that it did not become a full-fledged member of Europe-centred 'international society' until the period during which Japan was also achieving membership in the latter. Both the USA and Japan were 'admitted' to the dominant system of international relations during the declining years of the nineteenth and the early years of the twentieth centuries (Gong, 1984) – at a time when they were the two fastest-growing of the major industrial powers (Lehmann, 1982, p. 181) as well as encountering the problem of

'European modernity'. On the other hand, the simultaneity of their acceptance as the first significant non-European members of an international society which was largely government by 'the standard of civilization' (Gong, 1984) occurred against an historical background of considerable asymmetry concerning anticipations of the futures of the two societies. For whereas it had become widely accepted long before the American intrusion upon Japan in the 1850s – specifically, the attempt by Commodore Perry to 'open' Japan in 1853 – that the USA was destined to become a, probably *the*, major society in the world (Bell, 1980, p. 247), few had a sense even by the early years of the Meiji Restoration, which occurred some fifteen years later, that Japan might become a major power during the twentieth century.

In fact, however, Japan achieved rapid economic growth within a few years and, beginning with its defeat of China in the war of 1894–5, quickly became recognized as a significant national presence on the international scene and was released from the constraints of the 'unequal treaties' which 'civilized' nations, including the USA, felt entitled to inflict upon the 'uncivilized' (Gong, 1984, pp. 164–200). In 1902 it formed an alliance with Britain and in 1905 it was victorious in its fairly short war with Russia. During precisely the period of which I am speaking – about 1880 to about 1920 – the possibility of eventual serious conflict between the USA and Japan was becoming evident These were the two major non-European and increasingly the major Pacific powers and the potential for conflict was particularly evident in tensions occasioned by the growing presence of Japanese immigrants in California at the turn of the century and the formal discriminatory actions taken against them during the period 1900–24 – the high points of the trend being the 1922 decision of the US Supreme Court that Japanese were ineligible for American citizenship and the Quota Act of 1924 which completely terminated Japanese immigration (Kitigawa, 1987, pp. 324–5; Gong, 1984, pp. 197–200). During that same period Japan became increasingly involved in 'international society' – mainly via the problems of European, including Russian, encroachments upon China – while the USA had entered an imperialistic phase during which the revival of the doctrine of 'manifest destiny' was expanded so as to include the explicit national mission of 'civilizing' areas outside the Americas and competing in those places with major European nations.[1]

A central ingredient of the American sense of manifest destiny in this period was undoubtedly that of Anglo-Saxon racial superiority. This notion was encouraged by 'scientific racism' and Social Darwinism – which, in the form of their own readings of Herbert

Spencer, had also greatly affected Japanese intellectuals and political leaders (Blacker, 1964).[2] Japanese sensitivity to the racial issue was clearly sharpened and deployed during this period, not merely in terms of the immigration problem *per se* and the imperialistic moves of the USA into Hawaii, the Philippines, Samoa and Guam but also – in a way, more fundamentally – by the inflation of 'Yellow Peril' talk, which had originally been directed at the Chinese around 1880 but which had soon been applied to the Japanese (Dower, 1986, pp. 152–64). Sax Rohmer's Fu Manchu novels were popular in the USA from the beginning of the series in 1913 (Dower, 1986, pp. 158–9). On the other hand, the Japanese were sometimes directly inspired by forecasts of their own destiny: '[T]he visionary military writer Homer Lea . . . offered a forecast of Japan's destiny so apocalyptically compelling that the Japanese themselves were flattered and quickly prepared a translation' of his *The Valor of Ignorance*, which was first published in 1909 (Dower, 1986, p. 157) and then after 18,000 copies had been sold went out of print in 1922. It was to be reissued in 1942, shortly after the start of the Pacific War (ibid., p. 158).

Japan's growing international strength was greatly in evidence in the country's participation in the Paris Peace Conference following the end of the First World War. At that time Japan obtained from the other victorious nations (Britain, France and the USA) German territorial rights in China (which precipitated the 4 May Movement against the unstable Chinese regime). On the other hand, Japanese leaders were rebuffed in their attempt to have a clause inserted in the charter of the proposed League of Nations which would have prohibited member nations from discriminating against the nationals of other members. American resistance to that proposal was also to become a source of growing Japanese resentment against the USA. In spite of formal agreements with Britain, France and the USA, Japan became increasingly active in China in the late 1920s, leading to the invasion of Manchuria in 1931 and the establishment of a puppet state.

It is neither necessary nor possible in the present context to trace the mounting tensions between Japan and the USA during the 1930s, except to emphasize that racist attitudes towards the other further crystallized in both societies, as did economically motivated antagonism. Further incursions by Japan into Chinese territory, the conclusion of the Tripartite Pact with fascist Germany and Italy in 1940 and the announcement of the Greater East Asia Co-Prosperity Sphere in the same year set the immediate scene for the move towards war, which eventually came with the Japanese attack on the American naval base in Hawaii in December 1941. The Pacific War was, of course, terminated by the decision of the American government to drop atomic bombs on Hiroshima and Nagasaki in August 1945 and the subsequent surrender of Japan. There followed one of the more remarkable encounters between two societies in world history – namely the American (although officially the Allied) Occupation of Japan, which by the time it was concluded in 1952 (via the San Francisco Peace Treaty and the Japan–US Mutual Security Treaty of 1951) had resulted in what has been called 'the third turn' in Japan's very long history (Cohen, 1987) – the first turn having been the absorption of Chinese culture, writing, language and religion in the seventh and eighth centuries and the second the externally constrained dissolution of the Tokugawa regime, the Meiji Restoration – involving the enhanced centralization of Japanese society around the Emperor system – and the systematic response to the West in the last thirty years or so of the nineteenth century.[3] The American Occupation of Japan – more specifically the attempt by the Supreme Commander for the Allied Powers (SCAP), General Douglas MacArthur, to 'remake' Japan into an irenic and democratic nation – led to a formal relationship of alliance and co-operation between Japan and the USA, which was hastened by the communist invasion of South Korea in 1950. However, during the 1960s tensions occurred with respect, first, to the renewal of the security treaty (1960) and, second, the continuing occupation of Okinawa by the USA (1969). (Okinawa was restored to Japanese rule in 1972.)

Since the 1960s and in reference to Japan's remarkable economic expansion period there have been growing and diffuse problems between the two nations centred upon economic issues concerning investment, productivity and tariffs. These have ramified into a conflict over the core cultural features of the two societies. From the American side much criticism has been made of the cultural characteristics and social practices which allegedly enable Japan to be extraordinarily productive in economic terms – such as saving excessive percentages of individual incomes (at least by American standards), being too collectivistic and nativistic, not having large enough houses and apartments, operating with overly protectionist trading policies, and so on; while from the Japanese side there has been criticism of American concern for short-term economic gain, individual selfishness and, more intermittently, the allegedly debilitating consequences of American racial and ethnic hetero-geneity (which had actually been a basis for Japanese optimism at the onset of the Pacific War). Thus the problematic politics of the relationship between Japan and the USA in the recent period has consisted in what might be called an 'econocultural' clash, in the course of which the supposedly deep foundations of economic and political strength have been thematized.

With the apparent decline of USSR-led communism (although not, one riskily suspects at this time of writing, of Chinese communism) the situation of Japan and the USA facing each other directly as dominant powers has become more clearly outlined – against the background of debate about 'the decline of America' (considerably subdued, of course, precisely by the triumphalism of the seeming collapse of Soviet and European communism in 1989), and the discourse concerning possible Japanese dominance in the twenty-first century. Indeed public opinion polls in the USA in the late 1980s tended to show that Japan was regarded as the major national threat to the USA, as opposed to the USSR. More generally, the context of the relationship between the two nations is being reshaped by the concern of both with the restructuring and potential integration of Europe, a major component of which is, of course, 'the German Question' – which has, in turn, resurrected issues surrounding the formation of the pact involving Germany, Japan and (as a junior partner) Italy in 1940, in particular the issues of national-identity formation and racial homogeneity (Buruma, 1989).

It is in such respects that the interpenetration of American and Japanese identities had by the end of the 1980s reached almost 'fever pitch'. The clashes of the 1980s between the leaders – and indirectly the 'ordinary members' – of the two societies involved a considerable degree of questioning both of the identities of Self and Other and, in both societies, helped to create much discussion of the core cultural features of both Japan and the USA; although voices have not infrequently been raised against 'cultural explanations' on the American side (Johnson, 1988). The publication of Ezra Vogel's *Japan as Number One* in 1979 sparked off great – but of course different – reactions in the two societies. There was a Japanese tendency to speak, following publication of Vogel's book, of 'Japan *as* Number One'; while – as Ronald Dore (1987, p. 228) has remarked – the same book spoke to 'deep anxieties' in America, which were even 'more overtly' tapped in Vogel's later book, *Comeback America* (1985). In that regard Dore persuasively argues that 'the sense of a threat to America's natural and proper dominance of the world . . . is as much a factor in the continuing debates about Japanese trade as the penetration of particular American markets by Japanese imports and the threat to particular producer interests' (Dore, 1987, p. 228); while there is certainly a trace of wartime 'Greater East Asian' and, indeed, global aspirations on the Japanese side. In fact the kind of discussion which Vogel's writings did much to precipitate during the 1980s came to involve a considerable focus on the question as to what America could *learn from Japan* – thus to some degree reversing the old relationship between Japan and 'the outside world'. The fact also that a number of societies which Japan had previously controlled – notably (South) Korea, Taiwan and (if only briefly) Singapore and Hong Kong – have been remarkably successful in their economic growth has further enhanced the Japanese sense of superiority and, perhaps, exacerbated American anxiety. In these interpenetrating intra-societal debates – which, of course, have global politicocultural significance – there has also been considerable flourishing of national-cultural identities in relation to the general theme of 'internationalization'. In this sense the mounting interest in the latter theme in Japan from the late 1970s onwards has been matched by the prominence of *nihonjinron* – that is, 'teachings on Japan', 'Japanology', or, more generally, the cultivation of the idea of Japanese uniqueness and wholeness (Mouer and Sugimoto, 1986). In other words, the cultivation of the idea of the need for Japan – including its industrial corporations, its investment companies, its mass media, its prefectural governments, its educational system, and so on – to internationalize has gone hand in hand with the general attempt to provide insulation for a highly calibrated version of Japanese identity, which in its more extreme forms includes such claims as that the Japanese language is unique and not comprehensible in conventional linguistic terms, that Japanese people are biologically unique, and so on.

The phenomenon of *nihonjinron* is of importance in the present context because it is closely bound up not merely with American perceptions of Japan, but also – if less directly – with American perceptions of the USA, to the point that a literature has emerged which characterizes America largely in polar-opposition terms to the stereotyped images of Japan, which have been produced in large part by exponents of *nihonjinron*. For example, James Fallows has argued (1989) that America can be made 'great again' by capitalizing upon what he calls 'the American talent' for disorder and openness and by rejection of the 'Confucianism' which he says has taken hold of American society in the form of credentialism, reliance upon educational testing, and so on. Meanwhile, in the same year, Japanese representatives presented a wide-ranging critique of American society in response to the American government's insistence on Japan's opening its economy to more foreign investment and imports, including alleged mismanagement of the American economy and educational system. Even though much of the critique of some central aspects of American society on the part of the Japanese government has overlapped considerably with American *self-criticism*, the fact remains that the decade of the 1980s was one which witnessed the emergence of something like an American equivalent of *nihonjinron* with much debate about the ways in which American national culture could be enhanced and protected from global relativization. In certain respects the idea of American exceptionalism (Bell, 1980, pp. 245–71) is the equivalent of the idea of Japanese uniqueness. The critical difference in substance between the two appears to be that while the American emphasis upon the freedom of America and of its citizens has frequently been the basis of the argument that America is exempt from 'the laws of history' (particularly 'laws' concerning the rise and decline of great nations) and, indeed, that America's role is to release humankind from history itself, the Japanese emphasis upon its unique capacity to learn from other societies and from history generally leads it not to the anticipation of history and necessity but rather to the celebration of its potential own role in the twenty-first century as the leader of world history. Hence the remarkable proliferation in Japan of publications, both optimistic and pessimistic, about the twenty-first century and Japan's place in a future world when it has little to learn from other societies and civilizations for the first time in its long history. Thus the discourse of internationalization in Japan has only small areas of overlap with the less but increasingly explicit interest in that theme in the USA. Whereas the Japanese version primarily centres upon the ways in which Japan can become more involved in and utilize the material and human resources – material and sociocultural – of the world as a whole, internationalization in the USA – particularly the rapidly expanding field of 'internal' education – is as much concerned with learning about and accepting 'other culture' as it is about the purely instrumental issue of promoting American competitiveness.

Orientalism and occidentalism

Thematization of the Japan–USA relationship may well cast relatively new light on to the debate about orientalism. Orientalism has, in its most specific form, been considered as a particular patronizing and/or negative view of Middle Eastern societies on the part of European intellectuals; while even in its larger version the discussion of orientalism has mainly been confined to European perspectives on Asian, including West-Asian, and Middle Eastern societies. In his widely discussed *Orientalism*, Edward Said claims that 'the American experience of the Orient prior to [the] exceptional moment [of the Second World War] was limited' and that 'the specifically American contribution to the history of Orientalism' has been the conversion of the latter 'from a fundamentally philological discipline and a vaguely general apprehension of the Orient into a social science specialty' (Said, 1978, p. 290). In the latter circumstance 'an Orientalist begins . . . as a trained social scientist and "applies" his science to the Orient, or anywhere else' (ibid.). While mentioning, as inconsequential, 'cultural isolatos [sic] like Melville' and 'cynics like Mark Twain [who] visited and wrote about it' (ibid.) – as well as the founding of the American Oriental Society in 1843 – Said continues to insist that 'the imaginative investment was never made . . . perhaps because the American frontier, the one that counted was the westward one' (ibid.). As if Japan and China were not *west*, as well as east of America! As if the USA itself were not in part a by-product of a European drive *westward* to the Orient.[4]

Although it should be conceded that American orientalism did not pass through the stages of intellectual refinement and reconstruction which characterized West European orientalism, it must be pointed out that Said underestimates its presence in nineteenth-century America; for as Joseph Kitagawa (1987, p. 317) points out, many intellectuals 'shared their European counterparts' idealization of Eastern cultures and religions' – among them Emerson, Thoreau, Bigelow, Percival Lowell, La Farge and Henry Adams. Such people were, as Kitagawa emphasizes, 'spiritual heirs of the Enlightenment' – following in the footsteps of those who had often projected their own nostalgia on to alien, 'exotic' cultures (Baudet, 1965, p. vii). In any case, I have already indicated the significance of the clearly derogatory conceptions of, first, the Chinese as immigrants and, second, the Japanese as both immigrants and as comprising a potentially dangerous and threatening nation during the period lasting from about 1880 through to the mid-1920s. (After that period, most particularly following the Japanese occupation of Manchuria, the so-called, and still very active, China Lobby began, at first slowly and inconspicuously, to emerge in the USA as defenders of Nationalist China and China generally – against both Soviet communists and the increasingly militant Japanese regime.) Thus my principal point at this juncture is that American orientalism – certainly as far as the Japanese were concerned – had quite a long history prior to the Second World War, in both its highly negative and its nostalgic, patronizing forms.

While it is true that as the defeat of Japan became increasingly likely after the Japanese losses in the naval battle at Midway in 1942 – and even after the Japanese surrender in the late summer of 1945 – there was a shortage of experts with knowledge and language skills considered to be necessary for the task of the occupation of and the attempt to reconstruct Japan (Cohen, 1987), which tends to confirm part of Said's argument, he none the less still underestimates the extent of the accumulation of definite conceptions of Japan and the Japanese prior to the end of the war – indeed, prior to the war itself – on the part of academics and policy-makers. Much of the material relevant to the formulation of 'high-level' ideas about Japan has recently been discussed in some detail by John Dower (1986, pp. 118–44 and pp. 336–41). Dower (ibid., p. 118) emphasizes the significance of the 'larger vogue of interdisciplinary "culture and personality" studies that drew heavily upon the methodologies and vocabularies of anthropology, psychology, and psychiatry'. It was indeed during the Second World War that this vogue appeared in force as a result of what Dower (ibid.) calls 'unprecedented government support' not merely for the war effort itself but also for 'laying the groundwork for a more tolerant and peaceful postwar world' (ibid., p. 119). Among those who contributed to this effort were Margaret Mead, Gregory Bateson, Ruth Benedict, Clyde Kluckhohn and Geoffrey Gorer – each of whom focused in his or her own way on what Dower himself calls 'cultural character studies'. Ruth Benedict produced in 1946 her remarkably influential book on Japan – *The Chrysanthemum and the Sword* (Benedict, 1974) – based largely on research among Japanese Americans and Japanese living in the USA, many thousands of whom were incarcerated under the Civil Exclusion Order of March 1942 simply because they were of Japanese descent (Armor and Wright, 1988).

Although, as Dower argues, a basic premise of the national-character approach was 'the psychic unity of mankind', and that cultural differences should be respected, 'many writings in the national-character mode still tended, however unwittingly, to reinforce a whole series of assumptions about the Japanese that were also commonplace to racist thinking' (Dower, 1986, p. 122). In that connection Dower draws particular attention to the work of Gorer, who although an English social anthropologist delivered 'the single most influential academic analysis of "Japanese character structure" that was presented during the war' to an American audience in March 1942 – an analysis which was remarkably derogatory about the Japanese (ibid., p. 124 and pp. 124–8). Generally, the 'findings' about and interpretations of the Japanese centred upon the claim that they were immature and emotionally dependent – views which may well have been duplicated by policy-makers, but which, according to Dower, were *not* closely studied by those responsible for foreign or military policy.

Thus Dower produces strong evidence to the effect that whatever their declared intentions the general thrust of much of the work undertaken by social scientists, particularly within the Office of War Information, tended to be in line with populist, racist images of the Japanese; although it has to be made perfectly clear that social scientists did not directly promote the simian image of the Japanese which was a common feature of the American (as well as the British) media during the war years.

On the Japanese side – that is, from within Japan itself – there emerged statements and images which were as vitriolic as those produced in the media and by governmental propaganda efforts – but not, as I have emphasized, by a significant numbr of social scientists – in the USA. In brief, the characterizations of the Japanese as monkeys and apes was paralleled by the representation of Americans (and British) as devils and demons. But racism *per se* apart, the confrontation of images and stereotypes during the Second World War throws much light on the ways in which civilizations encounter each other. While undoubtedly much of the overall thrust of the American attitude did have its origns in a diffuse kind of orientalism (as indirectly confirmed by the fact that while there were 'good Germans' there were in the 'American mind-set' certainly no 'good Japanese'), it can be equally said that Japanese attitudes were embedded in an *occidentalism* which centred upon claims as to the selfish individualism, materialism, decadence and arrogance of westerners (particularly Americans). As far as East Asia is concerned, much of this way of thinking had its deep-historical and cultural roots in ideas about 'the middle kingdom' of Chinese origin, but which the Japanese came to attribute to themselves – particularly in view of the vulnerability of China to western intrusion, which made the Japanese responsible for the protection of Asian civilization.

Of considerable relevance to this theme is, of course, the large and much-discussed issue of the Japanese propensity to 'consume' ideas from outside its own geographical and cultural boundaries (Robertson, 1987). This cannot be the place to survey what is insufficiently known on this very important topic. But a few comments are in order. For a start, it should be pointed out that among the various contrasts which can be made between Japan and the USA is the fact that whereas the first has avidly – if also selectively – imported ideas but has resisted the immigration of people, the USA has tended in the opposite direction in both respects. In other words, the relationship between homogeneity and heterogeneity – which, it could be argued, is crucial in the persistence of any 'vital' society – is accomplished in opposite forms. In any case, as far as the theme of occidentalism in the case of Japan is concerned, it has to be emphasized that since its early thorough encounter with China, Japanese intellectuals and political leaders have tended to express the *content* of Japanese life in 'alien' *form* (Pollock, 1986) and thus Japanese identity has been continuously forged out of the relationship between the alien and the indigenous in a very systematic way. This has been the case – particularly during the periods when Japan has been 'open' to the world – ever since Chinese language and ideas were used to formulate a Japanese essence about 1,400 years ago. Thus Japanese identity largely rests on a form of occidentalism, since in functional terms China was the original 'Occident' for Japan and the concern with the west since the sixteenth century has been constituted by a generalization of 'China' so as to encompass the western world, particularly since the 1850s.

International relations and the construction of national identities

The debate about dominant ideologies, common cultures and so on, has proceeded with little attention to the international or, more diffusely, the global dimension of such issues. That circumstance is beginning to change with the increase in interest in the theme of identity in global perspective, but much more needs to be done before anything like the appropriate degree of analytical sophistication is achieved. The neglect of the extra-societal dimension – even in many discussions of nationalism – is in fact intimately related to the foundations of twentieth-century western social theory and of sociology as a discipline in particular. Notwithstanding certain global, international and universalistic interests of pre-classical sociology – that is, sociology prior to the period 1890–1920 – classical sociology itself was, particularly on the European continent, centred upon the strains attendant towards modernity. To a large degree sociology appeared in the form of *national* sociology – its leading practitioners being preoccupied with the integration of newly unified national societies, such as Germany and Italy, or with the restoration of integralness to a damaged societal fabric, as in the case of France. At the same time, the analytical apparatuses that such people as Emile Durkheim and Max Weber erected were clearly intended to restore or maintain distinctive features of their own societies' *Weltanschauungen* – although Durkheim was clearly more positively interested in what he called 'the international life' than was Weber.

The whole idea that sociology is focused, when all is said and done, primarily on *societies* and their viability thus derives from a particular period of world history – or, to put it another way, sociology itself is in part a product of a crucial shift in world order, a particularly important phase in the process of globalization (Robertson, 1987). That period was one in which a central ingredient of the remarkable compression of the world-as-a-whole was, indeed, the idea that the national society was the major unit both for the allegiance of individuals and of the global system *per se* and which also witnessed the flowering across much of the world of the appurtenances of national identity (Hobsbawm and Ringer, 1983). The idea of societal cohesion centred on shared values and beliefs – upon a common culture or ideology – came to fruition at that time, with societies vying with each other according to the perceived position of each in rapidly expanding 'international society'.

However, in spite of its being in part a result of a shift in world order, sociology – or more precisely the leading sociologists of the classical period – did not pay systematic attention to the degree to which the concern with national identity of the late nineteenth and early twentieth centuries was a highly contingent matter. And even if that is not an entirely fair comment the fact remains that subsequent concern with dominant ideologies, common cultures and so on has often been justified in relation to the writings of the classical social theorists. Recently, however, through such pioneering efforts as those of Eric Hobsbawm and his colleagues (Hobsbawm and Ringer, 1983) we have been made more conscious of the intentional, fabricative aspect of national-identity formation.

Japan and the USA entered the world scene at precisely the moment when there was considerable political activity along such lines and both experienced the challenge of European-type modernity (for America, see Marsden, 1982). Japan had a long experience in the systematic reconstruction of identity relative to a tradition of divine kingship and racial homogeneity – of reconstructing its 'civil religion' (Bellah, 1980) according to internal and, particularly, external circumstances. America, on the other hand, had possessed a more convenantal form of civil religion in combination with great ethnic and racial diversity. But it shared and continued to share with Japan the propensity and ability to release itself from '*the problem* of history' – to look directly ahead (Rubenstein, 1987); even though its 'constitutional fetishism' (Kammen, 1986) can be deployed in backward-looking directions (just as the Japanese Emperor system can be so used, in spite of American attempts to limit it in the Occupation years). In sum we may characterize Japanese culture and identity formation as an extreme form of universalistic particularism and American culture and identity as an extreme form of particular-istic universalism. Combined with other contrasts such as small–large, high population density–low population density, and so on, it is not surprising that it is difficult to conceive of any other pairs of nations which while sharing a few attributes are so different and which – particularly in interaction with each other – provide such stark alternatives for the future.

The general implication of this brief case study of the relationship between Japan and the USA is that the whole area of discussion of dominant ideologies, common cultures and national identities has involved the almost complete neglect of the inter-societal dimension. At the same time, there has been little or no attention paid to *the global circumstances* of the rise of concern with those themes during the most crucial phase in the rise of modern social theory – that is, the late-nineteenth and the early-twentieth centuries. The first lacuna has to be addressed because it is becoming increasingly clear that a central element of societal ideology, culture or identity (not to speak of 'civil religion') can only be accounted for in direct reference to the form and content of the interactions between one nationally constituted society and another. The second omission is just as serious, for it involves the overlooking of the world-historical terms in which the very idea of the cohesive national society arose. In sum, social theory has been held in thrall by the circumstances of a particular period and by the ideas which were produced in a particular phase of world history. We now need to attend in subtle ways to the whole question of dominant ideologies in terms of what I would call the world politics of the global condition. Dominant ideologies are produced and reproduced largely in the course of interactions between and politically structured comparisons with other societies, within the broad context of the shifting structure of the world system.

Notes

1   One of the major advocates of world power for the USA around this time
     was Captain Alfred Mahan, whose books – such as *The Interest of America
     in Sea Power* (Mahan, 1897) – were widely read and translated into a
     number of languages. He was 'studied assiduously in Japan' (Blum *et al.*,
     1963, p. 498).

2   It should be said that the American zoologist Edward Morse went to Japan
     as a short-term professor in 1877, which was a mere eighteen years after
     the publication of Charles Darwin's *Origin of Species* (Masao, 1985,
     pp. 378–85). It was Morse who introduced the theory of evolution to
     Japanese leaders and his dissemination of ideas about the survival of the
     fittest was relatively separate from the introduction of the sociology and
     philosophy of Herbert Spencer.

3   It is, perhaps, preferable to think of the Allied Occupation as constituting
     not the third but the fourth 'turn' in Japan's history – for during the second
     half of the medieval period (1185–1603) contact with China and other
     foreign countries was re-established in both cultural and economic terms
     (Ohnuki-Tierny, 1987, p. 15). The Chinese were later 'replaced as the
     principal foreigners by Westerners, beginning with the Portuguese, who
     introduced guns and Christianity to Japan in the mid-sixteenth century'
     (ibid., p. 145). In 1612 the Tokugawa shogunate banned Christianity and
     thus began the exclusion of all Europeans, with the exception of the Dutch
     – who were confined to a carefully monitored outpost. The Dutch plus
     licensed Chinese traders were to be virtually Japan's only links with the
     outside world until the mid-nineteenth century (Masao, 1985, p. 371).
     However, the tightness of Japan's two and a half centuries of 'isolation'
     has frequently been exaggerated by Japanese and non-Japanese alike.
     From 1720 foreign books, except those pertaining to Christianity, could
     be imported and, mainly via 'Dutch learning', a vast number of western
     ideas – particularly in the natural sciences – became available in Japan
     (Masao, 1985). For a specific study of Japanese learning in the Tokugawa
     period, with particular reference to the development of ideas about virtue
     and morality in relation to merchants and economic life in general and
     also to the relevance of Dutch studies, see Najita (1987).

4   For an interesting and sympathetic discussion of the relevance of Said's
     ideas to the American study of Japan, see Minear (1980). Minear pays
     particular attention to the major American 'orientalist' involved in
     Japanese studies – namely Edwin Reischauer, sometime American
     ambassador to Japan and of major importance in shaping American
     students' attitudes towards Japan. See Reischauer (1950 and 1988). Minear
     does not, however, have cause to touch upon the various ways in which
     American audiences were familiarized with Japanese thought, such as
     visits to America by Japanese intellectuals. One of the most influential of
     the latter was undoubtedly the Zen Buddhist D. T. Suzuki, who after
     attending the World Congress of Religions in Chicago in 1893 became
     directly or indirectly a promoter of Zen Buddhism on American soil
     (Dumoulin, 1979, pp. 4 ff.).

Bibliography

Armor, J. and Wright, P. (1988), *Manzanar* (New York).

Baudet, H. (1965), *Paradise on Earth, Some thoughts on European images of non-European man* (New Haven and London: Yale University Press).
Baudrillard, J. (1988), *America* (New York: Verso).
Bell, D. (1980), *The Winding Passage* (New York: Basic Books).
Bellah, R. N. (1970), *Beyond Belief* (New York: Harper & Row).
Bellah, R. N. (1980), 'The Japanese and the American cases', in R. N. Bellah and P. Hammond, *Varieties of Civil Religion* (New York: Harper & Row), pp. 27–39.
Benedict, R. (1946), *The Chrysanthemum and the Sword: Patterns of Japanese Culture* (Boston: Houghton Mifflin).
Blacker, C. (1964), *The Japanese Enlightenment* (Cambridge).
Blum, J. M. *et al.* (1963), *The National Experience: A History of the United States* (New York).
Buruma, I. (1989), 'From Hirohito to Heimat', *New York Review of Books*, vol. 36, no. 16, pp. 31–45.

Cohen, T. (1987), *Remaking Japan* (New York).

Dore, R. (1987), *Taking Japan Seriously* (London: Athlone Press).
Dower, J. W. (1986), *War Without Mercy* (New York).
Dumoulin, H. (1979), *Zen Enlightenment* (New York).

Fallows, J. (1989), *More Like Us* (Boston, Mass.).

Gong, G. W. (1984), *The Standard of 'Civilization' in International Society* (Oxford: Clarendon Press).

Hobsbawm, E. and Ringer, T. (1983), *The Invention of Tradition* (Cambridge: Cambridge University Press).

Johnson, C. (1988), 'The linkage of trade and defense', in R. A. Morse *et al.* (eds), *Japan and America* (Washington, DC: Woodrow Wilson International Centre for International Scholars), pp. 16–21.

Kammen, M. (1986), *A Machine That Would Go Of Itself* (New York).
Kitagawa, J. M. (1987), *On Understanding Japanese Religion* (Princeton, NJ).

Lehmann, J.-P. (1982), *The Roots of Modern Japan* (London: Macmillan).

Mahan, A. (1983), *The Interest of America in Sea Power* (New York).
Marsden, G. (1982), *Fundamentalism in American Culture: The Shaping of Twentieth-Century Evangelicalism* (Oxford: Oxford University Press).
Masao, W. (1985), 'Science across the Pacific: American–Japanese scientific and cultural contacts in the late nineteenth century', in *The Modernizers*, ed. A. W. Burks (Boulder, Colo.).

Minear, R. H. (1987), 'Orientalism and the study of Japan', *Journal of Asian Studies*, vol. 39, no. 3, pp. 507–17.
Mouer, R. and Sugimoto, Y. (1986), *Images of Japanese Society* (London: Routledge & Kegan Paul).

Nairn, T. (1988), *The Enchanted Glass* (London: Hutchinson).
Najita, T. (1987), *Visions of Virtue in Tokugawa Japan* (Chicago).

Ohnuki-Tierney, E. (1987), *The Monkey as Mirror: Symbolic Transformations in Japanese History and Ritual* (Princeton, NJ).

Pollock, D. (1986), *The Fracture of Meaning* (Princeton, NJ).

Reischauer, E. O. (1950), *The United States and Japan* (New York).
Reischauer, E. O. (1988), *The Japanese Today: Change and Continuity* (Cambridge, Mass.: Belknap Press).
Robertson, R. (1987), 'Globalization and societal modernization: a note on Japan and Japanese religion', *Sociological Analysis*, vol. 5, no. S, pp. 35–42.
Robertson, R. (1988), 'Globalization, internationalization and religion', *Journal of Oriental Studies*, vol. 27, no. 3, pp. 22–9.
Robertson, R. (1990 forthcoming), 'After nostalgia? Wilful nostalgia and the phases of globalization', in *Theories of Modernity and Postmodernity*, ed. B. S. Turner (London: Sage).
Rubenstein, R. L. (1987), 'Japan and biblical religion: the religious significance of the Japanese economic challenge', *Free Inquiry*, vol. 7, no. 3, pp. 14–20.

Said, E. (1978), *Orientalism* (London: Routledge & Kegan Paul).

Vogel, E. F. (1979), *Japan as Number One: Lessons for America* (Cambridge, Mass.)
Vogel, E. F. (1985), *Comeback America* (New York).

CHAPTER

8

Popular culture and ideological effects

NICHOLAS ABERCROMBIE

In its treatment of the ideological structure of modern Britain, *The Dominant Ideology Thesis* was limited in three important and related ways. First, its focus of analysis was relatively 'production' oriented, concentrating on those values, beliefs and practices to do with work or the class structure. The increasing significance of leisure was relatively ignored. Second, the analysis underrated the significance of pleasure in consumption. In many accounts of the role of culture, there is a reluctance to face up to the fact that people derive pleasure from their cultural pursuits and that this pleasure requires explanation. It is almost as if the experiences of cultural practice were forced on unwilling audiences and that cultural pleasures, especially *popular* pleasures, if they exist at all, are illicit. As Mercer (1983) points out, there is a kind of theoretical guilt in this, related, perhaps, to a generalized suppression of pleasure characteristic of western societies since the nineteenth century. For pleasure to be taken seriously, a theory of the consumer is needed which does not treat consumption as a residual category essentially explained by analysis of the mode of production.

The last limitation concerns the emphasis on public issues leading to a relative neglect of the private sphere. Clearly the fact that the bulk of leisure is taken in the private or domestic sphere (at least for most adult age-groups) is of great significance in the study of the ideological impact of modern culture. It must concentrate attention on the way in which households interpret, transform, or resist the ideological effects of dominant cultures. However, it is not just the position of households as intervening mechanisms that is at stake. Gender and generational relationships will have greater salience in cultural interpretation in privatized leisure. They are *relatively* less prominent in the public sphere where other social relations, those of class, for instance, are significant.

The study of popular culture is one way in which to incorporate these three points into an analysis of the ideological force of cultural forms. Popular culture, after all, represents a use of leisure, largely in the home, in which pleasure and consumption have to be central analytical categories.

Popular culture and ideology

There is no shortage of claims that modern, mass, popular culture in its various forms is ideological and that audiences appropriate it as ideology. Adorno is often taken as a standard reference point here. His view of the industries of culture is that they encourage mass deception and control consumers. They provide an 'affirmative culture' to 'regressed listeners'. Modern mass culture is standardized but pretends to be novel and can be contrasted with a genuine, pre-capitalist or early capitalist popular or folk culture. Most important of all, it encourages passivity in the audience and does not stimulate a critical social practice. 'By craftily sanctioning the demand for rubbish it [the culture industry] inaugurates total harmony' (Adorno and Horkheimer, 1979).

Modern sound movies, for example, stunt 'the mass-media consumer's powers of imagination and spontaneity' (ibid., p. 126) by making the moving images so real that spectators are drawn into the movie world without any real thought. Realism defeats criticism. Again, in his analysis of popular music, especially jazz, Adorno emphasizes the repetitive quality of the music. Jazz seems innovative but actually simply rehashes basic formulas with machine-like precision. Sameness blunts criticism in audiences. In this respect the essential sameness of jazz can be contrasted with the essential innovation of Schoenberg, whose music is always individual and demands of the listener 'not mere contemplation but praxis' (ibid., p. 150). Mass popular culture – certainly as represented in popular music and film – is, for Adorno, standardized and repetitive, and persuades the audience to effective obedience through inactivity. As a result 'The might of industrial society is lodged in men's minds' (Adorno and Horkheimer, 1979, p. 127).

This kind of account of the relationship of popular culture to ideology, reproduced in several different theoretical schemes (e.g. Fargier, 1980), incorporates rather crude, unidimensional views of the producers, the audience and the text itself. The production system is seen as coherently and smoothly generating the text, which is itself relatively homogeneous and invariant. Most important of all, the audience is presented as relatively uncreative in its responses to an ideological text. Some more recent views, often deriving their inspiration from Gramsci, set out to overcome these objections. My argument will be that this Gramscian turn, while important in itself, still has much in common with Adorno.

An influential statement of the Gramscian view of popular culture is represented in a collection of essays deriving from the experience of putting on in the UK an Open University course on popular culture (Bennett, Mercer and Woollacott, 1986). In the introduction to this volume, Bennett argues that: 'In Gramsci's conspectus, popular culture is viewed neither as the site of the people's cultural deformation nor as that of their cultural self-affirmation or, in any simple Thompsonian sense, of their own self-making; rather, it is viewed as a force field of relations shaped, precisely, by these contradictory pressures and tendencies' (p. xiii). In such a view, popular culture cannot be seen as a simple imposition of dominant ideology on subordinate classes. While cultural relations have to be understood in terms of the antagonistic relationships between the bourgeoisie and the working classes, bourgeois culture is not *simply* dominant. One cannot speak of domination here but rather the struggle for hegemony – that is, moral, cultural and political leadership. For Gramsci, the bourgeoisie can achieve hegemony only to the extent that it can accommodate subordinate class values. The establishment of hegemony is thus a case of *negotiation* between dominant and subordinate values. Dominant cultures have power because they can organize, in their own terms, the values of subordinate cultures. The trick is for the working classes to recognize themselves in dominant ideology. This means, in turn, that there is no pure bourgeois culture or, for that matter, working–class culture. Each is transformed by the other.

The Gramscian turn has a number of important advantages over the sort of approach to popular culture taken by Adorno. In particular, it takes audience pleasure seriously and seeks to *explain* involvement in popular culture rather than merely deride it. Secondly, it allows for the way in which dominant cultures have to accommodate subordinate cultures to be at all effective. Lastly, a Gramscian approach in practice does not insist that the messages of popular culture have to be homogeneous. There are, however, also theoretical disadvantages. The three moments, production, text and audience, are not well enough integrated, particularly the last. More important, however, is the question of indeterminacy. Gramscian analysts of popular culture see the social formation as composed of a set of conflicting social and cultural forces pushing in different directions, rather like vectors in mechanics. The outcome of these conflicts of forces is the assertion of hegemony. As Bennett says: 'Dominant culture gains a purchase in this sphere not in being imposed as an alien and external force, on to the cultures of subordinate groups, but by reaching into those cultures, reshaping them, hooking them and, with them, the people whose consciousness and experience is defined in their terms, into an association with the values and ideologies of the ruling groups in society' (p. 19). Or as Woollacott puts it in the same volume: 'Theories of hegemony make sure of the idea of articulation in a particular way to suggest that within a given mode of hegemony, popular consent is won and secured around an articulating principle, which ensures the establishment and reproduction of the interests of ruling groups while at the same time winning popular consent' (p. 213). The implication of these views is that the establishment of hegemony is the norm in modern capitalist societies. However, it is not clear what mechanisms will *normally* produce a hegemonic outcome out of the *mélange* of social forces; to have a principle that guaranteed such an outcome would reproduce the crudest features of a dominant ideology thesis. For present purposes, however, the point is that the truth conditions for this version of the theory of hegemony are very similar to those required by Adorno's theory of mass popular culture. For Adorno, popular culture is ideological and furthermore articulates a dominant ideology. For the Gramscians, popular culture typically takes a hegemonic form to which other cultures are subordinated, while being a site of struggle. For both positions, popular culture has ideological force and both have to submit to similar tests of that force. The disagreement is only about *how* that force is achieved.

What would be meant by saying that popular culture has ideological force? Provisionally the following four features are relevant.

(1)   Popular culture encapsulates a particular (hegemonic) view of the world, even if it has to accommodate other views.

(2)   This particular view of the world is widely available in society, perhaps the most widely available.
(3)   Popular culture conceals, misrepresents and secures an order of domination.
(4)   This concealment is in the interests of a particular (ruling) group, social formation or form of society.

What are the conditions for these propositions to be true? To illuminate this question it is useful, following Hall (1980), to distinguish three moments – production, text and appropriation – when carrying out a sociological analysis of any cultural form. Generally speaking, any analysis of this kind is initiated by a reading of the text which, as we all know, is notoriously difficult and controversial. That reading, whether it is a TV programme, film, book, or advertisement, establishes the dominant themes, codes, or discourses in the text. In so coding, a sociological problem is established, since the sociologist wants to know, on the one hand, *why* the text carries a particular discourse and, on the other hand, what an audience will *do* with the text. Therefore, a complete account has to *start* from the text but it should move on from there to consider the means of production and appropriation. As Hall points out, it is not simply a matter of looking at the three moments independently; it is actually the way that they fit together that is of chief interest in considering the relationship between cultural form and ideology. One can further distinguish three aspects of ideology which correspond to the text, production and audience moments. Textual ideology is thus the ideology encoded in the text whether it be film, television programme, photograph, piece of music, or novel. Ideology setting refers to those mechanisms within a production process which encode a particular ideology in the text. Ideological effect refers to the process whereby a textual ideology affects an audience in such a way that an order of domination is secured.

Obviously these three aspects are potentially connected although, equally obviously, the connection is contingent, not necessary; there is no a priori reason for their being connected in any particular way. These are three distinct social processes which intuitively seem likely to overlap but which do not necessarily do so.

Before looking at the three moments of ideology in detail, a methodological problem needs to be mentioned. Can one say that there is ideology in a text independently of any audience reaction? Are (1) and (3) above separable or can one reduce ideology to ideological effect?

The proposal that ideology is really a particular effect of a discourse is seductive. If we are able to say that a discourse is ideological, to the extent that it affects an audience so that the existing relations of domination are secured, we would at least avoid traditional hermeneutic problems. Instead of arguing over rival interpretations of a text, we would only have to find out how audiences appropriate the text. Such a point of view would also avoid the perils of an essentialist definition of ideology in which texts contain an invariant ideological core which can be read by audiences only in one way.

At first glance it might appear that the detection of textual ideology by an analyst is simply another audience reading without any special privilege. Any reading is a reading by someone and sociologists are no better than other social groups in this respect. An analyst's reading then functions essentially as an hypothesis about how audiences will respond. However, it is surely more than an hypothesis simply because it has to be possible to compare textual ideology and ideological effect. If there is a disparity between textual ideology and ideological effect then that is a matter requiring explanation. *In principle*, textual ideology and ideological effect are analytically separable. However, it is also very important to stress that an analytical separation of textual ideology and ideological effect does not entail that only a very narrow range of effects is possible. As I have already argued, that is the mistake that Adorno made in simply assuming that popular culture texts would all be read in the same way.

Textual ideology

In considering the relationship between popular culture and dominant ideology, there are two important aspects of textual ideology – coherence and dominance. It can be argued that for textual ideology to be a credible idea, there has to be some degree of coherence in the text and across texts. I do not mean here that all texts have to have some single, unambiguous message. However, some minimum coherence does seem to be necessary. That is, a text cannot be said to be ideological if it contains contradictory or contrary codings. Similarly, a set of texts is not likely to constitute an ideological formation if the texts are incoherent with each other.

The notion of dominance is unfortunately ambiguous. On the one hand, one can say of a text that there is a dominant or preferred meaning which is sufficiently powerful to organize other, subordinate meanings. On the other hand, one can say that a text expresses an ideology which is otherwise dominant in society. The first is a textual and the second a social dominance. It is by no means obvious that the two are always closely connected. Thus a text *may* be organized by dominant themes which bear little relationship to a socially dominant ideology.

The ideas of coherence and textual dominance are, however, connected since it is a reasonable hypothesis that the more one discourse organizes a text, the more coherent it will be and, at least potentially, the more possible it is for it to be ideological. A consideration of three case studies of popular culture texts may help to illuminate these distinctions.

Hurd (1981) seeks to understand how the 'ideological work' of police series on television functions. At one level this ideological work can be seen in what the dramas leave out. To start with, police series, though purporting to deal with the problems of law and order, actually leave two-thirds of the judicial process out, the courts and the prison system. It is as if the problems of conviction and imprisonment did not exist or, rather, were simply subsumed by the arrest of the villain. But it is not only these institutional sectors that are repressed. The typical plots function so that only policemen have characters. Everybody else – villains, the public, women – is presented as a series of stereotypes. Stereotyping encourages ideological treatment, especially by comparison with the police who are rounded characterful human beings. However, this still identifies only the 'more overt ideological results' in that it deals only with what lies on the surface.

Police series like *Z Cars* or *The Sweeney* are obliged to make their reality convincing. To be convincing they must 'incorporate the antagonisms and contradictions, real or perceived, of policing in England today' (p. 64) while at the same time displacing or concealing them. Police series must represent, but at the same time conceal, social contradiction. Hurd shows how representation-yet-concealment is achieved by considering the major oppositions identifiable within the programmes, the ways in which they are resolved within the drama and their relations to the social structural contradictions which they redefine. A variety of oppositions are identified including police versus crime, law versus rule, authority versus bureaucracy, intuition versus technology and comradeship versus rank, but it is the last which is probably the most important. So, the fictional police world is usually structured as an opposition between the comradeship of ordinary policemen on the one hand and the formal relationships of senior policemen on the other. This tension is psychologically plausible and therefore effective. Yet it diverts attention, in Hurd's view, from larger underlying conflicts in police work, 'by divorcing the activity of policing from any class analysis of power relationships within society' (p. 68). The police series perform their ideological work by portraying social conflict in a realistic way but by ignoring deeper contradictions; conflict is transposed fictionally from one place to another.

In a similar sort of way, the James Bond films can be said to manifest a textual ideology. Eco (1982) analyses the James Bond novels, and the method he uses can be extended to the films, in terms of binary oppositions between characters or events. For example, Bond can be opposed to the villain, Bond to M, the villain to the woman, love to death. However, and departing from Eco's analysis somewhat, some of these oppositions are more important than others. Three are especially significant, namely, villain versus hero, hero versus society, society versus villain, represented in the triangle below.

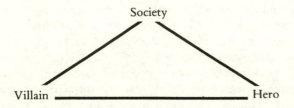

The antithesis between villain and society is relatively simple. Society at large is weak in the face of the villain. It is unable to fend for itself, either because it is unwilling, or because it generally lacks the resources. The relationship between hero and villain is also straightforward. These two are, ironically, very similar to each other in that they are both competent and powerful; in contrast to society, both hero and villain possess *will*. The difference between them is only that their wills are exercised on opposite sides. In James Bond films, as in many contemporary thrillers, the moral differences are underplayed. The crucial opposition is society versus hero. As I have already said, the important feature of society is its inability to act to solve its problems. The members of society may be virtuous – good honest folk – but they are unable to *do* anything. Notably free of any emotional or other constraining ties, Bond has the energy, skill and commitment to solve the problem *by himself.*

A number of features of the films emphasize Bond's individualism. For example, Bond's conduct is often contrasted with bureaucratic rules which the sheep follow but which Bond breaks as the only way to achieve his aims. Bond's relationship with M., for example, is one in which Bond represents the person who is always breaking rules and M. the person who imposes them ('It's time to do some work'). The same issue is raised more significantly in Bond's relationship with the villain who is usually seen as a bureaucrat in command of a vast army of organization men, planning his fantastic schemes down to the last detail. Bond's individualism depends on chance and initiative, not planning and organization. However, the relationship between Bond and bureaucratic rules is ambiguous. For, to an extent, Bond is an organization man. The films go out of their way to stress that he is a civil servant. Critically also, Bond is always set in motion by M., his bureaucratic superior. Bond's individualism is therefore almost professional. There are great similarities between the Bond films and the police series discussed earlier. In both the hero spends a great deal of time struggling against bureaucracy, a characteristic that helps him to win, yet, at the same time, he is essentially an organization man.

I want to suggest that the oppositions in the triangle that I have described overlap with one another to create a discourse of individualism. Each of the oppositions, or rather the combination of the oppositions, serves to stress the significance of individual action. Furthermore this discourse *dominates* and organizes other discourses present in the films and books. For example, there is a discourse of gender created by the overlapping of the oppositions Bond – villain – woman. However, this discourse takes much of its meaning from the relationship of the woman, often as inept if willing helper, to Bond's masculine individualism. Incapable of independent action herself, she is reduced to a minor supporting role. A similar relationship of dominance obtains between the discourses of individualism and nationalism. Persons of nations other than Great Britain function as foils for Bond's individualism. For instance, Americans (ironically) often act as technological helpers who do not have the essential qualities of enterprise and initiative.

In sum, the discourse of individualism organizes other discourses in Bond films and novels but it also takes much of its significance from them. The ideological force of this lies in the pretence that individual action is possible, especially in bureaucratic contexts when the reality of most people's lives is that bureaucracies stifle initiative of this sort.

A quite different example of textual ideology is provided by sport and its reporting in the media. Clarke and Clarke (1982) point out that sport appears an entirely natural activity, the zestful enthusiasm of the innately talented, with no meaning beyond healthful play. Actually, it is a socially constructed activity imbued with a variety of meanings which may be further enunciated by media reporting of sports events. The ideological force of sport comes not only from the meanings embedded in the activities, but also from the way that these meanings or values seem entirely natural and inevitable because of the association with 'uncontaminated' sport. Sport is ideologically successful because it can encode particular and distinct values by pretending to be something that it is not.

An important example that Clarke and Clarke cite is the involvement of sport with nationalism and, in Britain, specifically with Englishness. 'By national culture or nationalism, we mean an ideology which constructs "the nation" as a distinctive and unique set of characteristics, traits and habits which make up both a natural character and a national way of life. It identifies those things that we, as English, are supposed to have in common. But the construction of nationalism also involves suppressing internal differences and conflict in order to be able to present "us" as a unity' (p. 79). The presentation of sport involves not only a construction of national unity but also a unity structured in a certain direction. There is a close association between the idea of being sporting and the English way of life. Indeed the English often like to see themselves as the teachers of other nations, bringers of sports like cricket, tennis and soccer to the heathen. So sport involves self-control, respect for rules, reasonableness and fair play. Those who break rules or aim to win at all costs are actively disapproved of. Sport is, then, ideological in that it presents as natural and English a *particular* set of virtues and vices which is transferable to everyday life. The implication is that, to be a proper person, one should be sporting and always obey the rules.

These three examples drawn from different forms of popular culture all show the way in which textual ideology could be constructed. There is a certain coherence – themes hang together, even though there may be, at times, dissonance and disruption. To some extent there is a hierarchy of discourses in which one dominant discourse organizes the rest whether it be individualism or Englishness. Furthermore, this textually dominant discourse articulates well with discourses that are socially dominant.

However, perhaps the concentration on *content* is misleading and, considering textual ideology, we should really look also at more *formal* properties of the text. For instance, narrative realism is a textual convention frequently employed in popular culture. As a convention it has three features (Abercrombie, Lash and Longhurst, 1990).

First, it offers a 'window on the world'. In realist forms time and space are ordered and stable and the principles of that order lie in the language of scientific causation. This means that causes must be immanent either to everyday life or to the cultural object in question and that the cause must precede the effect. Second, the narrative has rationally ordered connections between events and characters. Realist cultural forms consist of a caused logical flow of events, often structured into a beginning, a middle and a closed conclusion. The important point is that for realist texts the narrative is the central organizing principle and the primary source of pleasure. The contrast is with those texts that are essentially 'spectacular', in which the pleasure lies in the images themselves; it is a visual, not a narrative, pleasure. Lastly, narrative realism conceals authorship and disguises the process of production of the text. Realist cultural forms present themselves essentially as well-formed reports upon external events. Authorship, and the fictional quality of the text, is suppressed and, as viewers or readers, we are not given any knowledge of the production process. For many analysts, this characteristic of realism makes the audience into passive observers. They are not invited into the text as active participants because they can see how it is constructed but are made to sit back and simply observe an apparently seamless whole.

These three features combine to give ideological force to the realist convention. It constrains audiences by concealing alternative views of reality; the world presented by realist popular culture becomes the only possible world. Realism presents its world as coherent and rational, disguises its fictional quality by suppressing the production process, and allows only one outcome of the narrative.

So far I have argued that there is a case for supposing that much popular culture encodes a textual ideology, especially if particular contents are allied with particular forms of representation – narrative realism, for example. This has to be seen as an *achievement*, for it depends on a level of coherence in the text and some coincidence of the textually dominant discourse with the socially dominant ideology, all together with a realist mode of representation. However, it is clearly not the whole story. There are texts where the dominant discourse does not coincide with the dominant ideology. In addition, much popular culture is clearly non-realist or at least contains elements that disrupt the realism, and there can be a permanent tension between a dominant discourse and dissonant subordinate discourses within the text. Furthermore, as I shall argue at the end of the chapter, these features may be becoming more common.

All this is, however, at the level of the single text. It is still the case that most textual analysis of popular culture is of single texts or groups of closely related texts such as police series. Doubtless this is partly related to the origins of this sort of analysis in the intellectual disciplines of aesthetic or literary criticism. This is obviously unrealistic, for our experience of popular culture is of a welter of very different texts. For example, on television we can watch adventure stories, police series, situation comedies, westerns, documentaries, current affairs, soap opera and the news. Indeed the data on audiences suggest that people's viewing habits are relatively undiscriminating. Viewers, on the whole, do not confine their television-watching to particular types of programme; they spread their attention relatively evenly over television's whole output (Goodhart, Ehrenburg and Collins, 1987). It is unlikely that the ownership and use of video recorders will make much difference to this pattern of viewing. On the whole, people employ video as an adjunct to their television, use it in much the same way and spend much the same amount of time watching television despite its use (Docherty, Morrison and Tracey, 1987). Furthermore members of the audience will often not stick to programmes they may like. For instance, on average only 55 per cent of the audience for one episode of a programme will watch the next episode. In addition, clearly the experience of popular culture is not restricted to television, even if it is the most popular medium. Even accepting a very narrow definition of popular culture, audiences experience television, film, music, literature, photography and advertising, all of which forms have radically different rules of composition. What is required is a theory that will make adequate sense of the diversity of texts and thereby reflect actual audience experience. Such a theory has to account for the relationships *between* texts and for the tendency, if any, for dominant meanings to migrate from one kind of text to another.

The theory of genre might provide a partial answer. Ryall (1975) defines genre in the following terms: 'The master image for genre criticism is the triangle composed of artist/film/audience. Genre may be defined as patterns/forms/styles/structures which transcend individual films and which supervise both their construction by the film maker, and their reading by an audience' (p. 28). On this view genres are a kind of agreed code between the film-maker and the audience. The conventions of a genre give the director a set of rules within which to work. At the same time, those rules enable the audience to recognize what it sees and to derive pleasure from that familiarity. To some extent, the pleasures of watching, say a Western, or a historical romance, derive from a knowledge of the genre and of seeing how *this* particular film or TV programme works within the genre. That is what makes parody effective. When we watch a spoof of a Western, we can laugh because we all know what the characteristics of a Western are. There are a number of means by which we recognize genres besides the manifest content. The iconography, for instance, is important. Within any one genre, objects function as icons or signs which are instantly recognizable as signs of that genre. These icons are often visual images – the horse and the six-gun for the Western, evening clothes for the musical, trench coats and machine-guns for the thriller.

There are, clearly, a large range of genres distinguished by rules of composition, iconography, or content. To stress the obvious, these genres are different, very different, from one another. Thus, while the notion of genres might propose a unity between certain texts of a similar kind, it serves, in turn, to emphasize the differences between groups of texts. The concept of genre does not, therefore, make adequate sense of the diversity of texts.

One solution might be to ask if there are any features that unify different genres however different they may appear on the surface. To some extent gender issues may fill this role. Thus it may be argued that a number of genres have similarities in that they are all what one could call males' tales. Westerns, adventures, police series, thrillers and science fiction are generally genres which have a central male hero, with patriarchal relationships with women, whose individual talents are employed to overcome great obstacles. The analysis of James Bond films given earlier in this chapter might stand for many texts of this kind. There is perhaps also an equivalent, female group of texts centred around soap opera which sees women as strong and men as relatively weak. Similarities of this kind do not, however, carry one very far into the variety of popular culture texts for there are many that do not conform even remotely to these two models.

The conclusion from these arguments is that the notion of textual ideology has its limitations. It is often possible to detect a dominant discourse within any one text which gives a certain coherence. However, the connection between this and discourses that have a social dominance is not always made and textually subordinate discourses are always present to provide a potentially discordant note. The real theoretical difficulties arise when taking into account the obvious point that audiences' experiences of popular culture are of a very large number of different texts. There is no reason to believe that a discourse dominant in any one text is dominant in another and, indeed, the three examples considered in detail earlier all have very different forms of textual organization. Texts do not overlap or they positively clash and the mechanisms that relate them to each other are weak or non-existent. It is difficult to see textual ideology in television as a whole let alone popular culture as a whole. The modern cultural experience is of a pluralization of texts which merely reflects Berger's diagnosis of modernity as a pluralization of life-worlds.

Ideology setting

Many different agencies are involved in the production of a film, television programme, or pop record. For instance, a television drama series will involve, amongst others, producers, directors, writers, actors, cameramen, lighting and sound technicians, musicians, film editors and costume specialists. Each of these groups of people will have its own occupational culture and artistic and commercial aims. In some ways, therefore, the problem is how such an apparently fragmented production process generates a product with an ideological coherence at all, a problem with obvious implications for the discussion of textual ideology earlier.

Euston Films is a film and television production company associated with Thames Television. Included in its output are well-known British television series such as *Minder, The Sweeney, Fox, Out, Widows* and *The Flame Trees of Thika*. Across this diverse output, the company has managed to maintain a distinctive house style which gives a measure of coherence to each series and also to the television work as a whole. In the case of Euston Films this coherence is apparently unlikely not only because of the complexity of the production process noted above but also because the company has a very small permanent staff and employs freelancers to make each programme (discussion based on Alvarado and Stewart, 1985). Ironically, however, the freelancers appear to enjoy this form of employment and in practice there is a greater continuity of employment at Euston than in the larger companies as freelance production teams return to make the same series time and again.

The stability of production teams is one reason for the development of a Euston house style. Also important is the strength of direction from the permanent staff especially the executive director of Production and the head of Scripts and Development. These people will discuss and refine initial ideas and formats and go over scripts so that ideas and documents can provide important reference points for

the production team. The importance of reference points of some
kind is obvious when considering individual series. In the case of *The
Sweeney*, for instance, the outline format of each programme laid
down very precise formal requirements for the production team. Part
of the intention of this was to standardize the product, to make it 'a
commodity built to precise specifications' (Alvarado and Stewart,
1985, p. 119). The rigidity of the format may make for standardization
and coherence but it also produces a certain tension within the
production team. Writers, for instance, have to innovate a little within
the format not least to maintain audience interest, and this innovation
might always threaten to produce dissonance. But the strong control
that the producer is given by a standardized format can also mean that
there are artistic tensions between producers and writers.

Analysis of another Euston series, *Minder*, also shows the centrality
of the producer in achieving a coherence and a distinctive series style.
The producer was the fixed point from episode to episode while both
writers and directors changed. 'On any series the producer has
responsibility for ensuring that individual episodes fit in with the rest
and therefore must have ultimate control' (ibid., p. 148). On occasion
the production crew would go over the head of the director to consult
the producer if it seemed as if the style of *Minder* was being
compromised. Such a relative demotion of the director and writer
(important figures elsewhere in television and in the film industry)
produced some of the same tensions experienced in *The Sweeney*.

Some of the coherence of Euston Film's output ironically derives
from the collaboration of a team organized by script editor and
producer and with points of reference in the script. The same is true
of a very different series put out by the BBC, *Boys from the Blackstuff*.
Like *The Sweeney* and *Minder*, this series was a highly organized
product, the result of endless discussion and meticulous planning.
The authors of a study on *Boys from the Blackstuff* (Millington and
Nelson, 1986) note that, to some extent, the coherence arises
informally and collaboratively: 'Such informality is not really leaving
everything to chance since directors take for granted the high degree
of standardisation in approach that exists within the various craft areas
across television . . . the style of a T.V. drama is not imposed simply
by the director, but arises in the course of production. It is the product
of team members responding to the particular features of the project'
(p. 123).

As with the Euston Films' products, coherence in *Boys from the
Blackstuff* is produced not only by team work but also by the
importance of certain roles within the team and of fixed points of

reference. In the case of a series like *Boys from the Blackstuff*, the writer and the director are central. British TV drama gives a particularly privileged place to the writer, an orientation perhaps deriving from the writer-centred British theatre. In the view of many, television actually favours the spoken word. As a medium it does not lend itself to large effects and the audience *listens* to television as a result. The director, the crucial figure in cinema, is therefore partly displaced by the writer and the script becomes a crucial point of reference for the production team. However, the script is not sacrosanct but becomes a working document which is revised as the programmes are produced. This does not reduce the importance of the author. Rather it yet further enhances the artistic coherence achieved through collaboration. Of course, the director is only partly displaced. He continues to have artistic control and 'all ideas and inputs for production are absorbed within his imaginative concept' (p. 128).

Television programmes and series often achieve their coherence through the adoption of a certain *style* which is instantly recognizable to audiences and which is jealously protected by the programme-makers. A case in point is *Dr Who*, the BBC's science fiction serial originally aimed at children. Coherence is a particular difficulty in this instance since the serial has been running for more than twenty years. During that time there have been changes in every department of the production team (Tulloch and Alvarado, 1983). Not only do writers and directors change as a matter of policy, and producers naturally move on to other projects, but there have also been six actors playing the role of Dr Who. Each of these actors naturally gave a particular character to the role, potentially threatening the continuity of style. Furthermore, the audience composition for the show changed over time becoming remarkably heterogeneous. Originally conceived as children's television, it began to attract adults in large numbers from all social classes.

The coherence of *Dr Who* is thus constantly under threat from a variety of sources and the production of the series is a struggle to maintain similarity while permitting difference. In this effort at continuity, as with the other television productions discussed earlier, certain positions are of central importance. In *Dr Who*, the producer is the most important guardian of the programme's style. In some phases of the series, he would actively intervene in the details of the production process, insisting on a particular way of playing a part or vetoing particular gestures from the actors (Tulloch and Alvarado, 1983, pp. 253 ff.). The director and the writer were correspondingly less important, not the least because the policy was to change them relatively frequently.

In this section I have been arguing that the notion of ideology setting requires that we take the coherence of the production process seriously. Given the fragmented nature of production in film and television, coherence is problematic and its achievement is likely to need constant *work*. However, in the studies of film and television that I have reviewed there are three important mechanisms which ensure coherence and hence have the potential for ideology setting. First, work in film and television is highly organized and collaborative. Second, there are always points of reference, usually the script or accompanying documentation and critical roles. These latter vary from production to production but writer, director and producer are the most important. Third, film and television production resemble industrial processes in that the programme or film has to *work* as a household machine might and the producers have to think of them as things that need to be *sold*. Television and film, in other words, are not self-justifying artistic objects but need to capture and hold an audience. Producers have to organize their productions in terms of a style or an image that appeals to specific audiences. Many writers refer to these processes as commodification. However, that term is not really appropriate if reference is being made to the usage adopted by Marx in *Capital* and by those influenced by him. Cultural goods have been sold in a market of sorts for a very long time. It is, rather, a distinctive *form* of commodification in which cultural goods are sold by producers who have in mind the tastes of consumers as well as the intrinsic qualities of the goods themselves.

The production process can, therefore, have a fair degree of coherence although it is perpetually under threat from the stresses within. As I have shown, this applies not only to individual programmes or films but also to series. There may also be some coherence over a wider area. For instance, film and television production teams will operate within the conventions of genre. Again large corporations may have artistic and commercial policies which give coherence of a kind to their products. However, we still do not have any reason for believing in relative coherence across TV output as a whole let alone across the field of popular culture. The problem for ideology setting is therefore similar to that of textual ideology.

Ideological effect

A crude dominant ideology thesis as applied to popular culture would suggest that audiences are relatively passive, absorbing the ideological content of television, film, or popular music without reflection. In such a scheme one would establish ideological effect simply by identifying textual ideology; the former is read off the latter. No sociologist now takes such a theory seriously, although it is still surprising how much audience reaction is taken for granted rather than seen as necessarily problematic.

In most of the literature audience passivity has been discarded in favour of audience activity. At the outset we have to note that such a move makes it more difficult to establish a coherent theory of ideology in popular culture; textual ideology and ideological effect now vary independently, necessitating an involved account of the way in which they may be related. Audience activity, however, turns out to be rather a complex notion. In the discussion that follows I want to draw out three aspects of this notion: choice, differentiation and creativity.

That audiences make active choices in their use of popular culture seems perfectly obvious. For instance, in their television-watching audiences decide what to watch. Indeed, in general, people are remarkably variable, even fickle, in their viewing. Thus, intuitively, one might imagine that in watching a series like *Dempsey and Makepeace*, or a serial like *Coronation Street*, audiences would stay with the programme episode after episode. Actually this is quite wrong. On *average*, of all television programmes, only 55 per cent of an audience for one episode watches the next (Goodhardt, Ehrenburg and Collins, 1987). There is not a great deal of variation between programmes either. For instance, 42 per cent of the viewers for any one *Match of the Day* watch the next programme, while for *This is Your Life* the corresponding figure is 68 per cent. That, in turn, might suggest that comparatively few people watch *all* of a series. Take the internationally popular *Brideshead Revisited*. Only 7 per cent of those who watched any one episode saw ten or eleven of the total number (eleven) of episodes. Of course, other evidence has shown that audiences do not sit glued to the television set. There is, for example, little channel loyalty. Viewers switch actively between channels. Furthermore, as is now well known, the degree of attentiveness to the television set varies widely. For much of the time, in many homes, although the set may be switched on, nobody is paying much attention to it; members of households will do all sorts of things in front of a television set besides watching it actively.

There are, of course, different ways of evaluating evidence of this kind. It could show a kind of systematic audience inattentiveness, an Adornoesque fickleness or mindlessness. On the other hand, it could demonstrate that audiences do make rational and informed choices about what they want to watch. In a sense it makes little difference to the argument developed in this chapter what interpretation is offered, for the lack of loyalty shown indicates that the television *experience* of audiences is not very likely to be coherent. A further illustration of this point is provided by the evidence on the loyalty of audiences to particular *types* of programme.

Commonsensically, one might think that viewers would have well-marked tastes in television which meant that, if they liked one programme, they would also tend to like the other programmes of the same type. Programme preferences would be linked so that there would be recognizable programme clusters. Very roughly, this turns out to be the case. Goodhart *et al.*'s analysis of data on viewers' preferences showed six programme clusters – sports, current affairs, light entertainment, adventure, children's, and, for want of a better word, what are called cult programmes. It would be natural to assume that clustering of preferences of this kind would give to viewers a certain coherence of experience. This is not the case, for *actual* viewing habits do not correspond to viewing preferences. Largely because of compromises within the family, people end up watching programmes that they do not particularly like. The result is that the clustering noted for viewing preferences all but disappears for viewing behaviour. As Goodhart *et al.* conclude: 'The striking finding here is how little the distribution of viewing time over the programme types varies for different audiences. For the viewers of *any* given programme, about 6% of the remainer of their week's viewing was of adventure/action programmes, about 5% of romance, about 15% of light entertainment and so on. There is almost no tendency for them to focus on programmes of the same or similar programme type' (p. 74). The implications of this finding are important. They suggest that, whatever are people's preferences, their viewing habits are very diverse. Typically, television audiences look at a wide variety of programmes, which must suggest an incoherent ideological effect. As I have said earlier, the use of video recorders does not seem to be altering this pattern much.

There is another reason for being suspicious of ideological effect in relation to audiences for television. As is again commonsensical, audiences for television are highly differentiated both in respect of social composition and, more important, of response. Two well-known studies by Morley illustrate this point. In the first (Morley, 1980), he got twenty-three different small groups together for discussions of a television programme, *Nationwide*, the groups being differentiated by factors such as ethnicity, occupation and gender. He classified the reactions of the audience into three types: dominant, negotiated and oppositional. If a section of the audience responds in the dominant mode, its members are using the values, attitudes and beliefs that are dominant in society. If they use oppositional modes they are, as the term implies, employing a way of thinking that contradicts the dominant mode. Other groups within the audience using the negotiated mode are neither oppositional nor dominant, but have a meaning system that can live with dominant values without necessarily believing or accepting them. Shop stewards took up oppositional codes, bank managers and schoolboys the dominant code, while negotiated meanings were adopted by teacher-training students and trade union officials. Even within these categories there were differences. For example, both black students and shop stewards had oppositional ways of thinking and saw *Nationwide* as biased against the working class. However, they were also very different from one another. The students essentially withdrew, considering the programmes to be irrelevant. The shop stewards, on the other hand, tended to be actively critical, seeing *Nationwide* from a radical working–class perspective.

In his second study, Morley (1986) found evidence of sharp differences between men and women in the *way* that they watched television. Thus men watched with great concentration, resenting interruption. Women, on the other hand, watched while talking or carrying out domestic tasks like ironing. Morley relates this finding to the way in which television is a domestic medium. In British society, the home is defined as a site of leisure for men by contrast with their work, while for women it is a place of work whether or not they also work outside. Furthermore, this difference is likely to become more acute as the home becomes defined as the 'proper' sphere of leisure by contrast with the decline of public places of entertainment.

These gender differences in the mode of viewing are related to other differences in the way that men and women use television. For instance, women talk about television far more than men, although they watch less television less attentively. Men appear embarrassed to admit to watching television at all, let alone discussing programmes, with the exception of documentaries and sport. Morley correctly attaches great importance to this point for the meanings of cultural events are partly created by talk about them, which suggests that the cultural experience of television must be greatly different for men and women. Masculinity and femininity are also reflected in the choice of programmes. Men watch factual programming while women actively prefer fiction. For men, this preference is accompanied by a feeling that watching television is a leisure activity greatly inferior to more active pursuits and that women's preferences are, in some way, improper. Even when watching fictional programmes, men prefer 'realistic' situation comedy to any form of romance.

Morley's work therefore shows substantial and, in the case of gender, crucial differences in audience responses to television. A study of Brazilian soap opera produces further evidence of audience differentiation, this time along social class lines which is also applicable to the British situation (Leal and Oliven, 1988). The authors of this study asked respondents from the working class and the professional middle class to retell the plot of a soap opera broadcast the previous evening. In describing the episode, middle-class viewers used the names of the actors to identify characters, while the working class relied on the characters' names themselves. In other words, the middle class tended to emphasize the fictional quality of the soap opera. Again, central themes of the story were interpreted quite differently, interpretations based on different views of marriage. For the working class, marriage is an alliance with a division of labour clearly demarcated. For the middle class, the goal of marriage is emotional fulfilment. The problems faced by the soap's characters are interpreted very differently by the two social classes in the light of these views of marriage.

I now turn to the third aspect of audience activity, that of creativity. It is clear from the previous discussion that central to the audience's experience of television is not only the programmes themselves but also *talk* about programmes. This is a crucial issue. In talk about television, in various different contexts, audiences create something of their own.

One way of looking at this question is to see audience talk as creative in the sense that people use television conversations to make sense of their own lives. For example, Buckingham (1987) shows the way in which working-class young people recognize their own lives in *EastEnders* in their talk about the programme. By perceiving middle-class characters as unsympathetic, they were able to give voice to their own frustrations and their own class–consciousness. A group of East End boys were able to use their pleasurable identification with one of the central characters, Dirty Den, to support a positive interpretation of their own experience as male, working–class Londoners. In other respects, though, many of the young people felt that the programme did not represent their lives. Some of the girls thought that its female characters were presented as unrealistically passive and they were frustrated by the characters' failure to assert themselves in a way that they would have wished in their own lives.

An even stronger view of audience talk as a sense-making activity is provided by Taylor and Mullan's *Uninvited Guests* (1986). As they say: 'in some cases it seems that television drama has only properly occurred, been thoroughly realised, when the plots and the moral messages they contain have been discussed and interpreted and re-dramatised in the company of friends or mere acquaintances' (p. 206). Taylor and Mullan's respondents showed no reluctance to talk and chiefly noticeable in the discussion of a wide variety of topics and programmes was the very great diversity of response. The use of television to make sense is a highly differentiated process. The study also brings out another notable feature of television talk. In order to use television to create meaning, viewers must invest programmes with a certain reality, especially fictional programmes; that is, the mechanism that connects up television with everyday life. It is, perhaps, this feature that leads so many social commentators to say that large numbers of viewers seem unable to distinguish reality from television fantasy; or write letters to fictional characters in soap operas; or talk about characters as if they were real people. Actually, as Taylor and Mullan's respondents indicate, viewers are, on the whole, perfectly able to perceive the fictional quality of television and, furthermore, spend much time discussing the acting style, special effects or camera tricks that all contribute to the experience. It is simply that some form of identification is necessary in order that television performs one of its functions in everyday life.

The notion that audiences are creative and give their own meanings to what they watch is hardly new in studies of television. Unfortunately, it is still the case that remarkably little is known about how these meanings are socially constructed in talk. From the point of view of ideological effect, the crucial point is how, or whether, audience talk is managed in *natural* settings to produce determinate outcomes. Again, discursive diversity is the obvious feature. We have already noted the way in which women and men talk about television in quite different ways; they appear to appropriate the experience differently. There are also likely to be age-group differences in the *modes* of audience talk as well as marked social class differences. Further, natural settings will surely vary in the 'rules' governing television talk. Although most television-watching takes place in the home, a good deal of talk about television takes place at work. Different settings with different discursive rules produce different forms and contents. Finally, one has to bear in mind the possibility that audience readings are relatively flexible, even protean, between settings and over time. Thus different audience members may participate in different discursive outcomes in different settings. For example, young people may read a programme in one way in the home, a different way at work and yet a third mode with their friends. This is important for the idea of ideological effect, for it suggests that such effects operate only in very limited settings and are not carried across to others. Ideological effect, if it exists at all, is not a solid nut that is carried around from context to context. It will only have any permanence to the extent that discursive rules producing particular discursive outcomes overlap between different social groups and social settings.

In trying to match up the concept of ideological effect to research, potential or actual, into audience talk, there are two theoretical issues that deserve mention. First, almost all existing research abstracts respondents from natural settings and explores their television responses in contrived small-group discussions. Of course, sociologists frequently claim that, in general, one cannot infer behaviour in natural settings from that shown in experimental contexts. There is also a specific problem arising with claims about ideology, that people will evince very different attitudes, beliefs and values when interviewed from those observed in natural settings. Interviews tend to call out responses that fit the dominant ideology rather better. Talk in natural settings is therefore likely to show even greater variability than that showing up in group discussions. This point raises the second issue, which is of even greater importance. In considering television talk from the point of view of ideological effect, the aim is to show how talk is *managed* to produce a particular *outcome*. Ideological effect has to refer to an outcome, a commonality of experience and practice, an agreement of sorts between the participants, even if it is not explicit. We have to know whether outcomes of this kind are produced at all and if so how. For example, in domestic talk about television, do men function powerfully discursively as well as controlling what is watched?

In discussing ideological effect I have been trying to show that audiences exercise choice, are highly differentiated and are creative in their responses, partly through talk about television. The net effect of these features is a great deal of diversity, pluralism and indeterminacy.

At the beginning of this chapter, I argued that to establish the truth conditions of the proposition that popular culture is ideological one had to distinguish three aspects – textual ideology, ideology setting and ideological effect. The discussion so far has shown that incoherence, diversity and pluralization characterize all three moments of the ideological process, making each difficult to secure. This makes the proper articulation of textual ideology, ideology setting and ideological effect, necessary for popular culture in any sense to be ideological, even more difficult to secure. There is no principle that organizes the three moments. I have argued that it is even difficult to find a dominant textual ideology, a dominant mechanism of ideology setting and a dominant ideological effect separately. Even if these were found, however, there is nothing that guarantees that they match up with one another, that, for example, a dominant textual ideology is represented in a dominant audience response. This is not to say that there never can be matching; there are social conditions that promote this outcome and those that hinder it and it is to this question that I now turn briefly.

Ideology and postmodern popular culture

So far I have given a fairly abstract analysis of the relations between ideology and popular culture. What is missing is some indication of how societies vary in the degree to which popular culture can be ideologically incorporating, or the way in which a society changes so that at one time popular culture can function ideologically while at another it does not. There is a need, in other words, for an historical or comparative analysis to complement the formal one. I am not, therefore, arguing that popular culture *never* functions ideologically. Quite the contrary; the point of the discussion so far was to indicate the conditions under which it does, or does not, work in this way.

In the remaining part of this chapter I am, very speculatively, going to consider some arguments about recent cultural change, largely since the Second World War in Britain, and to consider how they might relate to claims about ideology. The burden of what I want to say is that, if these arguments are accepted, changes in the form of popular culture are likely to lessen its ideological impact. I examine arguments about five closely connected processes of cultural change in the decades since the war – the arguments of Cultural Citizenship, the Authority of Producers, Fragmentation of the Audience, the Postmodernist Text and the Mode of Appropriation.

The distinction between popular and high culture is a familiar one. It is often suggested that high culture defines what is to count as a good cultural form and most popular culture fails to meet the standards. It is not only a question of cultural definitions that is at stake. In recent times, and especially in the interwar period, a greater deal of active hostility and fear has been directed towards popular culture. It has been variously accused of being vacuous, meaningless, encouraging of passivity, unchallenging, subversive, commercial, and too easy. Adorno, whose work was discussed early in this chapter, had a particularly bitter line in this form of cultural criticism. Cultural practitioners also evince hostility. So Betjeman (1937) says:

> Come, bombs, and blow to smithereens
> Those air-conditioned bright canteens
> Tinned fruit, tinned meat, tinned milk, tinned beans,
> Tinned mind, tinned breath.

Many descriptions of popular culture are, then, largely hostile and also, perhaps, fearful. At the same time, the distinction between high culture and popular culture functions as a *symbolic* boundary with appropriate transgression penalties (see Bourdieu, 1984). The boundary creates a social distance between the two cultural universes which it is almost painful to mix together.

It is possible to see the construction of a boundary between the two cultures as a process of social exclusion; cultural rules close off access to social groups. However, there is some reason to believe that the distinction in the postwar period is less marked and the boundary more permeable and less effective at maintaining social closure. Cultural producers feel themselves more free to mix cultural forms, popular culture is less likely to be a universal object of contempt and more likely, in certain cases at least, to receive artistic approval. Above all, *audiences* are not as likely to be restricted in their tastes and will admit to deriving pleasure from both high and popular culture forms.

If the description in terms of social exclusion or closure is at all useful, it might be possible to describe the breakdown of the boundary between high and popular culture as a process of acquiring cultural citizenship. This boundary functioned to exclude people from certain cultural rights; the acquisition of the rights means a reorganization of the boundaries. Marshall (1950) argued that the eighteenth century saw the acquisition of civil citizenship, the nineteenth century the development of political citizenship and the twentieth century the formation of the welfare state giving social citizenship. Cultural citizenship is simply an extension of the citizenship process, a democratization which undermines the authority of high culture as surely as the extension of the franchise undermined the authority of the ruling class.

A second process of postwar cultural change relates closely to the idea that high culture is losing its *authority* for this loss is also a diminution in the authority of producers *vis-à-vis* consumers; a consumer culture replaces a producer culture. This shift in authority means that the capacity to determine the form, nature and quality of goods and services has moved from producer to consumer. This represents a profound change in social relationships. The culture and institutions of a society in general define the relative positions of consumer and producer, definitions that cut across other forms of social differentiation. This is not to say that the producer/consumer relationship is more fundamental than any other, but changes in the relationship do have society-wide effects. Such shifts require relatively autonomous changes in both production and consumption sectors. It is unwise to put too much explanatory weight on the concepts of consumerism and consumer culture for it is not only a cultural shift that is at stake but a change in patterns of authority. This is partly a loss of authority *as* producer in determining form and content of production and consumption. It is also a loss of authority in a wider sense. Producers and regimes of production are associated with the forces of rationalization and order; the activities of production cannot be conducted without high levels of organization. Consumption, on the other hand, especially modern (or postmodern) consumption, is associated with undisciplined play and disorder. More institutionally, any increase in the importance of consumption and consumers involves a diffusion of authority which helps to explain the oft-remarked pluralism and fragmentation of the modern world; it is a change from a social organization dominated by a relatively small and well-structured group of producers to a more diffuse and much larger assembly of consumers (Abercrombie, 1990).

Fragmentation of the cultural audience is an aspect of a general fragmentation so often said to be characteristic of modernity. In the same way as producers of manufactured goods have, in the postwar period, to pay attention to the very different needs and wants of different groups of consumers, instead of relying on mass-marketing techniques, so also have the producers of cultural goods had to come to terms with a differentiation of audiences. Whereas in the fairly recent past, audiences might have had a degree of homogeneity, perhaps structured by social class, other social divisions, those of age and gender, have become more important, producing an audience cross-cut by different experiences and allegiances. The earlier discussion of ideological effect illustrates this audience differentiation of experience and response. For instance, Morley's (1980) *Nationwide* study shows that audience readings do not vary solely with social class but are also influenced by a variety of social positionings.

The fourth claim about recent cultural change concerns the nature of the text itself. It is unnecessary to repeat the now common postmodernist arguments about the way that contemporary texts, whether in television or literature, break down the barriers between popular and high culture, disrupt traditional narrative realism and fragment cultural experience. Spectacle, style and special effects become more important than narrative and plotting. Non-realist *forms*, like music videos or television advertisements, become significant elements of popular culture in their own right. Self-reference and irony are more or less mandatory even in apparently straightforwardly realist texts. So, the argument runs, contemporary popular culture is as much about disruption and play as it is about telling coherent stories. In a sense popular culture may always have had these characteristics in some measure. What may be happening, therefore, is that popular culture is becoming the dominant mode of textual organization, displacing the deeply serious narrative realism of high culture *as well as* itself changing in character.

Naturally enough, changes in textual organization will themselves be related to changes in audience organization, like the differentiation mentioned earlier. Thus, the qualities of spectacle and self-referentiality may appeal particularly to a younger audience which has become, in the postwar period, an important component of the market for popular culture. However, the relationship between changes in the nature of texts and alterations in audience composition and response may go deeper than that.

As many commentators have insisted, no analysis of culture is complete without an understanding of the audience. What is fundamental to that understanding, I would argue, is the mode of appropriation of the texts. This notion embraces a whole multitude of phenomena. For instance, modern viewers appropriate television by paying fitful attention, talking while the set is on, hopping between channels, not following a series episode by episode, and using a video recorder to watch their favourite scenes over and over again. Watching the television is not, in other words, remotely the same as reading a book or, even, going to the cinema.

There has been, until fairly recently, a 'correct' mode of appropriation of cultural objects which could be called the literary mode as book reading is its archetypical form. The literary mode insists, amongst other things, on uninterrupted appropriation, concentration on one object at a time, the critical importance of narrative and sequence, going through from beginning to end, the virtues of textual analysis and discussion and the salience of authorship. It is an educated, high-culture mode, perhaps also a possessive mode in Berger's (1972) formulation. However, the literary mode is losing its dominance as a way of organizing people's cultural experience at the same time as the less 'literary' forms of text – video, television, popular music, advertisements – become increasingly important in the repertoire of popular culture. 'Video' mode invades 'literary' mode.

These five arguments about cultural change in modern Britain – Cultural Citizenship, Authority of Producers, Audience Fragmentation, Postmodernist Text and Mode of Appropriation – are all very speculative and, if any of them are correct, they identify changes that are only just beginning. Furthermore, it is unclear what are the changes in *social* organization that correspond to these cultural shifts. However, from the point of view of this chapter, the important issues are the implications of the arguments for the ideological force of popular culture – and they all imply a diminution of that force.

Bibliography

Abercrombie, N. (1990), 'The privilege of the producer', in R. Keat and N. Abercrombie (eds), *Enterprise Culture* (London: Routledge).

Abercrombie, N., Hill, S. and Turner, B. S. (1980), *The Dominant Ideology Thesis* (London: Allen & Unwin).

Abercrombie, N., Lash, S. and Longhurst, B. (1990), 'The crisis of classic realism', in S. Lash (ed.), *Culture and Identity; Tradition, Modernity and Post-Modernity* (London: Verso).

Adorno, T. (1967), *Prisms* (Cambridge, Mass.: MIT Press).

Adorno, T. and Horkheimer, M. (1979), *Dialectic of the Enlightenment* (London: Verso).

Alvarado, M. and Stewart, J. (1985), *Made for Television: Euston Films Limited* (London: BFI/Thames Television/Methuen).

Bennett, T. (1986), 'Introduction: popular culture and "the turn to Gramsci" ', in T. Bennett, C. Mercer and J. Woollacott (eds), *Popular Culture and Social Relations* (Milton Keynes: Open University Press).

Bennett, T., Mercer, C. and Woollacott, J. (eds) (1986), *Popular Culture and Social Relations* (Milton Keynes: Open University Press, pp. xi-xix.

Bennett, T. and Woollacott, J. (1987), *Bond and Beyond: the Political Career of a Popular Hero* (London: Macmillan).

Berger, J. (1972), *Ways of Seeing* (Harmondsworth: Penguin).

Bourdieu, P. (1984), *Distinction* (London: Routledge & Kegan Paul).

Buckingham, D. (1987), *Public Secrets: Eastenders and its Audience* (London: BFI Publishing).

Campbell, C. (1987), *The Romantic Ethic and the Spirit of Modern Consumerism* (Oxford: Blackwell).
Clarke, A. and Clarke, J. (1982), ' "Highlights and action replays" – ideology, sport and the media', in J. Hargreaves (ed.), *Sport, Culture and Ideology* (London: Routledge & Kegan Paul).

Docherty, D., Morrison, D. and Tracey, M. (1987), *The Last Picture Show?* (London: BFI Publishing).

Eco, U. (1982), 'Narrative structure in James Bond', in B. Waites *et al.* (eds), *Popular Culture: Past and Present* (London: Croom Helm).

Fargier, J.-P. (1980), extract from *Cinéthique*, no. 5, 1969, in C. Williams (ed.), *Realism and the Cinema* (London: Routledge & Kegan Paul), pp. 171–86.

Gershuny, J. and Jones, S. (1987), 'The changing work/leisure balance in Britain: 1961–1984', in J. Horne, D. Jary and A. Tomlinson (eds), *Sport, Leisure and Social Relations* (London: Routledge & Kegan Paul), pp. 9–50.
Goodhart, G. J., Ehrenberg, A. S. C. and Collins, M. A. (1987), *The Television Audience* (Aldershot: Gower).

Hall, S. (1980), 'Encoding/decoding', in S. Hall *et al.* (eds), *Culture, Media, Language* (London: Hutchinson), pp. 128–30.
Hurd, G. (1981), 'The television presentation of the police', in T. Bennett *et al.* (eds), *Popular Television and Film* (London: BFI/Open University Press).

Jay, M. (1984), *Adorno* (London: Fontana).

Leal, O. F. and Oliven, R. G. (1988), 'Class interpretations of a soap opera narrative: the case of the Brazilian novella "Summer Sun" ', *Theory, Culture and Society*, vol. 5, no. 1, pp. 81–99.

Marshall, T. H. (1950), *Citizenship and Social Class* (Cambridge: Cambridge University Press).
Mercer, C. (1983), 'A poverty of desire: pleasure and popular politics', in *Formations of Pleasure* (London: Routledge & Kegan Paul).
Millington, B. and Nelson, R. (1986), *'Boys from the Blackstuff: the making of TV drama* (London: Comedia).
Morley, D. (1980), *The Nationwise Audience* (London: BFI).
Morley, D. (1986), *Family Television: Cultural Power and Domestic Leisure* (London: Comedia).

Neale, S. (1980), *Genre* (London: BFI).

Ryall, T. (1975), 'Teaching through genre', *Screen Education*, no. 17.

Social Trends (1988) (London: HMSO).

Taylor, L. and Mullan, B. (1986), *Uninvited Guests* (London: Chatto & Windus).

Tulloch, J. and Alvarado, M. (1983), *Doctor Who: The Unfolding Text* (London: Macmillan).

Woollacott, J. (1986), 'Fictions and ideologies: the case of situation comedy', in T. Bennett, C. Mercer and J. Woollacott (eds), *Popular Culture and Social Relations* (Milton Keynes: Open University Press).

Young, M. and Willmott, P. (1973), *The Symmetrical Family* (London: Routledge & Kegan Paul).

9

Conclusion: peroration on ideology

BRYAN S. TURNER

Introduction: the fragmentation of sociology

The Dominant Ideology Thesis was written at a time when British sociology was profoundly influenced by structural Marxism, and especially by the scientific Marxist theories of Louis Althusser and Nicos Poulantzas. Our argument accepted much of the spirit of Althusser's anti-humanism in *For Marx* (Althusser, 1969) and the Althusserian reading of the works of Marx (Althusser and Balibar, 1970). Althusser's conception of science was at the time influential in our approach to ideology, because we wanted to go beyond a merely descriptive account of the nature of beliefs in British society to present an explanation of social stability in capitalism. It is hardly surprising therefore that our approach to the problem of ideology was conducted under a shadow cast by Althusser's materialist reading of the concept of ideology (Althusser, 1971). However, our work should not be interpreted as overtly and directly a contribution to the Marxist sociology of ideological structures, because we in fact contradicted much Marxist theory.

The relationship of our study of the dominant ideology to Marxism may be expressed in the following fashion. On the one hand, in our approach to the periodization of the analysis of ideology we accepted an historically materialist account of the economic structure of society. On the other hand, our critical evaluation of the 'ruling ideas' in Marx and Engels's *The German Ideology* had the consequence of turning conventional Marxism on its head, as Stephen Hill's statement of our position in Chapter 1 of this volume demonstrates.

In the decade following the publication of our argument, there has been a major decline in the intellectual authority and significance of Marxism both as a theory and as a social movement, in particular as it influences intellectuals within the universities. For a great variety of political, social and intellectual reasons, Marxism as a theory of society no longer has any significant purchase within the academic system (Callinicos, 1988). A number of influential Marxist thinkers (Ernesto Laclau and Chantal Mouffe, 1985) have recognized an urgent need for a major redirection of Marxist theory in response to postmodernism (Laclau, 1988), but also in response to changes in capitalism and to the vitality of the new social movements. The result is that there is a theoretical vacuum at the core of contemporary social science. No dominant paradigm has in sociology, or more broadly in social theory, replaced structuralist Marxism and contemporary sociology is characterized by its fragmentation and absence of cumulative theorization (Smelser, 1988). At least one aspect of the absence of a more dominant and authoritative paradigm is that sociology in particular, and the social sciences generally, have undergone a long period of change, division and dispersal.

Capitalism as a socioeconomic system has also, since the oil shock of 1973, gone through a period of instability marked by periodic recessions, in association with an increasing globalization of the capitalist economy which some writers have referred to as 'the end of organized capitalism' (Lash and Urry, 1987). Throughout this period of disruption and relative economic decline in Britain, where there have been exceptionally high rates of unemployment, de-industrialization and bankruptcy, there is little or no evidence, at the level of the street as it were, that the dominance of industrial capitalism as a system has been in any sense at all challenged by working-class political movements in the 1970s and 1980s. Indeed, the gradual erosion, both relatively and absolutely, of the working class has been the most significant aspect of transformation of the class structure in this period (Abercrombie and Urry, 1983; Wright and Martin, 1987).

Although no single dominant paradigm has emerged in contemporary sociology, the last decade has witnessed both a remarkable revival of Parsonian sociology (Alexander, 1984 and 1985) and a growing interest in the importance of cultural sociology (Archer, 1988; Robertson, 1988; Wuthnow, 1987). In the light of these developments, it is interesting to ask how our treatment of ideology stands in relationship to both the so-called new theoretical movement (Alexander, 1988) and the revival of cultural sociology. On the surface, there would appear to be good reasons for believing that *The*

Dominant Ideology Thesis was simultaneously anti-Parsonian and opposed to the idea of cultural sociology as the analysis of a separate and quasi-autonomous realm, namely the cultural sphere.

Our analysis of ideology implies an economistic theory of social and cultural relations, since, although we criticized the metaphor of base and superstructure, the argument concerning the 'dull compulsion of economic relations' appears to suggest an analysis in which social solidarity is explained by economic constraint. Yet *The Dominant Ideology Thesis* should also be read as a text which gave decisive prominence to cultural analysis for the following reasons. First, we tended to equate ideology with culture, partly because we rejected many previous definitions of ideology in terms of false beliefs, false consciousness, or the fetishization of commodities. We abandoned, more by implication than by overt argument, the idea of ideological critique in which the beliefs or values of dominant groups were criticized as false or distorted in order to secure the continuity of the rule of capital. Just as social anthropologists had argued that culture functions to produce social solidarity, so we argued that the function of ideology was to produce an integrated dominant class rather than to produce a subordinated working class. This function of ideology in relation to the coherence of the dominant class is supported by the evidence from Britain in Stephen Hill's chapter. The implication was that the coherence of society was an unintended consequence of an integrated dominant class, in a context where all other classes were constrained by their economic subordination.

Secondly, we did not reject outright functionalist arguments and we suggested that much of the Marxist critique of functionalism could be redirected at Marxism itself. After the publication of our study of ideology, there has been independently a major re-evaluation of the nature of Parsons's functionalism. Current interpretations of Parsons have focused on Parsonian sociology as an account of pluralism and structural complexity in advanced social systems rather than as a theory of consensus. It is now also clear that the distance between critical theory and Parsonian sociology had been exaggerated in the 1970s (Sciulli, 1986 and 1988). Functionalist arguments are in fact ubiquitous in all social science explanations. In most cases there is little difficulty in retranslating Marxist terminology into structural functionalism; for example, it is the function of ideology to bring about the subordination of the working class either by falsifying their understanding of reality or by obscuring reality. To this functionalist discourse, we added an historical account of the origins of certain types of ideology and historically examined the changing relationship between the mode of production, the means for the distribution of ideas and the changing class structure.

Thirdly, this historical analysis led us to the conclusion that the cultural was becoming increasingly autonomous from the economic requirements of late capitalism. As the system of inheritance by primogeniture declined, the capitalist family became less and less important in the ownership of the means of production and thus most of the traditional ideologies surrounding family life, sexuality and inheritance were no longer significant, or at least no longer 'conditions of existence' of the mode of production. Some aspects of our argument about the legal conditions which are necessary for capitalism are disputed in Anthony Woodiwiss's chapter. To some extent this changing relationship between the family and capitalism had been already analysed in Daniel Bell's *The End of Ideology* (1960). This argument about the decline of sexual ideology in the reproduction of capitalism also meant that we disagreed, at least by implication, with the prevailing feminist views of patriarchal power because there is no specific relationship between capitalism and patriarchy, and indeed the development of capitalism may in fact under certain conditions transform the pattern of sexual repression.

The paradox was that, as the means of ideological manipulation increased (with the growth of mass media), the requirement for the cultural integration of the dominant class declined, because that class itself was being fundamentally reorganized by the changing character of capitalist ownership, production and distribution. These arguments about the relationship between particular ideologies, classes and modes of production were developed at considerable length in the sequel to *The Dominant Ideology Thesis*, namely in *Sovereign Individuals of Capitalism* (1986).

In this study of individualism, we argued that an individualistic culture was not a necessary requirement of capitalism under all circumstances, but rather that it played a specific role in competitive capitalism in reflecting, for example, the needs of property owners for the legitimization of wealth. However, we argued that in late capitalism there is in fact a gap or hiatus between individualistic ideologies and the requirements of capitalism, and that indeed in the Japanese case capitalism may well function far more effectively with collectivist rather than individualistic beliefs. Anthony Woodiwiss is critical of some aspects of our original argument in his chapter on Japan in this volume. Although he presents a powerful argument against our view of contingency, it is not self-evident that law is an *ideological* condition of existence, or whether it is a coercive institution for the enforcement of contracts. Further, we believe our argument about contingency is potent. We retain our view that it is difficult to develop a general theory of ideology or to establish that there are necessary relationships between ideology, capitalism and property. Capitalism as an economic system appears to be compatible with a wide range of different types of belief systems. Liberalism, far from being the dominant ideology of capitalism, may turn out to be an exceptional case. In societies such as Germany, the Netherlands and Australia where the state has historically regulated the economy, the connection between liberalism and capitalism is weakened. Scott Lash's chapter on Germany and my study of Australia show that the relation of the state to capitalist development has varied considerably between different societies in different periods. Therefore, our apparent economism allowed us to explain the very *autonomy* of culture in late capitalism. This paradoxical conclusion is compatible with recent views on the importance of the analysis of culture as not only a specific and special activity in sociology, but an autonomous feature of social structure (Wuthnow, 1987).

Historical case studies: from feudalism to baroque culture

Our historical analysis was again significantly influenced by the work of Althusser, particularly in his interpretation of a particular passage from Marx's *Capital*:

> that the mode of production determines the character of the social, political and intellectual life generally, all this is very true for our own times, in which material interests preponderate, but not for the middle ages, in which Catholicism, nor for Athens and Rome, where politics, reigned supreme. (Marx, 1974, p. 86)

Following Althusser, we considered the proposition that in the Catholic Middle Ages the economic was determinant but not dominant. Of course, we gave this a special meaning, since we argued that Catholicism played a major role in the distribution of property in land through the regulation of family and sexual life in a society based upon primogeniture (Ariès and Béjin, 1985). In a feudal system, overt violence by men–at–arms was a particularly crucial feature of social control of the peasantry, but some 'extra economic factor' was necessary for regulation in feudalism, since the peasants may always have been able to support themselves on some common land or small peasant plot, particularly when there was a shortage of labour in relation to land. However, yet another paradoxical consequence of our argument was to suggest that in feudalism we find a society in which culture (ideology) is an essential aspect of the economic and political organization of a dominant class. In this section, I wish partly to confirm that argument, but also to add certain refinements and extensions in terms of more recent work. Our argument about the transition to capitalism can then be made both more problematic and more precise.

I believe that one weakness in the original argument of *The Dominant Ideology Thesis* was its failure to recognize the coherence of Christendom as a dimension of the ruling classes. The main burden of our chapter on ideology in feudalism was negative, that is to refute the idea of a 'Golden Age' of religious practice from which there was a process of secularization with the development of a capitalist industrial society. Against the conventional wisdom of both Marxism and sociology, we argued that there was considerable evidence that in the Middle Ages the great majority of the population existed outside the urban cultural world of the Church and that much of the pre-Christian magic, superstition and heretical world-view persisted in the common popular culture. This argument is supported by a wide range of historical research (Anglo, 1977; Corrigan and Sayer, 1985; Dobbelaire, 1987; Ginsburg, 1966 and 1976; Gurevich, 1984; Larner, 1982; Le Roy Ladurie, 1981). The historical evidence suggests that, prior to the development of modern means of communication, the Christian Church managed to retain, as it were, a foothold in the city centres of medieval society, where it exercised an important influence over the literate elite, whereas in the hinterland the peasantry were relatively immune from the orthodox belief and practice of the Christian core. In general, communication between the ruling class and its subjects was limited by the absence of any effective means of communication other than the elementary means of proclamation by bills or posters (Richmond, 1988). Our original argument probably presupposed too sharp a division between popular and official culture. Furthermore, there were important divisions within popular culture; for example, between rural and urban cultures (Burke, 1978).

Having argued that the spiritual means of communication (the sacraments, preaching, religious drama and other means of spiritual instruction) in medieval Christendom were relatively under-developed and failed to provide the societal cohesion necessary for incorporating all sectors of society within the same religious framework, we demonstrated that the function of Christian culture, especially concerning women, the family and reproduction, was to provide a familial ideology compatible with the economic requirements of a patriarchal household system. The legacy of medical guidelines for reproduction from the classical world still functioned to control women in the interest of a patriarchal economic order (Rousselle, 1988). A further aspect of this argument was to deny that there was any 'great divide' between the feudal period and early capitalism, because early capitalism (especially English capitalism) also depended upon the coherence and integration of family wealth in order to secure a financial basis for future investment in the absence of a sophisticated banking system. The consequence of this argument was to suggest that the dividing line between Catholic and Protestant teaching on the family was insubstantial, because both ideological systems in fact supported the patriarchal household which was crucial for the continuity of wealth in land and capital. In *Sovereign Individuals of Capitalism*, we supported this argument by a discussion of the continuities within a confessional culture across the division between Catholic and Protestant, despite the overt emphasis on individualism within the Protestant reformed tradition. This study provided further elaboration of my work on the historical development of a confessional culture in the historical sociology of religious change (Hepworth and Turner, 1982). These studies have been further reinforced by the contributions of historians working in the tradition of Michel Foucault on the development of the western notion of the self as the result of a discourse of truth (Martin, 1988).

In retrospect, while these arguments appear to be historically valid, the original thesis can be strengthened and reinforced through an examination of the rise of the nation-state and the political and cultural fragmentation of Christendom. The political organization of Christendom was not adequately considered in our original research and we may have by implication underestimated the politico-societal integration of Christian Europe prior to the Reformation, the development of nationalism and the rise of separate and competitive nation-states. In neglecting the political organization of Christendom, we may have underestimated the coherence of Christianity at the super-national level and thereby failed to grasp the cultural impact of Christianity across the entire range of dominant classes in pre-Reformation Europe. Prior to the political fragmentation of Europe, there existed a common intellectual class (the clergy), who were trained within a more or less unified educational system; there existed an international official language (Latin); there was a more or less uniform set of sacramental practices (such as baptism); there was a uniform calendar (for the organization of religious life and business); and there was a considerable flow of information and migration of persons within the system (Le Goff, 1984). Although our original argument was perfectly correct in suggesting that the subordinate classes by and large existed outside this unified reality, we understated the degree of cultural cohesion among the ruling class as a whole across the European continent in the medieval period. Following Saint-Simon's *De la réorganisation de la société européenne* of 1814, Durkheim in *Socialism* (1962) argued that Roman Catholicism had provided the primary moral coherence of the European states prior to the development of industrialism. Within this context, for example, the Church provided the moral basis for the development of the notion of chivalry, honour and prestige for a noble stratum of militarized men (Bush, 1983; Keen, 1984).

It is important to make this argument clear in order to prepare the theoretical context within which to claim that there was a major discontinuity between the Catholic Middle Ages and Europe in the Reformation era, namely a fragmentation of political unity. We can, of course, find incipient nationalistic tensions in the Catholic Middle Ages; for example, in the thirteenth century there were tensions between French, German and Italian societies within Christendom. Dante in his *Monarchia* appealed to an idealized, global monarchy in order to provide the political cement for these competing national groups and to contain the emergence of national sovereignty (Ullman, 1975). Michael Mann in *The Sources of Social Power* (1986) divides the emergence of the European nation-states into two periods, namely 1155–1477 and 1477–1760, arguing that the struggle to achieve a fiscal basis for military activity was a crucial factor in the emerging autonomy of state power. These changes in political structure had their counterpart in religious struggles:

> Up to the seventeenth century, grievances expressed in religious terms were paramount in social struggles; yet they took on an increasingly state-bounded form. The break up of Europe's religious unity in the sixteenth century was predominantly into politically demarcated units. Religious wars came to be fought either by rival states or by factions who struggled over the constitution of the single, monopolistic state in which they were located. (Mann, 1986, p. 435)

While the Protestant Reformation provided much of the ideology for national leadership of state and church, Protestantism also had to provide a legitimization for state power as that instrument necessary for the subordination of the unruly and the ungodly. Godly discipline became a necessary component of any subservient citizenry (Walzer, 1965). In his *Institution de la religion chréstienne* of 1536, Calvin argued that the aim of government is to force us into conformity with the law of the land in which we live, in order, through a system of civil justice, to establish peace and tranquillity (Calvin, 1939, p. 199). In particular, Lutheranism came to deny that there was a Christian right to oppose princes and thus the Protestant Reformation, having legitimized various nationalistic conflicts against Rome, came eventually to provide the ideological foundations for political apathy and Christian obedience to the centralized authority of the nation-state.

One further cultural consequence of the Protestant Reformation was to undermine the global authority of Latin as the language of both intelligentsia and the court. By translating the Bible into various vernacular languages, the Protestant churches both legitimized regional languages and provided one ingredient for the growing union between ethnicity and nationalism (Smith, 1986). The notion that citizens as common members of a political body should share the same language as an essential criterion of membership within the societal community began to emerge as a central feature of nationalism. Of course, while the use of the common language in the translation of the Bible had created a new national basis for the nation-state, the specific association of language with nationalist revival was developed much later by romanticism, following the language theories of Johann Gottfried Herder (1744–1803). In the nineteenth century, romanticism played a critical role in a reformation of a secular mythology of the nation as a community with a specific historical trajectory based upon a common culture, which meant essentially a common language. Dictionaries, grammars and scientific tracts on pronunciation played an important part, especially among the intelligentsia, in creating the sense of the national identity linked to a reformation of languages. For example, the Flemish Movement came to regard language as the expression of a unified national identity and P. Blommaert's *Aenmerkingen over de Verwaerlozing der Nederduitse Tael* (Observations on the neglect of Dutch) of 1832 is characteristic in proclaiming that the language of the people is the foundation of the nation (Brachin, 1985). Struggles for independence and national self-determination were inextricably involved in a quest for a common language. For example, the struggle of the Greek communities against the Ottoman Empire was also a quest for a common language and a common religion as the cultural basis of a new nation (Beaton, 1988).

The recent interest in the sociology of the state has produced some important research on the historical development of nationalism as a unifying cultural force in the formation of separate, independent nation-states. The formation of a national identity owes a great deal to the involvement of elites (especially university intellectuals) in the development of a national mythology, which, rather than necessarily unifying the nation as a whole, provides the dominant class with a new discourse of national commitment. Oppositional cultural movements for regional or national autonomy characteristically require the involvement of an intelligentsia, often working in the context of the university, to give literary expression to radical or dissenting movements. Scottish cultural nationalism is no exception. By concentrating on the *economic* functions of ideology in the historical part of our original work, we neglected the complicating relationship between politics, economics and culture in the break-up of Christendom and the formation of separate nation-states, partly as a consequence of the Puritan Reformation. This leads me to conclude that our division between feudalism, capitalism and late-capitalism (which was of course the conventional wisdom at that time) was too simple as a periodization of the development of European society. In particular, it may be the case that the development of absolutism and the creation of a baroque culture provide a more telling confirmation of our general argument than the more elementary division between feudalism and capitalism.

The baroque culture of the seventeenth century was the cultural expression of the absolutist states, which in turn were political responses to the crisis faced by the dominant class of the old regime in the face of the emerging economic and political power of mercantile capitalists. The absolutist state represents the attempt of a traditional ruling class to reassert its authority over both the peasantry and the urban merchant capitalists (Anderson, 1974). The baroque represented an attempt through absolutism to maintain the system of feudalist states, the rigid stratification of the traditional system and the authority of the landowning classes, including the Church, over new competitive groups. Leibniz's argument, that we live in 'the best of all possible worlds', perfectly expressed the ideological aspirations of the dominant classes of the baroque world (Buci-Glucksmann, 1986, p. 77). The baroque was therefore an essentially conservative culture responding to a period of insecurity and change and to a sense of decay, crisis and decline.

The development of baroque culture is particularly relevant to any debate about the existence of a dominant ideology, because the baroque period can be seen as the first modern attempt self-consciously to create a mass culture in order to subordinate the lower orders in the interests of the continuing control of a dominant class. In order to appeal to the emotions as the main means for the social control of the masses, baroque culture stimulated the senses, created an elaborate public spectacle, developed religious architecture in order to convert the masses by a display of opulent and luxurious symbolism and organized an entire musical world which again sought to lull the masses into acquiescence. Although, following Adorno (1984), it is common to identify 'the culture industry' with the mass markets which were made possible by Fordism in the twentieth century, we can also identify a nascent culture industry in the cultural commodification of the baroque epoch. The baroque combined kitsch and high culture for an urban market-place. The powers of baroque society (the Church, the monarchy and the landed aristocracy) who

> felt the need for acceptance by the masses and made use of means to address them. Baroque culture, in all of its aspects, required a way to approach the popular masses; thus, without taking away from the variety offered by the resources, those manipulating them always attempted to spread them beyond the circle of the aristocratic minority . . . 'to get to the motivations (*Resortes*) of popular emotion' (many writers have noticed) the tendency of the baroque to address the masses so as to bring them together and integrate them, prompting their admiration by means of pomp and splendor. (Maravall, 1986, p. 92)

The public art of baroque attempted through pomp and splendour to incorporate the masses into a new relationship of political loyalty through the exploitation of an aesthetic sense (Buci-Glucksmann, 1986).

The creation of baroque culture provides, therefore, an important additional example for the study of the construction of dominant ideologies around an organized, and in this case defensive, dominant class. Of course, in the long run the absolutist states failed and with them baroque culture went into decline, to be replaced by more liberal forms of politics, by less authoritarian forms of administrative power and by an artistic culture which was more pietist, individualistic and austere in its attempt to communicate with the populace. In more fashionable upper elites, the public spectacle of the baroque was briefly replaced by the more intimate interior style of rococo. As the court society (Elias, 1983) declined and was slowly but inexorably replaced by a bourgeois culture, a new individualism was created as the central feature of the process of civilization, where an individual is expected to control himself or herself by following a particular life-style based upon restraint. This transition to liberal–bourgeois culture did not occur evenly or inevitably across Europe. Authoritarian monarchies in Germany, Austria and Russia survived into the twentieth century until the destructive impact of total war erased them from the outside (Mann, 1987).

Individualism

In attempting to answer the question (What is the relationship between individualism and capitalism?) in *Sovereign Individuals of Capitalism*, it was necessary to clarify a number of related ideas and issues which typically go under the single umbrella of 'individualism'. First, we identified the notion of the individual; that is, a separate subject or person with a consciousness, continuity and social identity. The development of the idea of the individual, specifically within western society, can be traced over many centuries under the impact of Greek philosophical ideas, Christian notions of the soul and Roman legal conceptions of the individual as the bearer of rights (Martin, 1988). Clearly this long development of the individual over many centuries cannot be explained by reference to capitalism alone, since the history of the concept of the individual predates the emergence of capitalism.

Secondly, we separated the discussion of the emergence of the individual from the more conventional discussion of individualism, which we identified as a specific doctrine which describes the individual, the allocation of rights and duties, and specifies the relationship between the individual and other entities such as the state and society. We argued that individualism was a doctrine which came to fruition in the seventeenth century, particularly in the work of Hobbes, Spinoza and Locke, and that there was a specific interaction between individualism and capitalism such that capitalism pushed individualism towards possessive individualism, while individual-ism pushed capitalism towards a highly individualistic conception of property rights. The individualism of Locke's political philosophy was a justification of the political settlement of 1688 and, more importantly, a critique of Filmer's defence of absolutism and royal prerogative. It was in the period of competitive capitalism, therefore, that there was a specific conjunction of individualism as a doctrine and capitalism as a socioeconomic system; however, we argued that, with the development of late capitalism, these two systems (individualism and capitalism) drifted apart.

Thirdly, the idea of individuality is a romantic view of the educational development of the special individual, emphasizing the aesthetic judgement of the individual, the creativity of the separate person and the emotionality of human existence. As a theory of the interior development of the individual, individuality in the Romantic movement was an oppositional idea critical of the central institutions of bourgeois society. This tradition gave rise in Germany to an oppositional notion of inwardness (*innerlichkeit*) and romantic isolation (*einsamkeit*) and loneliness. Goethe's *Wilhelm Meister* perfectly expressed the anxieties of the educated middle classes in their quest for *Bildung* (cultivation) and their powerlessness within the German political context. While individualism supported capitalism in the seventeenth century, the individuality of romanticism in the nineteenth century was a critical position.

Finally, individuation refers to the bureaucratic regulation and surveillance of individuals, perceived by the bureaucracy as mere units of equal value within a system. The individuation of individuals is brought about by bureaucratic means to achieve bureaucratic goals such as the regular and routine taxation of a population. The process of individuation is greatly enhanced in contemporary society by the development of such means as the computerization of information. Although the process of individuation may be important for the development of an administrative infrastructure for capitalism, individuation is not produced by capitalism and furthermore individuation is as important for state-socialism as it is for competitive capitalism. This overtly simple scheme proved invaluable in clarifying many confused arguments regarding the relationship between individualism and capitalism. For example, Susan Kirkpatrick (1988), in an interesting article on Spanish romanticism, asserts that

> Romanticism helped to elaborate the ideology of individualism that facilitated and buttressed the new social and economic structures: a language for the experience of the individuated self was worked out in exuberant complexity . . . The Church remained the hegemonic force in Spanish culture until the beginning of the nineteenth century, effectively limiting the inroads of a secular, bourgeois mentality that might undermine the traditional world view. (Kirkpatrick, 1988, p. 261)

She claims that the distinctive feature of romanticism everywhere was its special emphasis on the individual consciousness. In short, Kirkpatrick makes the classic (in our view) confusion between a bourgeois theory of individualism as a doctrine of individual rights in opposition to absolutist theories of state, and the romantic notion of individuality which was a discourse about the inner consciousness and its development. German individualism emphasized the aesthetic appreciation of reality by a cultivated individual; romantic individualism did not involve a critique of the state.

Individualism on the one hand was the underlying ideology of social contract which negated the traditional view of authority, whereas individuality describes a particular romantic mentality in opposition to all forms of social life which restrict the development of an heroic personality. While the classic authors of individualism were Hobbes, Spinoza, Locke, Bentham and James Mill, the classic exemplars of individuality in its romantic form were Byron, Keats and Shelley, and in philosophy Schopenhauer and Nietzsche. Although individualism might be thought to support capitalism, individuality does not. In fact, romantic forms of individualism appear to flourish under political conditions of authoritarianism, in, for example, Tsarist Russia and nineteenth-century Prussia. Scott Lash's discussion of Germany would seem to support our argument about individualism in its romantic and subjective forms.

The bases of social order

One important feature of *The Dominant Ideology Thesis* was that it combined a certain amount of theoretical eclecticism (Parsons's Hobbesian problem, Marx's ruling-ideas thesis and Weberian notions of legitimation) with a unified analytical purpose: how do social systems survive class conflict and value differentiation? Since the publication of the original statement of our thesis, there has been a transformation of social science paradigms and a shift in empirical emphasis in sociology. The problem of ideology has, however, remained a critical issue in sociology and cultural studies, where the question of the effects and efficacy of cultural symbols has remained a perennial issue (Schudson, 1989). The definition of ideology also continues to cause frustration and confusion (Ashley, 1984; McLellan, 1986, p. 1). There have also been a number of important translations of (primarily French) social theorists – in particular Charles Lefort (1988) and Cornelius Castoriadis (1987) – which have redirected sociological interest in ideology towards the idea of the imaginative self-reconstruction of society in ideological structures which transcend individual beliefs and practices (Thompson, 1984).

The idea behind these theories is that every society, as it were, reconstitutes itself on an imaginary plane. A society cannot exist unless it is able to represent itself as a unity at the ideological level of the imaginary. The human body has been historically an essential feature of this unificatory imagination by representing the differentiated social system as an organic unity (O'Neill, 1985). Furthermore, the whole methodology of deconstruction and the growing influence of Paul de Man (1989) have begun to influence sociology via a renewal of interest in the idea of rhetoric (Simons, 1988).

While the debate about ideology is intellectually robust, many of the problems which were originally identified in *The Dominant Ideology Thesis* continue to plague contemporary debates. Although these theories of the imaginary are stimulating in their conceptualization of the problems of political unity (whether in American democracy or in Soviet dictatorship), almost no evidence is presented to demonstrate who experiences society as a unity, whether society is seen as a unity, or how such images have their effects. As Nicholas Abercrombie's chapter points out, reception theory alerts us to the very complex ways in which media messages are received. These theories of the imaginary reconstruction of society are in fact post-Marxist attempts to understand the dilemmas of Stalinist power within a framework, which covertly retains a strong commitment to Marxist orthodoxy.

The erosion of Marxism as a theory and as a set of beliefs is related to broad changes in the composition of the class structure of capitalist societies, namely a relative and absolute decline of the working class. It is increasingly evident that radical changes in capitalism will, if they occur at all, be brought about by a variety of social groups rather than by a single class. More importantly, Marxism, or more specifically organized communism, has become less and less politically credible as a consequence of the turmoil in central, Soviet Europe, in China and in the USSR itself. Jan Pakulski's chapter is particularly important in its documentation of the ossification and final erosion of Marxist-Leninism as an ideology. The commitment of many Polish workers to some form of socialism contrasted sharply with the cynicism of party officials. As Polish, Chinese, Hungarian and Yugoslavian intellectuals now look towards the western democratic tradition for inspiration, it is hardly credible for western bourgeois intellectuals to be exporting Marxism. By comparison with the 'forced consent' of Soviet-style societies of eastern Europe, the 'mere liberalism' of the capitalist West now 'appears as the embodiment of human freedom' (Feher, Heller and Markus, 1983, p. 203). The recent history of Polish society, which is analysed in this volume by Jan Pakulski, is a dramatic illustration of the precarious nature of 'forced consent' within an authoritarian regime. Finally, the authoritarian dimension of Marxist-Leninism is increasingly under attack as a form of modernist 'grand narrative', which disguises a repressive rationalism behind the façade of socialist progress. While there is much talk of a crisis in western capitalist society, the *real* crisis is in communism and Marxism.

What are the consequences for post-Marxist social theory of these extraordinary changes in the politics of the modern world and its fragmented intellectual climate? Given the re-evaluation or demolition of Marxism in the 1980s, it is now more than ever difficult to sustain the language of false consciousness, hegemony, fetishism, or inverted consciousness. When the whole apparatus of Marxist theory and ideology is being demolished, there is for many social theorists no longer any valid or scientific theory of reality against which alternative belief systems could be held to be false or inverted. In a period where, for example, many Yugoslavian intellectuals believe that capitalism is the only solution to the general problems of socialism and that the specific economic solution for Yugoslavia would be membership of the European Community, it is difficult for English Marxists to regard, for example, the policies of the Trades Union Congress as reformist, or to criticize the working class for its adherence to trade-union consciousness. To take another example, it is difficult for Marxists to adopt a critical perspective on those members of the working class who vote Conservative when Mrs Thatcher has been welcomed in Poland as a heroine of the people. As we come towards the end of the twentieth century, it is now more than ever clear that there will be no working-class revolution in the advanced industrial capitalist societies. It is also uncertain whether we should continue to use the traditional terminology of capitalist and socialist societies, or whether we have arrived at the 'end of organized capitalism' (Lash and Urry, 1987). It is equally unclear what sort of hold, if any, communism will be able to retain over those societies which came under Soviet control in the aftermath of the Second World War. The incorporation of non-communist political forces into the political process in Poland and Hungary, and the dismantling of the Berlin Wall, are visible signs of the decay of old-style communism in the political and economic institutions of Eastern Europe. It is hardly surprising that there is much talk of post-Marxism and *fin-de-siècle* socialism (Jay, 1988). Jan Pakulski's chapter forcefully demonstrates the great difficulty of successfully imposing a dominant ideology over Polish society.

These global changes pose problems for Marxist theory which may prove to be as terminal as Darwinism was for the Christian certainties of the late nineteenth century. Are they also terminal for *The Dominant Ideology Thesis*? The answer is negative, because our argument, while partly drawing on the Marxist tradition, was addressed to problems which are fundamental to social science as such and which as a consequence are not subject to changes in intellectual fashion or the specific political conjuncture of a given period. The original argument was an attempt to clarify two fundamental issues. The first was the classical Hobbesian problem of order (namely how is social stability possible?) which forced us to provide an answer to the sociology of Talcott Parsons as much as to the historical materialism of Karl Marx. The second issue was the nature of human agency in relationship to the character of the social sciences as sciences of action. Here again Parsons's analysis of action in *The Structure of Social Action* was as important as Marx's stipulations about action in the theses on Feuerbach. These analytical problems (order and agency) are not specific to particular paradigms, because they lie at the root of any attempt to provide a theory of society (Alexander, 1982).

In terms of a theory of social order, the existence of shared values or a common culture does not appear to be empirically a necessary requirement of the existence or continuity of actual societies, because there is considerable historical evidence to suggest that societies are not in fact organized around common cultures which are able to embrace different social classes. Stephen Hill's chapter has drawn on much contemporary evidence to show that Thatcherite Britain is not based on any general consensus over values, but there is a definite commitment of business leaders to the ideology of capitalism. We also raised doubts about the possibility that either nationalism or patriotism is capable of providing a basis for social cohesion by transcending class conflicts. To be more precise, from the empirical evidence we deduced that common values or a dominant ideology are not *necessary* conditions of social order. Various contributions to this study, for example, Ephraim Nimni's study of Argentina, have also provided contemporary evidence that a dominant ideology is not a necessary feature of social order. If there is any cultural coherence in society, it is more likely to express itself through the cultural and ideological integration of the dominant classes rather than through the ideological incorporation of the working class or subordinate social groups into society; commitment is at best likely to be pragmatic. We did not argue that ideology *never* provides the social cement of class-divided societies, but the historical evidence suggested that such a state of affairs was unlikely.

Furthermore, it would be wrong to assume that there was some resemblance, however remote, between our theory and the end of ideology thesis (Clegg, 1989, p. 164). We did not suggest that a welfare consensus had replaced the old divisions between left and right. Stephen Hill's chapter throws doubt on the assumption that the postwar period was one of political or welfare consensus, and he also draws upon new evidence to show the importance of a dominant ideology in the dominant class of contemporary capitalism. We noted the continuing importance of class struggles and indeed the idea that in capitalism there is a pluralization of life-worlds suggests that there will be more rather than less disagreement about values. We did not take a particularly optimistic view that civic cultures (Almond and Verba, 1963) would permit successful compromises between competing sections of the western democracies, and to some extent the permanent sense of social confrontation which has characterized the ten-year history of the Thatcher regime has supported the argument that value consensus and political legitimation are not essential requirements of democratic orders under capitalist conditions. The Thatcher regime has not secured its rule on the basis of consensus and compromise. Roland Robertson's chapter illustrates the intense nature of the ideological conflict between national elites at the global level over social identities. The growth of pluralism, cultural diversity, multiculturalism and value differentiation which is a feature of complex societies does not, contrary to the anxieties of cultural conservatives, necessarily spell the end of civilization as we have known it. But it does not suggest the possibility of an imminent revolution as a consequence of a crisis of legitimacy either.

The solution of the Hobbesian problem of order is a materialist one. Because human beings are forced to work to live, there is a dull compulsion of everyday economic realities which forcefully binds them to social order. We also argued that this 'dull compulsion' gave a certain facticity to everyday life which provides a sense of stability. If it is possible to reinforce this pragmatic involvement in society by political and ideological means, then of course it would be rational for ruling classes to seek out such reinforcement. For example, Michael Mann has argued that in the modern period the extension of citizenship is a ruling-class strategy to incorporate the working class (Mann, 1987). Baroque culture can also be regarded as an attempt by a threatened dominant class to win the hearts of the masses by a culture of sensual display. Whether or not these attempts at political or ideological incorporation were successful or effective must, however, be a matter of empirical inquiry rather than simply of theoretical speculation alone. One must be deeply critical of any attempt to posit or stipulate a dominant ideology as merely a *theoretical* solution to the Hobbesian question.

The Dominant Ideology Thesis suggested that this economic explanation of social order was an explanation fundamentally compatible with classical Marxism and the early writings of Durkheim. This thesis, though, was mainly a negative explanation; it conceived of economic compulsion as a restraint on the individual and social groups. However, there are also positive economic relations, namely those of consumption. If capitalism both exploits workers and gives them material advantages through rising standards of living, then 'dull compulsion' is only one side of the economic equation. It then becomes important to ask the question: is it in the rational interest of the working class to overthrow capitalism if the net rewards of socialism are either uncertain or potentially below those of capitalism? Stephen Hill has presented recent evidence from Britain which supports this view that material standards of living are more significant than ideological incorporation. The *relatively* high standard of living for working-class Australians is also pertinent to this argument. Here again the image of empty Russian shops and Polish workers in long queues waiting for basic commodities has reinforced the idea that, on grounds of economic self-interest, a revolutionary overthrow of capitalism would not necessarily be in the workers' interests. Because there is little evidence that socialism has significantly improved the standard of living of the workers more effectively and continuously than capitalism, there is, to put it mildly, room to doubt the idea that socialism is a rationally preferable option over capitalism in simply economic terms. Of course, the problem with capitalism is that these rewards are distributed in a way which is grossly unequal and unjust. However, in the context of the economic growth which took place in the postwar reconstruction, the standard of living of workers continued to rise, and the crises since 1973 have not yet brought about a total reversal of the gains which were achieved after 1945.

In general terms, precisely because Marxist theory has focused attention on production, the whole question of consumption has been neglected (Otnes, 1988). Of course, some radical critics of capitalism would suggest that consumerism and television have trivialized life to such an extent that workers can no longer distinguish between fantasy and reality. Adorno's criticisms of the culture industry and mass society have been resurrected in various postmodern versions of the modern world. While the world falls apart, we are amusing ourselves to death (Postman, 1982). In the hyper-reality of modern society, the system works through the erosion of reality and fantasy (Eco, 1987); the density of commodity symbolism is such that reality has been imploded (Baudrillard, 1983). In fact 'the real' has disappeared to be replaced by simulations. The result is that oppositional and alternative ideals cannot flourish, either because the majority of the population is bought off by the false glamour of consumerism or because opposition is undermined by its very incorporation into consumption. Thus, the oppositional music of punk and rap is eventually commodified and appropriated by the culture industry. These arguments can be regarded to some extent as a modern version of Marcuse's notion of 'repressive tolerance' (1969). However, one curious feature of some theories of contemporary culture, especially Jean Baudrillard's writing on television and the world of commodified signs (Baudrillard, 1983), is that they have reverted to an outdated technological determinism in which there is no mediation between technological source and ideological effect. As a general rule, these theories are characteristically lacking in any systematic evidence or empirical backing, or they ignore the findings of mass media studies which suggest that no *general* conclusion as to the effectivity of messages is plausible on the basis of existing research, because the results are too complex or too contradictory to permit any simple conclusion. Again the implications of postmodernism for traditional theories of ideology have been analysed by Nicholas Abercrombie in his chapter on popular culture in Britain.

Contemporary theories of ideological incorporation – whether expressed in the language of postmodernism, or semiotics, or neo-structuralism, or deconstructionist theories of rhetoric, or modern film theory, or contemporary studies of the aestheticization of everyday life – face a similar and perennial theoretical dilemma, regardless of changing fashions in sociological vocabulary. If a theory has a strong view of the efficacy of cultural symbols, in either causal or hermeneutic terms, as influencing or directing behaviour, then the human agent either disappears or becomes merely the carrier or recipient of ideological messages. The human agent is converted into a *tabula rasa* on which the media inscribe messages. The stronger the theory of ideology, the weaker the agent. Because, so to speak, we had a very weak theory of ideology in *The Dominant Ideology Thesis*, we had a correspondingly strong theory of agency. This issue is the well-known dilemma of the 'two sociologies' (Dawe, 1970) and 'the oversocialized conception of man' (Wrong, 1961). In our analysis of economic constraint, far from seeing the social actor in a position of subordination to social structure or incorporation in an overarching set of values, we pictured the human agent as knowledgeable and practical. Rather than being duped by the system, *homo ideologicus* was deviant, prone to strike, rebellious, cynical and cunning. His proneness to revolt or revolution was, however, tempered by a realistic appraisal of his life chances under various systems. Anthony Giddens (1979, p. 72) has correctly recognized that the position we had developed was in fact a contribution to the agency/structure debate, because our thesis was based on a premise about the knowledgeability of the social actor.

Giddens has argued that both normative functionalism and Marxist structuralism exaggerate the degree to which social actors internalize normative obligations (Giddens, 1984, p. 30). We had not assumed that capitalism, or any other social system, depended ultimately on the stupidity of the masses. We thereby avoided not only the theoretical problems of a theory of false consciousness, but also the implicit moral and intellectual elitism of both right-wing and left-wing criticisms of working-class culture and consciousness. Because we had reduced the stability of the social system to a minimum set of conditions which were primarily economic, we had, as it were, liberated the actor from ideology. As Nicholas Abercrombie shows, reception theory has elaborated this basic argument by claiming that it is never possible to assume that a text has obvious, direct and immediate effects, or a unitary meaning.

Ideology and postmodernism

Perhaps one of the most significant developments in social theory in the last ten years has been the debate over modernism and postmodernism which had been a familiar issue in architecture, fashion and literature since the 1960s and suddenly became very influential in social theory in the 1980s. The exchanges between Foucault, Lyotard and Habermas have brought about a significant shift of topic and approach in sociology. We do not intend here to enter into the core of this issue; there is now a major publishing industry around postmodernism. Indeed, the more difficult it is to define the term, the more extensive the debate (Featherstone, 1988). Whether or not this fashion will leave behind it a substantial contribution to the development of sociological theory remains to be seen. However, the issues raised by postmodernism are particularly germane to *The Dominant Ideology Thesis*.

The implications of postmodernism for the sociology of ideology will depend significantly on how we define postmodernism and on how we see it arising historically. If, however, we regard post-modernism as the fragmentation and diversification of modern cultures by the forces of consumerism and global markets, then postmodernism means that it is impossible to have a dominant ideology in an advanced capitalist system. Postmodernization is the break-up and collapse of unitary paradigms in science, of unitary patterns of architecture, of standardized forms of fashion, and of coherent political platforms. We are here interpreting post-modernism as a version of the notion of pluralization of life-worlds which is an effect of the complex differentiation of societies; postmodernism is in this sense the logical conclusion of modernism. By making this connection between postmodernism and pluralism, I am of course adopting a controversial standpoint, and one which is obviously congenial to the argument of *The Dominant Ideology Thesis*. Since there is no authoritative view on postmodernism (and since postmodernism would rule out a unified definition of itself), I feel justified in adopting this perspective. In summary, the existence of a postmodern culture means that by definition there cannot be a single, dominant, or coherent ideology.

Political culture

The Dominant Ideology Thesis may be criticized for failing to analyse ideology in relation to politics, by concentrating too exclusively on the relationship between economics and ideology; the same criticism might be levelled at *Sovereign Individuals of Capitalism*. For example, the precise nature of individualism and individuality will vary across cultures according to the relationship between the state and the citizen, that is, in terms of the development of the notions of the public, and the political (Maier, 1987). In societies where the state enjoys a certain moral as well as political prominence, and where the private life of the family, religion and the individual are also strongly emphasized, then the public arena is underdeveloped and there is little scope for a politically active notion of citizenship and of political individualism. There appear to be therefore important contrasts between the *Bildungsburgertum* tradition of Germany, the British notion of the citizen as a loyal subject of the monarchy, and the

American conception of democratic participation (Lefort, 1988). Scott Lash's chapter has addressed the complex history of the *Bildungsburgertum* in German social history, adopting a sceptical view of many conventional interpretations. There are rather important differences between the type of individualism described by de Tocqueville within the political conditions of colonial America, and the very limited idea of democratic individualism in Max Weber's political writing on Germany. The different legacies of German political authoritarianism and Tocquevillian democracy are still evident in different conceptualizations of the private and public, the state and the citizen in the German and American traditions. In America, the emphasis on the individual is combined with a view of the political as morally suspect and, therefore, political commitment in America tends to be directed towards private participation in voluntary associations. Within American public discourse therefore, it if often difficult to hold a meaningful discussion or analysis of the political as the public; these issues formed an important part of Bellah's *Habits of the Heart* (Bellah *et al.*, 1985).

In retrospect, therefore, I suggest that one problem with the original discussion of ideology in both *The Dominant Ideology Thesis* and *Sovereign Individuals of Capitalism* was a failure to pursue the analysis of politics with the same rigour with which we analysed the economic and the cultural. In this third volume in our analysis of dominant ideologies, we hope some of these issues have been solved and some of these gaps have been filled by these comparative studies of political ideology in Argentina, Australia, Poland, Japan and Germany. We have also attempted to address more directly the problem of citizenship in relation to political stability and social solidarity. Stephen Hill has taken up critically my challenge that the original argument failed to consider the importance of citizenship for social solidarity. Roland Robertson's chapter can also be read as a sustained criticism of local, society-centred analyses of ideology.

In this brief review of the debate around *The Dominant Ideology Thesis*, I have suggested that our argument attempted to avoid the simplicity of the conventional dichotomy between materialism and idealism, between the base and superstructure and between agency and structure. Although it was argued that in capitalism it is largely the dull compulsion of economic relations which produces social order, in practice our account of both feudalism and capitalism was a good deal more complex. First, in our view culture plays a crucial role in a production of class solidarities, but not necessarily in the integration of entire social systems. Secondly, our argument had the paradoxical consequence of making cultural analysis very prominent, since we conceptualized the relationship between culture and economics as historically contingent. Furthermore, our argument carried with it an implication that, in late capitalism, there is a divorce between culture and economic necessity such that the cultural becomes increasingly independent from the requirements of capitalism as an economic system.

In this conclusion I have suggested that a number of additional refinements to the original position, which centre primarily on the nature of the political in relation to both the economic and the cultural, may serve to extend and clarify the original thesis. For example, the original analysis needs to be supplemented by an account of the nation-state and nationalism. Again, Roland Robertson's chapter has addressed some aspects of this issue of the formation of nationalism. Anthony Woodiwiss's chapter on Japanese society also suggests that an account of the stability of capitalism requires an explication of the role of law in securing capitalist possession. We also neglected the importance of absolutism and baroque culture in the development of early political theories of legitimacy. In the modern period, our argument has neglected politically different traditions in relationship to the connection between the individual and state. Although these and many other refinements, changes and additions could be made with respect to *The Dominant Ideology Thesis*, it can also be argued that this approach to the study of ideology established a particular way of *doing* sociology which is deeply grounded in a historical appreciation of the contingent, and therefore changing, relationships between the major institutions of any given society. Doing sociology therefore necessarily involves doing empirical, comparative, historical research, and the existence of an ideology (dominant or otherwise) can never be established merely by theoretical assertion, or by depending parasitically on guidelines developed in the classical Marxist literature – such as the *Prison Notebooks of Antonio Gramsci* (Gramsci, 1971) – which were located and written in highly specific historical contexts. These present studies of dominant ideologies have attempted therefore to develop sociological analysis in a globally comparative and historical perspective, that is away from arid theoretical elaboration and conceptual specification.

Bibliography

Abercrombie, N. (1980), *Class, Structure and Knowledge* (Oxford: Blackwell).

Abercrombie, N., Hill, S. and Turner, B. S. (1980), *The Dominant Ideology Thesis* (London: Allen & Unwin).

Abercrombie, N., Hill, S. and Turner, B. S. (1983), 'Determinacy and indeterminacy in the theory of ideology', *New Left Review*, vol. 142, pp. 55–66.

Abercrombie, N., Hill, S. and Turner, B. S. (1986), *Sovereign Individuals of Capitalism* (London: Allen & Unwin).

Abercrombie, N. and Urry, J. (1983), *Capital, Labour and the Middle Classes* (London: Allen & Unwin).

Adorno, T. W. (1984), *Aesthetic Theory* (London: Routledge & Kegan Paul).

Alexander, J. C. (1982), *Theoretical Logic in Sociology*, Volume One, *Positivism, Presuppositions and Current Controversies* (London: Routledge & Kegan Paul).

Alexander, J. C. (1984), *Theoretical Logic in Sociology*, Volume 4, *The Modern Reconstruction of Classical Thought: Talcott Parsons* (London: Routledge & Kegan Paul).

Alexander, J. C. (ed.) (1985), *Neofunctionalism* (Beverly Hills, Calif.: Sage).

Alexander, J. C. (1988), 'The new theoretical movement in sociology', in N. J. Smelser (ed.), *Handbook of Sociology* (Beverly Hills, Calif.: Sage), pp. 77–101.

Almond, G. A. and Verba, S. (1963), *The Civic Culture: Political Attitudes and Democracy in Five Nations* (Princeton, NJ: Princeton University Press).

Althusser, L. (1969), *For Marx* (Harmondsworth: Penguin).

Althusser, L. (1971), *Lenin and Philosophy and Other Essays* (London: New Left Books).

Althusser, L. and Balibar, E. (1970), *Reading Capital* (London: New Left Books).

Anderson, P. (1974), *Lineages of the Absolutist State* (London: New Left Books).

Anglo, S. (ed.) (1977), *Of the Damned Art, Essays in the Literature of Witchcraft* (London: Routledge & Kegan Paul).

Archer, M. (1988), *Agency and Culture* (London: Routledge).

Ariès, P. and Béjin, A. (eds) (1985), *Western Sexuality: Practice and Precept in Past and Present Times* (Oxford: Blackwell).

Ashley, D. (1984), 'Historical materialism and ideological practice: how do ideologies dominate people?' *Current Perspectives in Social Theory*, vol. 5, pp. 1–20.

Baudrillard, J. (1983), *Simulations* (New York: Semiotext(e)).

Beaton, A. R. (1988), 'Romanticism in Greece', in A. R. Porter and M. Teish (eds), *Romanticism in National Context* (Cambridge: Cambridge University Press), pp. 92–108.

Bell, D. (1960), *The End of Ideology* (London: Collier, Macmillan).

Bellah, R. N., Madison, R., Sullivan, W. M., Swidler, A. and Tipton, S. M. (1985), *Habits of the Heart, Individualism and Commitment in American Life* (Berkeley, Calif.: University of California Press).

Brachin, P. (1985), *The Dutch Language, a Survey* (Cheltenham: Stanley Thorns).

Buci-Glucksmann, C. (1986), *La folie du voir, de l'esthétique baroque* (Paris: Galilée).
Burke, P. (1978), *Popular Culture in Early Modern Europe* (London: Maurice Temple Smith).
Bush, M. L. (1983), *Noble Privilege* (New York: Holmes Maier).

Callinicos, A. (1988), *Making History: Agency, Structure and Change in Social Theory* (Ithaca, NY: Cornell University Press).
Calvin, J. (1939), *Institution de la religion chrétienne*, Volume 4 (Paris: Société des Belles Lettres).
Castoriadis, C. (1987), *The Imaginary Institution of Society* (Cambridge: Polity Press).
Clegg, S. R. (1989), *Frameworks of Power* (London: Sage).
Corrigan, P. and Sayer, D. (1985), *The Great Arch: English State Formation as Cultural Revolution* (Oxford: Blackwell).

Dawe, A. (1970), 'The two sociologies', *British Journal of Sociology*, vol. 21, pp. 207–17.
de Man, P. (1989), *Critical Writings 1953–1978* (Minneapolis, Minn.: University of Minnesota Press).
Dobbelaire, K. (1987), 'Some trends in European sociology of religion: the secularization debate', *Sociological Analysis*, vol. 48, no. 2, pp. 107–37.
Durkheim, E. (1962), *Socialism* (New York: Collier).

Eco, U. (1987), *Travels in Hyper-Reality* (London: Picador).
Elias, N. (1983), *The Court Society* (Oxford: Blackwell).

Featherstone, M. (1988), 'In pursuit of the postmodern, an introduction', *Theory, Culture and Society*, vol. 5, nos 2–3, pp. 195–216.
Feher, F., Heller, A. and Markus, G. (1983), *Dictatorship Over Needs: An Analysis of Soviet Societies* (Oxford: Blackwell).

Giddens, A. (1979), *Central Problems in Social Theory: Action, Structure and Contradiction in Social Analysis* (London: Macmillan).
Giddens, A. (1984), *The Constitution of Society* (Cambridge: Polity Press).
Ginsburg, C. (1966), *I Benandanti-stregnenia e culti agrari tra Cinquecento e Siecento* (Torino: Giulio Einandi).
Ginsburg, C. (1976), *Il Formaggio e Iverni il Cosmo di un Nugraio del 1500* (Torino: Giulio Einandi).
Gramsci, A. (1971), *Selections from the Prison Notebooks of Antonio Gramsci* (London: Lawrence & Wishart).
Gurevich, A. J. (1984), *Categories of Medieval Culture* (London: Routledge & Kegan Paul).

Hepworth, M. and Turner, B. S. (1982), *Confession: Studies in Deviance and Religion* (London: Routledge & Kegan Paul).

Jay, M. (1988), *Fin-de-siècle Socialism and other essays* (New York and London: Routledge).

Keen, M. (1984), *Chivalry* (New Haven, Conn. and London: Yale University Press).

Kirkpatrick, S. (1988), 'Spanish romanticism', in R. Porter and M. Teich (eds), *Romanticism in National Context* (Cambridge: Cambridge University Press), pp. 260–83.

Laclau, E. (1988), 'Politics and the limits of modernity', in Andrew Ross (ed.), *Universal Abandon? The Politics of Postmodernism* (Minneapolis, Minn.: University of Minnesota Press), pp. 63–82.

Laclau, E. and Mouffe, C. (1985), *Hegemony and Socialist Strategy, Towards a Democratic Politics* (London: Verso).

Larner, C. (1982), *The Thinking Peasant, Popular and Educated Belief in Pre-industrial Culture* (Pressgang); reprinted in *Witchcraft and Religion, the Politics of Popular Belief* (Oxford: Blackwell).

Lash, S. and Urry, J. (1987), *The End of Organized Capitalism* (Cambridge: Polity Press).

Le Goff, J. (1984), *La Civilisation de l'Occident médiéval* (Paris: Artaud).

Le Roy Ladurie, F. (1981), *Carnival in Romans, a people's uprising at Romans 1579–1580* (Harmondsworth: Penguin).

Lefort, C. (1988), *Democracy and Political Theory* (Cambridge: Polity Press).

Maier, C. S. (1987), *In Search of Stability, Explorations in Historical Economy* (Cambridge: Cambridge University Press).

Mann, M. (1986), *The Sources of Social Power*, Volume 1, *A History of Power from the Beginning to AD 1760* (Cambridge: Cambridge University Press).

Mann, M. (1987), 'Ruling class strategies and citizenship', *Sociology*, vol. 21, no. 3, pp. 339–54.

Maravall, J. A. (1986), *Culture of the Baroque, Analysis of a Historical Structure* (Manchester: University of Manchester Press).

Marcuse, H. (1969), *An Essay on Liberation* (New York: Beacon Press).

Martin, L. H. (1988), 'Technologies of the self and self-knowledge in the Syrian Thomas tradition', in Luther H. Martin, Huck Gutman and Patrick H. Hutton (eds), *Technologies of the Self: a Seminar with Michel Foucault* (London: Tavistock), pp. 50–63.

Marx, K. (1974), *Capital: a Critical Analysis of Capitalist Production*, Volume 1 (London: Lawrence & Wishart).

McLellan, D. (1986), *Ideology* (Milton Keynes: Open University Press).

O'Neill, J. (1985), *Five Bodies: The Human Shape of Modern Society* (Ithaca, NY and London: Cornell University Press).

Otnes, P. (ed.) (1988), *The Sociology of Consumption: an anthology* (Oslo: Solum Forlag, A.S., and New Jersey: Humanities Press).

Postman, N. (1982), *Wir amusieren uns zu Tode* (Frankfurt am Main: Suhrkamp).

Poulantzas, N. (1973), *Political Power and Social Classes* (London: New Left Books).

Richmond, C. (1988), 'Hand and mouth: information gathering and use in England in the later middle ages', *Journal of Historical Sociology*, vol. 1, no. 3, pp. 233–52.

Robertson, R. (1988), 'The sociological significance for culture: some general considerations', *Theory, Culture and Society*, vol. 5, no. 1, pp. 3–23.
Rousselle, A. (1988), *Porneia: on Desire and the Body in Antiquity* (Oxford: Blackwell).

Schudson, M. (1989), 'How culture works, perspectives from media studies on the efficacy of symbols', *Theory and Society*, vol. 18, pp. 153–80.
Sciulli, D. (1986), 'Voluntaristic action as a direct concept: theoretical foundations of societal constitutionalism', *American Sociological Review*, vol. 51, no. 6, pp. 743–66.
Sciulli, D. (1988), 'Foundations of societal constitutionalism: principles from the concepts of communicative action and procedural legality', *British Journal of Sociology*, vol. 39, no. 3, pp. 377–408.
Simons, H. W. (ed.) (1988), *Rhetoric in the Human Sciences* (London: Sage).
Smelser, N. J. (1988), 'Introduction', in Neil J. Smelser (ed.), *Handbook of Sociology* (Newbury Park: Sage), pp. 9–19.
Smith, D. A. (1986), *The Ethnic Origins of Nations* (Oxford: Blackwell).

Thompson, J. B. (1984), *Studies in the Theory of Ideology* (Cambridge: Polity Press).

Ullmann, W. (1975), *Medieval Political Thought* (Harmondsworth: Penguin).

Walzer, M. (1965), *The Revolution of the Saints, Study in the Origins of Radical Politics* (Cambridge, Mass.: Harvard University Press).
Waters, L. and Godzich, W. (eds) (1989), *Reading de Man Reading* (Minneapolis, Minn.: University of Minnesota Press).
Wright, E. O. and Martin, B. (1987), 'The transformation of the American class structure 1960–1980', *American Journal of Sociology*, vol. 93, pp. 1–29.
Wrong, D. (1961), 'The oversocialized conception of man in modern sociology', *American Sociological Review*, vol. 26, pp. 183–93.
Wuthnow, A. R. (1987), *Meaning and Moral Order, Explorations in Cultural Analysis* (Berkeley and Los Angeles, Calif.: University of California Press).

Index

newspapers
  Australia 170–1
Nimni, Ephraim J. 130–57, 245
nobility 67–8, 70–1
  medieval 236

occidentalism 183, 190–3
ocker culture 163–5
Offe, C. 45, 86–7
officiers 67–9
oligarchy, agrarian 131–41, 143–4, 146, 148–9, 152–3, 155–6
Ongania, General 149
oppositional ideology 6, 9
order 245–6
orientalism 183, 190–3
Ottawa Conference 140
ownership
  enterprises 11–12
  and voting 26

Pacific War 185–6, 191
Pakulski, Jan 38–64, 243–4
panopticism 160
Paris Peace Conference 185
parliament, German 78
Parsons, Talcott xv, 230–1, 242, 245
particularism 78–82
pastoralists, Australian 162, 164
patriarchy 103–4, 106, 110–12, 117–18, 170–1, 232, 235
patriotism 245
  Australia 165, 174
Patterson, Banjo 168
Peasant Party 53–4
Perón, Eva *see* Duarte, Maria E.
Perón, Juan Domingo 144–8, 150–2
Peronism 142–51, 154–6
pleasure, cultural 199
pluralism 231, 246, 250
  cultural 174, 246
Poland 38–64, 243–4
police series, television 205–6
Polish Socialist Party 53
political
  citizenship 27–33
  culture 18, 250–2
  ideology 251
  participation 31
  process 7, 32
  rights 73–5
popular culture 199–228, 248
  and ideology 200–4
  postmodern 222–6
populism 168
positivism 167, 174

possession 100
  capitalist 100, 103–4, 112–13, 123
  personal and impersonal 11–12
postmodernism 84, 93–5, 230, 248–50
  popular culture 222–6
Poulantzas, Nicos 169, 229
pragmatism xv, 3, 46, 55–8, 175
press
  Australia 170–1
Primo de Rivera, José Antonio 141
private
  education 16–17
  medicine 17
Proceso, El 152–3
producer authority 224
production, television 212–15
profit 4, 7–10, 33
proletarian internationalism 47–8, 51
propaganda 42–3, 45, 53, 55, 57–8
property 4, 10–11, 100, 109, 111, 174
  right to 17
  and voting 26
protectionism
  Australia 175
  Germany 80
Protestantism 235–7
Prussia 67–9, 72, 79–80, 242
Pufendorf 73–4

racial superiority 184
racism 162, 185, 191–2
  scientific 184
radicalism 4, 7, 22, 138, 163
  Argentina 150
  egalitarianism 6–7, 9–10, 19
  working-class 136
railways, Argentina 134
rational choice xv, 24–5
rationalism 167
reactionary modernism 81–6, 89
realism, narrative 208–9
reception theory 243, 249
Rechtsstaat 75, 109
Rechtsstaatlichkeit 80, 85–7
Reformation 236–7
Regierungen 68–9
religion
  Australia 164–5
  civil 165, 194
  Germany 79–80
  Japan 107
  Middle Ages 234–6
  Poland 46, 49, 53, 55
  Reformation 236–7
rentier capitalism 106
repression 56